CRICUT FOR NEWBIES

How to Use Your Cricut Machine with Confidence

Master Design Space, Build Your Skills with In-Depth Project Tutorials, and Enjoy a Treasure Trove of Cricut Tips & Tricks

SECOND EDITION

by Delara Chowdhury

CRICUT FOR NEWBIES SECOND EDITION, PUBLISHED IN 2023

(First edition published in 2022)

For Zabed and Aliya.

Nothing would be possible without you two.
Love you—always.

Claim Your **FREE** Gift Right Now

Hello, fellow Cricut crafter.

Thank you so much for investing in this book. As a token of my gratitude, I'd like to **send you a FREE Design Space guide**. It's the perfect companion booklet that will help you understand the basics of Design Space in an easy and fun way. Visit the website below to tell me where I can send your copy of *The Must Have Design Space Cheat Sheet for Cricut Newbies.*

www.cricutfornewbies.com

Happy reading and crafting!

TABLE OF CONTENTS

INTRODUCTION

WELCOME TO THE EXCITING WORLD OF CRICUT CRAFTING

Creativity is inventing, experimenting, growing, taking risks, breaking rules, making mistakes, and having fun.
—Mary Lou Cook

Have you ever opened a box with uncontainable excitement only to find yourself staring at its contents with the feeling that a tsunami had just crashed down on you?

That was my first Cricut experience.

As an avid crafter, who had never wanted to do anything but create, going through such immense overwhelm was discouraging and frustrating, so much so that it pushed me into a period of creative limbo.

To make things worse ... the machine turned me into a liar. Months after I had bought my Cricut Explore Air 2, my husband asked if I was still as excited about my machine as I had been at the beginning.

"Oh, I'm absolutely in love with it!" I replied with all the enthusiasm I could muster and said I had just been too busy to experiment with it. But I promised he would soon receive a gift from me—one I would craft with my Cricut machine, of course.

I felt terrible.

Long before that moment, I had seen a Facebook post from a coworker where she showed off a cool sign she had made with her Cricut. I didn't know what a Cricut was, but I was so charmed by that post that I immediately did some research and got pulled into a fascinating world where I saw endless and exciting possibilities. My enthusiasm grew and led to many conversations with my family and husband. Seeing how Cricut had given a new spark to my imagination and creativity, my husband encouraged me to invest in my own Cricut machine. It took a lot of contemplation on my side and some loving nudging from his side, but we finally went out and bought one. When I got home and opened that box, though ... well, that's when the tsunami hit.

But overwhelmed and scared as I felt, I was determined to make good on the promise I gave my husband, no matter what.

As if by fate, I stumbled upon a how-to video about using Cricut for crafting a couple of days later. It's been five years, but the memory of discovering how easy it was to make a customized mug with my sister's name on it is so vivid, it's as if I had my "Aha!" moment just two minutes ago. The tutorial also helped me realize my Cricut machine looked way more intimidating to operate than it actually was.

As humans, most of us shy away from the unknown. But when we choose to brave the unknown, that choice just might end up being the best decision ever. For me, it certainly was; and if you allow me to take your hand and lead you into the enthralling world of crafting with Cricut, I'm confident you'll feel the same.

I'd also like to dedicate this book to you, the absolute Cricut Newbie. In these pages, you'll find guidelines to make the first steps of your Cricut journey fun, memorable, and easy.

I've gone through every trial, error, and downright laughable "Oops! Was that supposed to happen?" scenario you can't even imagine. With your burning passion and the knowledge you'll gain from Cricut for Newbies, you'll be crafting whatever your heart desires (and more) in no time.

When I finally handed over my husband's gift, my life changed forever. I realized then that my Cricut had not turned me into a liar—I am, to this day, absolutely in love with it, and it's a source of indescribable fun and fulfillment.

Nice to Meet You

I'm Delara Chowdhury, an unapologetic craft addict. Don't ask my mom, but I'm pretty sure I could craft before I could sit up straight. Thousands of hours of my life have gone into various projects—from pottery to woodwork, to knitting, to paper crafting, and more. The latest crafting trends have always fascinated me, and I'll be the first to admit: nothing comes close to Cricut. It's the proverbial magic button every experienced and aspiring crafter needs, especially in the ever-changing, go-go-go world we live in. No matter how hectic your life is, you can pursue your desire to create with your Cricut machine. All you need is your passion, your machine, a bit of patience while learning, and as little as 30 minutes a day to become a confident, experienced Cricut crafter.

What You'll Learn

I wrote this book for people who know little to nothing about Cricut. Maybe you bought your machine because it was on sale and it looked cool, but you now don't know what to do with it. Perhaps you inherited it from someone else or got it as a gift but experienced intense overwhelm the first time you peeked inside the box. Or maybe you don't own a Cricut yet, and you're just curious to know if it is worth the investment.

Whatever path brought you here, you're in the right place, and this book is for you. If you're still on the fence about getting a Cricut, you'll find all the information you need right here to make an informed decision. If you already have a Cricut but you're not using it, you'll learn all about your machine and gain confidence to create, create, and create some more.

We'll talk about what Cricut is, how it started, and how it has changed over the years. We'll dive into every Cricut model and discuss how to choose the best option for your needs. I'll also show you how to set up your machine with step-by-step instructions, whether you use an Apple or Windows computer, or an Android or iOS device.

After watching that tutorial I told you about earlier, my creative mind switched into overdrive. In my haste to create, I learned valuable lessons by hitting my head more times than I can remember. Although I persisted, those roadblocks were discouraging and wasted so much time. I'd hate for the same thing to happen to you. So, once you have set up your machine, we'll chat about important things you need to consider before you start with your first crafting project.

Along the way, I'll share some little-known tidbits to make your journey as smooth as possible. We'll dive into the different materials you can use with your machine, as well as the tools and accessories available to make your job easier and your craftwork more unique. I dedicated an entire chapter to Design Space, Cricut's very own design software. For most Newbies, Design Space is the mountain standing between them and finished projects, and, sadly, it is one of the top reasons they give up on Cricut. But you have nothing to fear. I'll walk you through the program's interface, functions, and features to help you feel ready and comfortable when you create your first projects.

Speaking of projects, we'll do three of them together from start to finish. This will empower you to take on new projects on your own like a pro. You'll learn useful tips and techniques for operating your machine and have access to cheat sheets for quick referencing whenever you work on something new. There is also a troubleshooting guide you can consult in case your machine doesn't play nice. You shouldn't experience major issues with your Cricut, but, as with any technology, hiccups may occur on the odd occasion.

Soon after delivering on my promise to my husband, I started creating gifts for friends and family members. Later, I became confident enough to sell my creations, and today I own a successful craft business. Over the past couple of years, I have had the amazing opportunity to share my knowledge with a few acquaintances, which helped me to identify my second passion: showing others how they can unleash their creativity and use it to build lives centered on doing what they love. Even if you discover Cricut is not for you, I guarantee what you'll learn here goes way beyond learning a skill or how to operate a machine. You'll walk away empowered and determined to pursue your creative passion, whatever it may be.

What's New in the Second Edition?

Since the first edition's release, Cricut's design software, Design Space, has undergone many changes. The interface is different and there are new features to enrich your creation process. Thus, the entire Design Space chapter (Chapter 9) has been updated to reflect the changes.

Chapter 10 has also undergone extensive updating. The project tutorials have been rearranged according to the level of simplicity involved in the design process and rewritten for even more clarity.

The book's overall design has been updated to create more consistency between this book and my newest release, *Cricut Design Space Handbook for Newbies*, and to give you a better reading experience.

Cricut Design Space Handbook for Newbies is the perfect next step you can take to up your Cricut crafting journey after you have read this book. While this book has a pretty big chapter on Design Space basics, my new book delves much deeper. It's a comprehensive guide that, as the name implies, covers every aspect of Design Space in detail, but in a straightforward way any Newbie can understand and appreciate.

If you had told me *Cricut for Newbies* would become an immediate Amazon best seller upon its release, I would have smiled, thanked you for your enthusiasm, and politely told you to be realistic.

"This stuff just doesn't happen to ordinary people," I would have said.

Well, it turns out I was wrong.

You, I, and billions of other ordinary people can indeed achieve marvelous results. All we need is faith in ourselves, tenacity, and a willingness to put in our everything. Remember that as you work your way through the book.

Now, it's not that I didn't believe in my book's potential to change new Cricut crafters' overwhelm and uncertainty into confidence (that's why I wrote it!), but I honestly thought that 'best seller' status was reserved for celebrities and influencers. I am awed, humbled, and indescribably grateful that *Cricut for Newbies* has been a best seller in multiple Amazon categories for around a year now. And it's all because of you, my valued reader. So, THANK YOU. *Thank you* from the bottom of my heart.

Now let's get started!

CHAPTER 1

CRICUT HISTORY & INTERESTING FACTS

Creativity doesn't wait for that perfect moment.
It fashions its own perfect moments out of ordinary ones.
—Bruce Garrabrandt

The What: A Crafter's Dream

Cricut is an innovative brand that offers specialized die-cutting machines. These machines look a lot like cool printers, but that's where the similarities end. A Cricut machine works with a blade that can cut through paper, vinyl, thin sheets of metal, leather, and many more materials. There are different blades you can install on your machine, depending on the material you're working with, and your machine can even perform more specialized tasks like writing with a pen, scoring, and making perforation marks. What your Cricut cuts (whether it's shapes, pictures, or words), depends on the instructions you give it via its specialized design program, called Design Space.

In Chapters 3 to 5, you'll learn everything about the different Cricut models and the materials they can cut, and in Chapter 9, you'll learn everything you need to know about using Design Space.

Cricut machines are easy to use with proper guidance, making them a dream come true for Newbies. With determination, patience, and by practicing what you learn in this book, you can become a Cricut pro and wow your friends and family sooner than you think.

Be warned, though: once you get the hang of things, you'll become totally and unapologetically addicted to Cricut crafting.

But What Is Die-Cutting Anyway?

These days, "die-cutting" is a buzzword in crafting communities the world over. Its origins, however, lie in another craft altogether: shoemaking. Before the 1800s, making shoes was a tricky, labor-intensive business. Holes had to be punched manually, and it was difficult to cut identical leather pieces to produce matching soles. Let's just say new shoes were an expensive, somewhat rare commodity back then.

These difficulties gave rise to die-cutting machines, a means for cobblers to use standardized shapes to cut soles out of leather. In time, the technology advanced and allowed cobblers to use differently shaped and sized dies to produce any shoe parts they needed, which made shoe production more efficient and reliable. Die-cutting opened the doors to the mass production of shoes and is the reason we have standardized shoe sizes today.

The technology continued to advance, and various industries implemented it because it offered speed and mass production capabilities. Thanks to creative companies like Provo Craft & Novelty, the inventor behind Cricut, die-cut technology eventually made its way into crafters' homes.

A "die" is a metal or plastic mold with sharp edges that can cut through a sheet of material to produce precise duplicates of a specific shape. Think of it as a crafter's cookie cutter.

However, Cricut helped redefine what die-cutting meant in the world of crafting. Instead of using standardized shapes, all new Cricut machines can communicate with a digital program (Design Space) and cut out whatever design you can imagine.

The When: A Fascinating Stroll through History

Once upon a time, there was the Provo Craft Cuttlebug—an innovative little crafting tool that allowed users to cut out shapes and emboss paper. It was a revolutionary technology in a world where schools and businesses had to rely on expensive, heavy-duty machines if they wanted special letters and shapes made for signage.

If you were the creative type who enjoyed making special greeting cards and similar things for your friends and family, you had to rely on scissors or settle for the same generic stuff as other people. Not fun.

The Cuttlebug was just the latest invention by Provo Craft & Novelty, who had been on a mission to re-imagine industrial die-cut technology since its founding in 1969. Their mission was to bring the technology into ordinary people's homes, and they succeeded wonderfully. A few years later, they introduced one of the crafting world's most popular brands: Cricut.

The Cuttlebug required no electronic connections or steep learning curves. All you had to do was place a plastic die on top of a sheet of paper and arrange them in between two cutting plates (kind of like how build a sandwich).

Then you had to feed the "sandwich" through the machine by cranking the handle. A few seconds later, you would have perfectly cut shapes to use for a crafting project, which typically entailed card making or scrapbooking. In a time when things like these were not available to the masses, the Cuttlebug was pure magic.

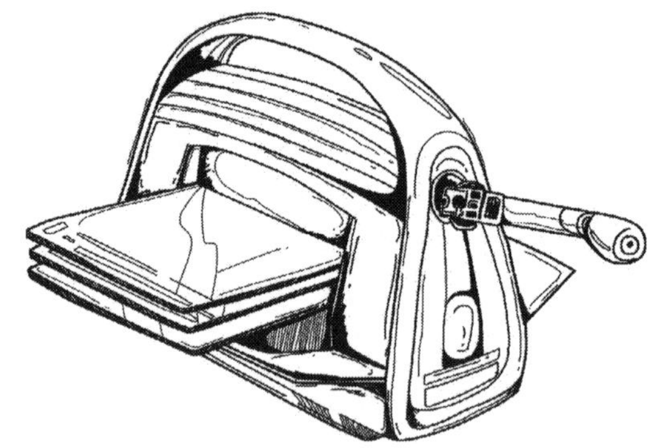

Despite its popular and catchy name, the Cuttlebug would be the first and last to bear it. Its successor, released in 2003, was the Cricut Personal Cutter (CRV001). Soon after, the Provo Craft Cuttlebug received a minor makeover and became the Cricut Cuttlebug.

This once state-of-the-art machine is still available today. However, Cricut announced its discontinuation in 2019—much to the dismay of its users. Luckily, there are still accessories available to use with it, and it will be a long while before Cuttlebugs become obsolete.

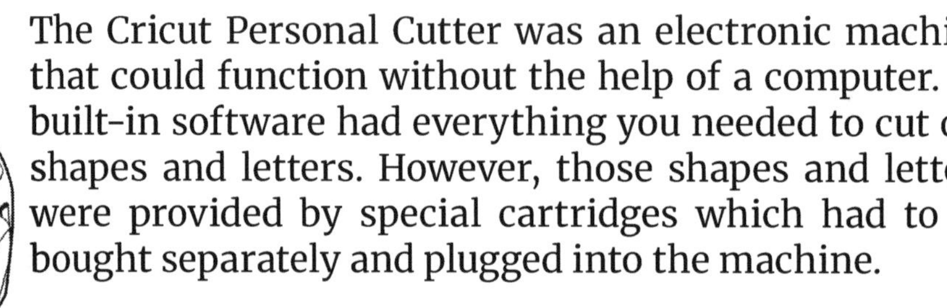

The Cricut Personal Cutter was an electronic machine that could function without the help of a computer. Its built-in software had everything you needed to cut out shapes and letters. However, those shapes and letters were provided by special cartridges which had to be bought separately and plugged into the machine.

Each cartridge contained a set of designs that the Personal Cutter could read and cut according to the settings you wanted. For example, a cartridge with a specific font set could give you outputs with uppercase, lowercase, bold, regular, condensed, or cursive letters, together with a few distinctive design elements. The Personal Cutter now falls under the category of "legacy machines" at Cricut. They no longer manufacture or give technical support for legacy machines. That said, many crafters still use the Personal Cutter.

The Personal Cutter laid the foundation for subsequent Cricut inventions. First, it allowed for the cutting of more materials, including vinyl and vellum. One of the latest Cricut models, the Maker, can cut up to 300 different materials. Second, the machine's built-in software was the beginning phases of what would later become a specialized design software. Today, we Cricut crafters use Design Space, which gives us the freedom to design and cut whatever we want. Third, and probably the most important in terms of technological advancement, the Personal Cutter worked with a blade that could cut out whatever design the machine received instructions for. It was one of the first machines that no longer needed dies to cut out shapes.

The Cricut Personal Cutter's successors continued to add value to the growing Cricut crafting community. From a machine that could both print and cut to one that was made specifically for cutting cake decorations, Cricut made them all. Most were raving successes, others got scrapped soon after their introductions. Since its inception, Cricut has perfected their brand and products. Today, their specialized technology offers all crafters, from Newbies to pros, the perfect solution. All current Cricut cutting machines work with a computer or mobile app (or both), an Internet connection, and Design Space.

The Why: What's the Big Deal with Cricut?

Let's face it: time is always an issue.

We're moms, wives, sisters, friends, professionals, and more. Anything that saves time is a bonus. But anything that saves time *and* guarantees fun is hands-down worth an investment. Cricut offers immense enjoyment and relaxation without demanding hours you don't have. More than that, it has created the possibility for super busy people to explore their creative sides and discover their hidden passions.

If you're someone who loves making special gifts for others, have a special interest in crafting, or even dream of starting your own business, you *need* a Cricut. It's accurate, relatively easy to learn, and will introduce you to a vast community of like-minded people. And it's fast—way, way faster and less frustrating than battling with a pair of scissors. Even with the smallest model, the Cricut Joy, you can cut over 50 different materials. On top of that, the project ideas you can come up with are endless, because the right Cricut machine can handle whatever cool ideas you can think of (I'll help you decide which one is best for your needs in Chapter 6).

Apart from Cards and Scrapbook Stuff, What Can You Make with a Cricut Machine?

The simpler question would be: what *can't* you make with Cricut?

These machines are amazingly versatile for all kinds of gift and DIY projects. And, if you're more entrepreneurially inclined, you can employ your machine to help you make extra money. Here are a few things you can do with your Cricut machine, but the list is by no means exhaustive:

- Basswood or balsa wood signs.
- Stencils.
- Leather crafts, like journal covers and earrings.
- Stickers.
- Iron-on designs for t-shirts, mugs, and more.
- Foam crafts, like bookmarks.
- Vinyl decals for walls.
- Foil artworks.

- Typography art, like quotes.
- Labels.
- And much, MUCH more.

The Big Question: How Do You Pronounce "Cricut?!"

Many people who read about Cricut for the first time assume the pronunciation is "cry cut" because the company offers cutting machines. However, the correct way to say it is "cricket," like the insect.

Also, as you get to know the brand, you'll notice the "C" in "Cricut" sometimes has little bug antennas attached to it. It's a useful reminder of the connection between the pronunciation of the brand name and the cricket insect.

Are you ready to learn how Cricut machines work? Head over to Chapter 2 to find out.

Chapter 1 Notes

Use this space to jot down the best take-aways you learned from Chapter 1. Use these notes as your personal quick-reference guide whenever you want to refresh your memory ons something specific.

CHAPTER 2

HOW YOUR CRICUT MACHINE MAKES MAGIC

Invest time in yourself to have great experiences
that are going to enrich you.
—Steve Jobs

Cricut makes life so much easier for crazy crafty people—ahem—people who are crazy about crafting. But it can be scary and overwhelming the first time you lay eyes on your machine. Now that I have met many fellow crafters and listened to their stories, I know my first experience with Cricut was one most (if not all) new Cricut crafters go through.

Love at first sight is both exciting and scary. If that was your first Cricut experience, this chapter will reintroduce you to your Cricut so you can get to know each other without those hard feelings from your previous meeting. If you haven't bought a Cricut yet, reading this chapter will save you from an awkward first meeting altogether.

I have learned that people feel more comfortable when they understand things before trying to use it, and working with a Cricut is no different. When I first saw a tutorial that explained how to use this magical machine, I thought, *Huh! That doesn't seem so hard to operate*. With a renewed spark, I saved my Cricut from the dark closet. And ... well ... My first attempt at using it was not exactly successful. Neither was the second. The issue, though, was not operating the machine. That part turned out to be the easiest.

No, really.

In fact, cutting a project with your Cricut machine happens in five simple steps, and I'll tell you all about it in a moment. Most of my struggles were related to a general lack of know-how; things like:

- Which materials to use.
- Which mats work best with which materials.
- How to not waste material (because, you know, money doesn't grow on trees yet).
- How to store supplies.
- How to master the Design Space beast (this is a big one for most Newbies!)

As my Cricut journey progressed, I met fellow crafters whose struggles mimicked mine. Back then, Cricut crafters were few and far between, so the way forward was through trial and error for most of us. But you don't have to worry about any of that because you'll learn everything (as in *everything*) you need to know. You'll be the most knowledgeable Cricut Newbie ever by the time we're done hanging out in these pages!

How to Use a Cricut Machine

The following basic steps are applicable no matter which Cricut model you own (excluding the legacy machines we talked about in Chapter 1). The aim of this chapter is to help you get familiar with the technical aspects of operating your machine. (Don't worry, we'll skip the nitty-gritties under the hood and just focus on the fun stuff.)

Step 1: Finalize and Confirm Your Design

Whenever you want to cut projects with your Cricut, you will use Design Space to give your machine all the information it needs for the cutting process. Remember, we'll dive into Design Space in Chapter 9, so don't worry if the following information doesn't make sense right now.

After completing your design, you will double-check that everything is in the right place and, if there are words in your design, check the spelling. Then, when you're happy, you will commit your design by clicking on the *Make It* button in the upper-right corner of the Canvas interface.

Step 2: Follow the On-Screen Prompts from Design Space

Design Space will open a Preview screen where you can review your design one last time before the cutting process. From there, you will click on the *Continue* button in the bottom-right corner of the screen. Next, the program will prompt you to choose which material you want to cut and guide you through more steps so your machine can start the cutting process.

Design Space is so cool that you never have to scratch your head over which blade (or other tools) to insert into your machine. It will tell you exactly what's needed.

The Cricut Explore and Maker series machines can house two tools at the same time and some of the tools are interchangeable between the two machines. The Cricut Joy, being smaller than the other machines, works with its own tools that are incompatible with the other machines, and it can house one tool at a time.

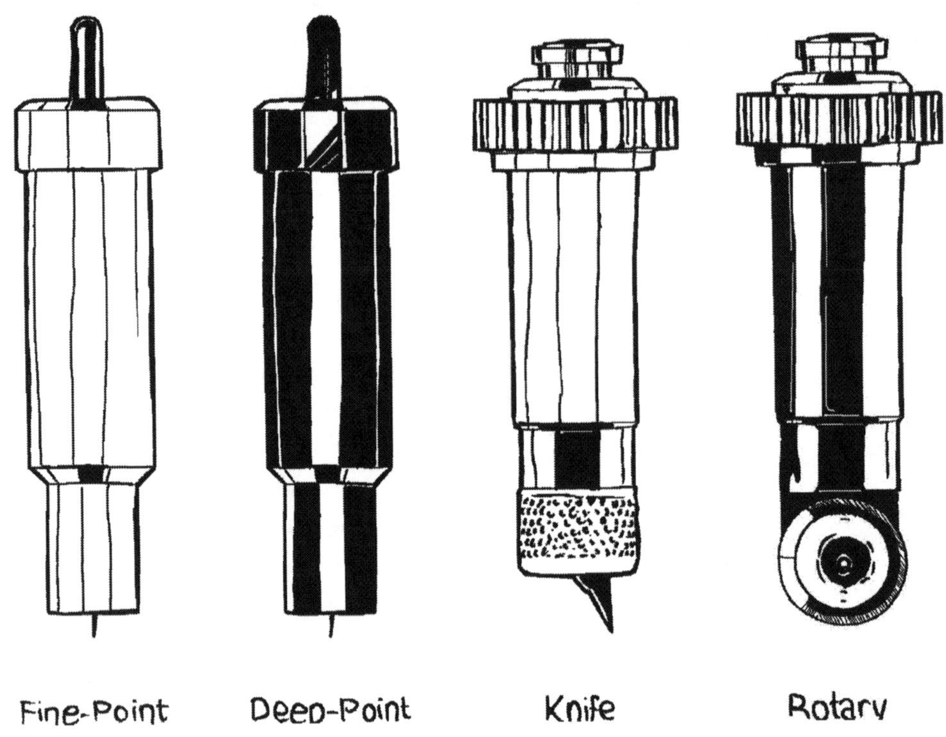

How to Install Blades and Specialty Tools

Cricut machines have housing units for their tools. The housing unit is called the tool holder on the Cricut Joy, or the double tool holder on the Explore and Maker series machines. The component looks a little intimidating, but it's actually easy to operate. With the Explore and Maker series machines, Design Space will even tell you which of the two holders to insert your tool into.

To install a blade or tool, first open the tool holder's clamp by gently pulling it away from the holder (toward yourself). Remove the tool inside the tool holder by lifting it out of the holder. Now you can insert the new tool by dropping it inside the empty holder. One it's in place, close the clamp again. You'll know everything is secure when the clamp locks squarely with the tool holder.

Step 3: Place Your Material on the Cutting Mat

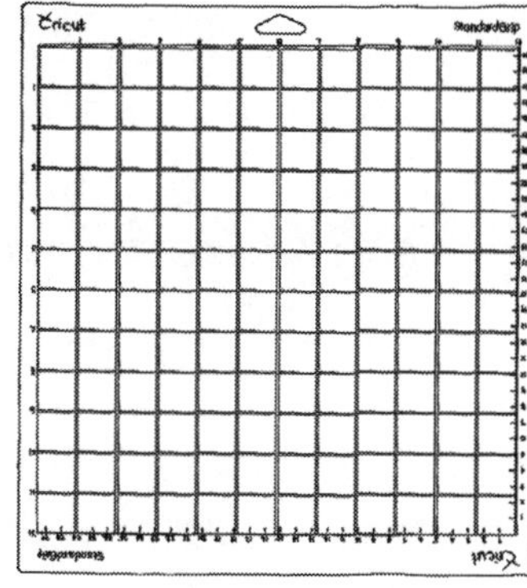

A cutting mat (also known as a Cricut mat) is essential for most digital die-cutting machines like Cricut. It's a sticky mat on which you place the material you want your machine to cut. Once the material is secure, you can insert the mat into your Cricut, using the guides at its opening to make sure the mat lines up with the machine's rollers (these will grip and control the mat as your Cricut cuts). Cutting mats are important for the following reasons:

- A cutting mat provides a stable surface for your machine to cut on. Without this stability, your Cricut would not be able to make accurate cuts.
- A cutting mat protects your machine's cutting blade from blunting prematurely by providing it with a soft surface to work on.
- You can use the measurements on your mat, together with the Preview screen of Design Space, to optimize how much material you use during a cutting session. This is especially useful when working with scraps (leftover material from your previous projects).

Apart from the Cricut Joy, all Cricut machines use 12" by 12" or 12" by 24" cutting mats, and the size of your design will determine what size mat you'll need. The Cricut Joy uses 4,5" by 6,5" or 4,5" by 12" mats. In addition, it has a special mat called the Cricut Joy Card Mat, made specifically for greeting card projects.

In 2020, when the Cricut Joy was released, the company introduced a cool feature: the ability to cut materials without a cutting mat. However, this feature requires the use of Cricut Smart Materials. Cricut's introduction of Smart Materials proved so popular that they built the feature into their latest generation of machines, the Explore 3 and Maker 3. We'll talk more about Smart Materials in the upcoming chapters.

Apart from choosing the right mat size for your project, you'll want the right amount of tackiness for the material you'll cut. This is important—you don't want your material to rip because it's stuck too tight *or* shift around because it's too loose while your machine cuts out a project. Luckily, with Cricut's color-coded mats, it's easy to choose the right one for your projects. Let's have a quick look at each mat.

Blue for *LightGrip*

If you're working with materials you consider flimsy, the blue mat is perfect. It has the least amount of adhesive grip for projects that require paper, vellum, lightweight cardstock, and other materials that can tear during the cutting process or when removing it from the cutting mat after a cut.

Green for *StandardGrip*

Some materials require a stronger grip to keep them in place while your Cricut works. For those, such as vinyl, Iron-On (or heat transfer vinyl), patterned and textured paper, and other heavier materials, you can rely on Cricut's *StandardGrip* cutting mat. This is also the most popular cutting mat under Cricut crafters. As a Newbie, you'll probably use it a lot, too.

Purple for *StrongGrip*

The Cricut Maker and Cricut Maker 3 are the brand's heavy-duty machines. Although they can also cut lightweight materials, they are also capable of applying a lot of pressure when cutting. Thus, these two models can cut over 300 different materials, from leather to wood, to craft foam, to thick cardstock. We call those materials heavy-weight materials, and they require a mat with enough stickiness to hold them in place for the cutting process. The *StrongGrip* mat offers just that.

Pink for *FabricGrip*

Cricut offers a special cutting mat with a perfect blend of density and adhesiveness for a variety of fabrics. It's strong enough to hold fabric in place for the cut but allows you to release the fabric easily enough without causing damage to your design.

The good news is that you don't have to remember which color works for which materials. All you have to do is look at your cutting mat's upper right-hand corner and read the mat's name.

How to Place Material on the Cutting Mat

All Cricut mats have one-inch grids printed on their sticky sides. (They also have centimeter measurements for those who don't work in inches. So, when you place material on your mat, just be sure you're working with the right orientation for your needs.) The grid's border indicates where the mat's adhesive layer ends, so be sure to stick your material within the border. Another reason it's important to stay within the border is so that there are no obstacles in your machine's way while it cuts out your design. Trust me, you don't want to jam your precious Cricut!

Use the upper-left corner of the grid on the mat as the starting point to place the material on your cutting mat. Once you have placed the material, use your palm, a brayer, or a Cricut Scraper to smooth everything out before feeding the mat into your machine.

Good to Know

- Cricut mats are reusable.
- Keep your hands off the sticky area of your mats whenever you handle them. Your fingers give off oils that can break down the mats' adhesive coatings.
- Keep the plastic sleeves that your mats came with and re-apply the sleeves when you don't use your mats. This will allow you to use your mats for a longer time.
- I'll share more cutting mat tips and tricks, including how to clean and store them, in Chapter 11.

Step 4: Load Your Cutting Mat into Your Cricut

Once you have selected the relevant material in Design Space, you'll see a blinking light on your Cricut machine, indicating that it's waiting for the mat. Use both your hands to align the mat with the guides at either side of the machine's opening. When you're happy, press the blinking light. Your machine will measure the mat and the material's size to double-check that it can cut according to the size instructions you gave in Design Space. If there was a slight misalignment when you inserted the mat, your machine will try to realign it automatically. You'll know your machine is ready to cut out the project when the *Go* button starts blinking after it has measured the mat.

On the Cricut Explore Air 2 and Cricut Maker, the *Go* button is the "C", while on the newer models, the Cricut Explore 3 and Cricut Maker 3, the *Go* button is the one with a "play" sign on it.

Step 5: Press That Button!

When you're ready, go ahead and press the blinking *Go* button to start the cutting process. The Cricut Joy has no buttons at all. To tell you it's ready for the cutting mat, you'll see a blinking light on top of the machine. When you insert the mat, your machine will grip and measure it automatically and the light will stop blinking. From there, you can press the *Go* button on your Design Space app to initiate the cutting process.

You can keep yourself busy with something else while you wait for your Cricut to cut the project, but—fair warning—you won't be able to resist staring in a trance as your machine works. And no, it never gets old.

How long your machine will work to cut a design depends on the material and intricacy of the project, but it's always a fairly quick process. Once done, the button with an up/down arrow on your machine will blink to tell you it's time to unload the mat. To release the mat from the machine, press the button. The last step is to click the *Finish* button in Design Space to let the program know the project is complete. With the Cricut Joy, you'll unload the mat using the Design Space app, just like you used it to initiate the cut.

See? Operating a Cricut machine is as easy as counting from one to five, but way more fun and rewarding. Design Space makes the process intuitive and, as long as you choose the right cutting mat for your material, there's really not much that can go wrong. If you experience issues, though, consult the troubleshooting guide in Chapter 12 or contact Cricut support to help you.

In the following three chapters, we'll explore everything there is to know about the different Cricut cutting machines. If you already have your Cricut, feel free to page to the chapter that deals with the model you own (Chapter 3 deals with the Cricut Joy, Chapter 4 deals with the Cricut Explore series, and Chapter 5 deals with the Maker series).

If you're still undecided and feel unsure about which machine will serve your needs, take your time studying Chapters 3 to 5 and make notes along the way to help you remember which machine's features stand out to you.

Chapter 2 Notes

Use this space to jot down the best take-aways you learned from Chapter 2. Use these notes as your personal quick-reference guide whenever you want to refresh your memory ons something specific.

CHAPTER 3

MEET THE CRICUT JOY

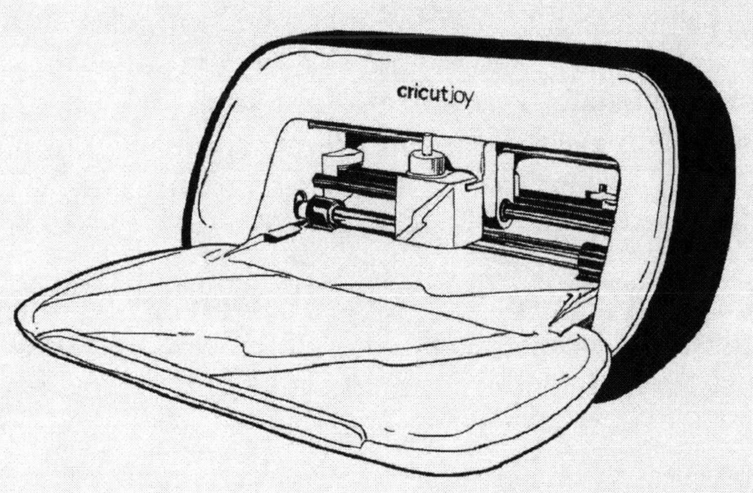

Cricut calls the Joy "Your DIY Best Friend," which is a perfect description for this tiny but mighty cutting machine. More or less the length of your forearm and slightly shorter than the height a classic coffee mug, Cricut's smallest machine is in a league of its own.

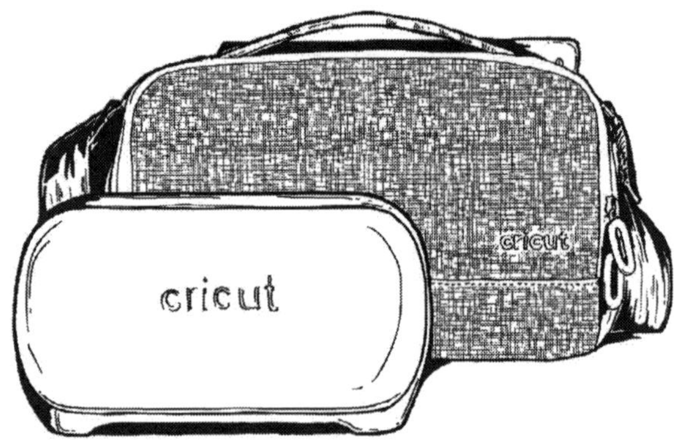

Features

Portability

This machine is not only small; it's light, making it easy to travel with you wherever you go. We crafters have a problem: inspiration and the need to create can hit at the weirdest (and sometimes awkward) moments.

But that's OK. Those closest to you know (or will know soon enough) that us artsy types are, well ... different. Weird and wonderful—that's us.

Now picture this: you get to work and everyone is in higher spirits than usual. You pull your colleague bestie to the side and ask what's up. An incredulous expression is followed by "Um, it's the boss's birthday. Don't tell me you forgot!"

Oh. No.

But wait ...

You can create a stunning birthday card in just a few minutes. And, hands-down, it's going to be the most impressive one among the lot. You can even get a cool Cricut Joy carry bag for the easy and safe transportation of your little companion. The bag has two compartments: one for the machine and another for the power cord and tools.

No Buttons

The Cricut Joy connects to your computer, tablet, or phone via Bluetooth. From there, you can operate it using the Design Space app. Once plugged into the wall, the machine will automatically switch on and be ready to bring your project ideas to life. It works with a standard power cord that needs to be plugged into the wall, and it doesn't even have a USB port.

Unique Tools and Accessories

The Cricut Joy's tools are specific to it and cannot be interchanged with any of the other Cricut models' tools. This is because the Cricut Joy is so much smaller than the other machines. Let's explore the Cricut Joy's tools.

Cutting Blade

The Cricut Joy works with a single, all-purpose fine-point blade. It can handle lightweight materials like cardstock, various adhesive and Iron-On vinyls, and a range of papers. The Cricut Joy comes out of the box with a pre-installed blade. In time, though, your blade will become dull with use and lose its ability to make crisp cuts. When the time comes, you'll need to install a replacement blade from Cricut.

Cricut Joy Foil Transfer Tool

Together with foil transfer sheets, you can use the Cricut Joy foil transfer tool to add a professional-looking foil effect to paper and cardstock projects. You won't find this tool in the box when you buy your Cricut Joy, so you have to buy it separately if you have a need to use it for your projects.

Cricut Joy Pens and Markers

Cricut offers a decent range of pens and markers for all kinds of writing and drawing projects. The best part is that all Cricut pens and markers are non-toxic and acid-free. You can buy them in sets online from Cricut.com or from certain craft stores that supply Cricut products.

Cutting Mats

The Cricut Joy uses *LightGrip* and *StandardGrip* mats in two sizes: 4.5" by 6.5" and 4.5" by 12." Since the machine is small and does not exert the pressure needed to cut heavy materials, there is no *StrongGrip* mat for it. However, the Cricut Joy does have a specialized Card Mat unique to this model, which allows you to create greeting cards effortlessly.

Smart Materials

With Cricut *Smart Materials*, your machine does not need a cutting mat to cut out designs, as the *Smart Materials* come with thicker backings that the machine blade cannot cut through. (The backing is the sheet to which your crafting material is attached and is also known as the carrier sheet.).

However, the range of *Smart Materials* is limited, so you still need cutting mats for specialty projects. And, as with everything in life, Smart Materials come with the good and the bad. Let's see what they are.

Smart Materials Pros

- They're not limited by the length of a cutting mat, so you can cut a continuous shape up to 4 feet long or repetitive shapes up to 20 feet long in one go.

- The materials are thicker than their regular equivalents and have a high quality look and feel.
- They cut fantastic.
- It's easy to weed *Smart Materials.*

Smart Materials Cons

- It's a little harder to apply *Smart Materials* to surfaces than it is to apply regular materials.
- Some people have had issues transferring *Smart Materials* with transfer tape.

Smart Materials are more expensive than regular materials, and, once they've lost their width (from being used), you'll need your good old cutting mat to use the scraps for other projects. Whether you'll have use for *Smart Materials* depends on what you want to use your machine for. That said, the introduction of *Smart Materials* to the Cricut Community was met with a lot of excitement. Cricut will definitely continue to develop the technology and add more options. In the world of crafting, it pays to be bold and try new stuff, so don't hesitate to try out these innovative materials.

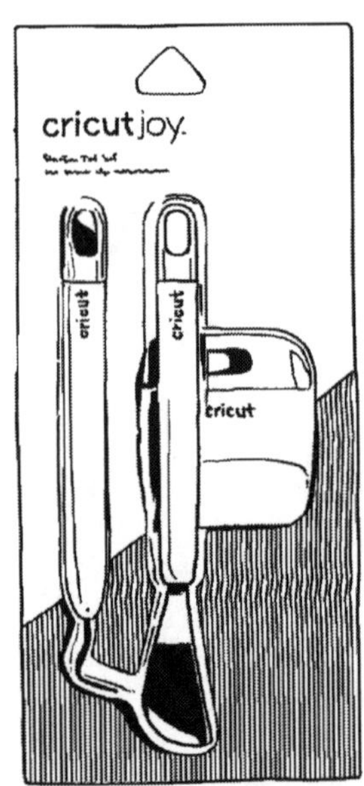

Cricut Joy Starter Tool Set

To complete your projects with ease, you'll need help from a few handheld tools, which Cricut offers in a cool little bundle. The tool set includes:

A Spatula: Use this tool to lift materials from your cutting mat after the machine completes a cutting project. You'll especially appreciate this simple but effective tool when working with delicate materials like paper.

A Weeder: Remove unwanted scraps from a newly cut project easily and fast. In the old days, you'd have to block off the entire afternoon just to weed! (We'll chat about weeding later.)

A Scraper: The scraper serves two purposes. One, it helps to clean up your cutting mat after a cut; and two, you'll use it to apply vinyl decals to surfaces.

How to Change Cricut Joy Tools

As mentioned earlier, the Cricut Joy works with a Foil Transfer Tool and pens, too. However, it has space for only one tool at a time. Whenever you work with projects that require another tool, making the change is easy. Simply open the tool holder clamp by pulling it toward yourself.

Take out the current tool (probably the cutting blade) by lifting it out of the tool holder and replace it with a pen or the Foil Transfer tool by slipping it into the same space. To secure the new tool, push the clamp toward the machine until it clicks and rests tightly against the too holder again.

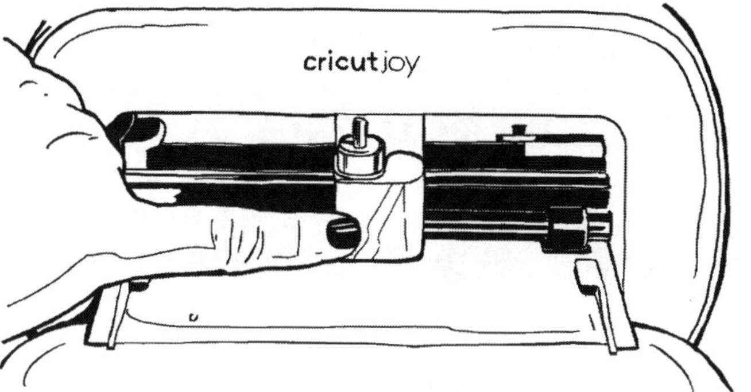

Cricut joy Must-Have Tools, Accessories & Materials

Although you can buy the Cricut Joy as is, there is not much you'll be able to do with it unless you stock up on the things you'll need to complete your first projects. Through the years, I have learned that it's better to be prepared and have the essentials in place, rather than discovering you need something in the middle of a project. It's kind of like taking your baby on an outing ... It's all fun and games until you realize you forgot the diapers.

Tools

- Replacement blades. Whether or not you'll craft often, your machine's cutting blade will eventually become so dull, it just won't do you any favors anymore.
- Cricut Joy Starter Tool Set (includes the spatula, weeder, and scraper as on the previous page).

Accessories

- An extra set of *LightGrip* and *StandardGrip* cutting mats in all sizes.
- At least one extra black pen and at least one black marker. If you can, you might just as well invest in a set of colored pens and markers, as you will probably want them once you start making more projects anyway.

Materials

- Cricut Joy Smart Vinyl.
- Transfer Tape (a see-through adhesive tape that you use to transfer adhesive materials like vinyl and Iron-On from their backings onto their intended surfaces).
- Cricut Joy Insert Cards (to make amazing greeting cards).

Note that although you need materials to cut your first projects, it doesn't make sense to go on a shopping spree, either. Invest in one to three colors of vinyl and one to three colors of cardstock to start with. Those materials will last you long enough to get comfortable using your Cricut Joy. When you're ready to take on new projects, you'll know exactly what to get and how much of it you'll need. Cricut products are easy to come by, as they're available from many brick-and-mortar and online craft stores.

Materials You Can Cut with the Cricut Joy

Despite its cuteness and size, this machine can cut many materials for almost any DIY project you can think of. Let's see what you can work with for your projects.

Material Category	**Material Name**
Art Board	Corrugated Cardboard Flat Cardboard Foil Poster Board
Cardstock	Glitter Cardstock Insert-Card Cardstock Medium Cardstock (80 lb, 216 gsm)
Iron-On	***Everyday Iron-On*** - Regular - Mesh - Mosaic - Glitter Mesh - Holographic - Holographic Mosaic - Holographic Sparkle ***Infusible Ink*** - Infusible Ink Transfer Sheet ***Smart Iron-On*** - Regular - Glitter - Holographic - Patterned - SportFlex
Leather	Faux Leather (Paper Thin)

Material Category	Material Name
Paper	***Deluxe Paper*** - Regular - Adhesive Backed - Foil Embossed Foil Paper – 0.36mm Pearl Paper Shimmer Paper Smart Label Writable Paper Sparkle Paper True Brushed Paper
Plastic	Foil Acetate
Vinyl	Adhesive Foil Chalkboard Vinyl Dry Erase Vinyl Holographic Sparkle Vinyl ***Premium Vinyl*** - Regular - Frosted Glitter - Frosted Gray - Frosted Opaque - Holographic (Regular) - Holographic 3D Textured - Holographic Art Deco - Holographic Bubbles - Holographic Crystals - Holographic Threads - Mosaic - Pearl - Textured - Textured Metallic - True Brush Smart Label Writable Vinyl

Material Category	**Material Name**
Vinyl	***Smart Vinyl*** - Holographic Patterns - Matte Metallic - Permanent - Removable - Shimmer Stencil Vinyl
Other	Party Foil Window Cling

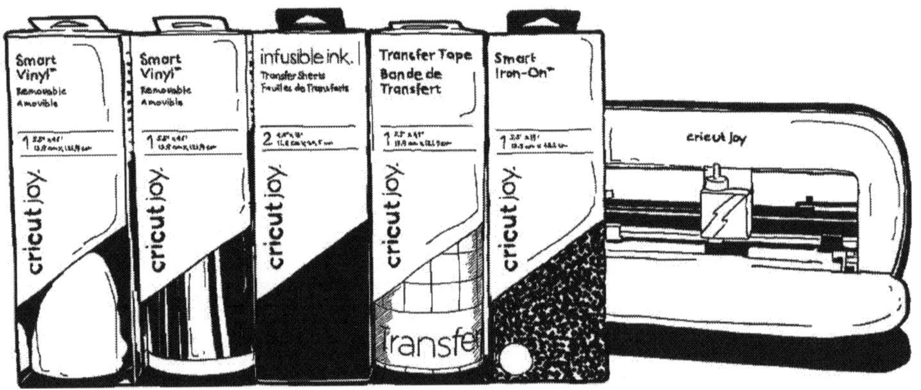

Who Needs the Cricut Joy?

If you are new to the world of crafting and would love a stress-free way to dip your toes in the vast ocean of arts and crafts, the Cricut Joy is yours. Even if you (highly unlikely) discover crafting is not for you, investing in this cute little digital cutter will never be a waste. There will always be something you need it for, whether it's to make labels for organizing your life or to spice up a room with vinyl decals.

Also, I really think this is the perfect machine to get your kids interested in crafting and a way to bribe them into spending time with you. Hey, Mom's gotta do what Mom's gotta do, right? Seriously, though, despite its small size, The Cricut Joy will provide hours of fun and you'll have something to show for it at the end of the day. But, please, don't leave your kiddos alone with this or any cutting machine. That blade is incredibly sharp and can cause havoc if those little fingers go exploring where they're better off not doing so.

If you are a seasoned crafter, you won't regret adding the Cricut Joy to your ever-expanding collection of crafting tools. And, let's face it—we're not always in the mood to start up our bigger machines for small stuff. With the Cricut Joy in your home or crafting space, you'll have just the right tool for quick and easy projects. The best part is that the machine is tiny, so "I have no more space" is no excuse for not getting one.

The Cricut Joy is indeed anyone's DIY best friend. Its amazing versatility, backed by its small size and portability, makes it a must-have for Newbies and pros alike. That said, if you're new to crafting and this is your first and only machine, I have a hunch that you'll outgrow it pretty fast. Once the crafting bug bites, you'll grow an insatiable desire to create new things all the time. Soon, you'll want to experiment with more than what the Joy can offer, and that's where Cricut's other machines, the Explore and Maker series, can help.

Chapter 3 Notes

Use this space to jot down the best take-aways you learned from Chapter 3. Use these notes as your personal quick-reference guide whenever you want to refresh your memory ons something specific.

CHAPTER 4

MEET THE CRICUT EXPLORE SERIES

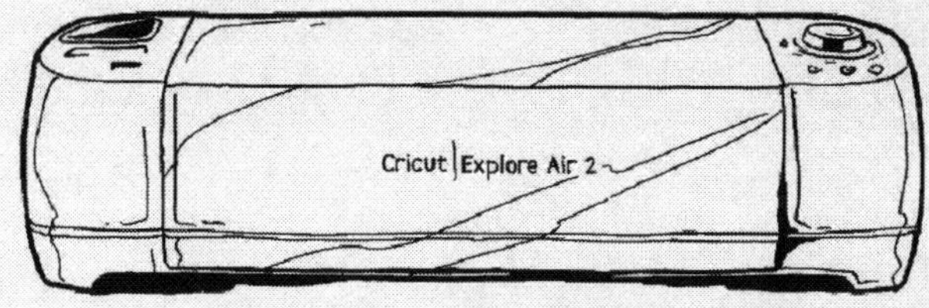

If the Cricut Joy is your DIY best friend, the Cricut Explore series represents your *all-you-need-and-more* crafting bestie. There are actually five machines in the Explore series, but we'll be focusing on the two latest models, the Explore Air 2 and the Explore 3. The explore machines are 22.17" by 7.01"—a convenient size that can fit somewhere in your home or in your craft room with ease; and with the ability to cut fairly large projects, it will suit most of your crafting needs.

Meet the Cricut Explore Air 2

I am particularly fond of the Explore Air 2, as this was my very first Cricut. It's a wonderfully reliable, user-friendly, and downright beautiful machine. It's also the most popular Cricut among newbie and pro crafters alike. If you already have your machine, there's a fair chance this is the one. And if you're still deciding which one will be best for you, this might be it. Although the Explore Air 2 came out in late 2016, it's still a fabulous choice in 2023.

Features

Colors Galore!

The Explore Air 2 is the only Cricut machine that comes in a stunning variety of colors. We arty folk are always looking for an excuse to let our personalities shine through, which makes this simple feature cool and exciting.

From wild rose to emerald, to sunflower, to mint, to matte black and everything in between, there are 22 colors to choose from. The machines on Cricut's website aren't available in all the colors, though, so be sure to shop around online and offline until you find your match.

The Smart Set Dial and Other Buttons

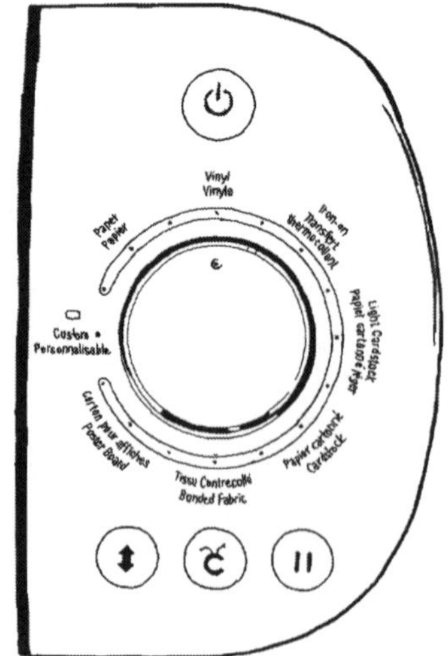

A trademark of the Explore series is the *Smart Set Dial*, which was introduced with the release of the Cricut Explore (the first machine in the Explore series) upon its release in 2014. The Smart Set Dial is a round knob on top of the machine. It has different options that represent the most common materials you'll cut with your machine but in reality, you can make projects made from over 100 materials. The options on the Smart Set Dial are:

- Paper
- Vinyl
- Iron-On
- Light Cardstock

- Cardstock
- Fabric
- Poster Board
- Custom

The last option, *Custom*, is the one you'll choose whenever you want to cut materials other than the ones on the dial. These can include things like felt, fabric, or wood (yes, wood!). You'll have a chance to tell your Cricut exactly which material it will cut when you confirm your project in Design Space. By simply turning the knob, your machine will use just the right amount of pressure and speed for your projects. So, even if you're not technically inclined, the machine is a breeze to operate.

Above the *Smart Set Dial*, you'll see the power button. Underneath the dial are three more buttons:

- One with arrows facing up and down, which you'll use to load and unload your cutting mat.
- Another one with the Cricut logo on it, called the *Go* button, which you'll press to start the cutting process once you have loaded the cutting mat into your machine.
- The last one has two vertical strokes, which you'll use to pause the cutting process if the need arises.

On top of the left side of the machine is a button that says *Open*. You'll press that one to make the top and front panels of your machine open in the most satisfying way. The little flap just above the open button is a nod to Cricut's older machines, which worked with cartridges. If you're familiar with Cricut and are looking for an upgrade, you'll be pleased to know you can still insert your cartridges into the Explore Air 2, into that compartment underneath the flap. If you're a brand new Cricut crafter, you need not be concerned about cartridges at all, as you'll never use them. Design Space has replaced all previous methods of giving a Cricut machine instructions to cut projects.

Double Tool Holder

The Explore series can house two tools at the same time. Not all projects require two tools, and the machine can still work magic if one holder is empty.

Storage Compartments

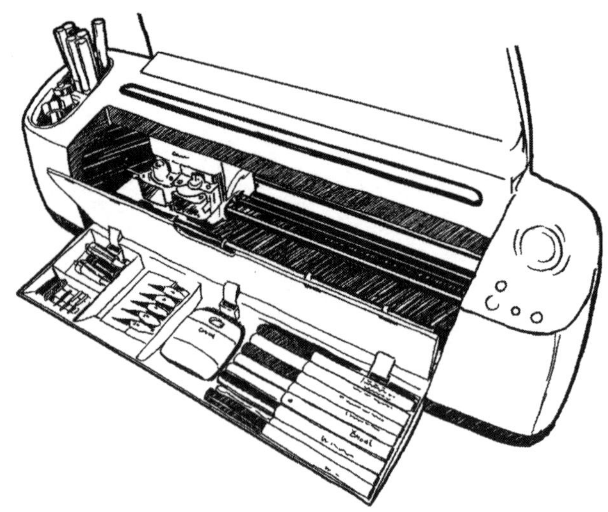

OK ... Hands up! Who has crafty stuff ALL OVER the place? Yeah, I can't help it, either. But we're in luck because Cricut has our backs. First, although you can achieve so much with these machines, they don't have a ton of tools. That said, the larger your machine, the more capabilities it offers, and with that comes more goodies.

Both the Cricut Explore and Cricut Maker series help you stay organized with storage compartments built into the machines. They all have a storage hole on top of the machine (to the left when you're in front of it). These holes are slightly larger on the Explore 3, Maker, and Maker 3 than on the Explore Air 2. The storage hole on top of your machine is perfect for tools you use regularly need easy access to. The front panel (or front door) that covers the opening where you insert your cutting mat has flaps you can lift when its open. Underneath those flaps are extra storage compartments for things you don't use all the time, like replacement blades.

Wireless and USB Connectivity

If having too many wires around tends to disrupt your creativity, you can pair your machine to your computer, laptop, or mobile device using the machine's built-in Bluetooth. The Bluetooth activates the moment you switch on the machine, so all you have to do is go to your computer or mobile device's Bluetooth setting to make the connection. If you're asked for a password, it's 0000.

If you're not into wireless connections or you're having Bluetooth connection issues, you can use the USB cable that came with your machine to connect it to your computer or laptop. If you only have a cell phone to operate Design Space, you'll need to connect the machine and cell phone via Bluetooth.

Fast Mode

The Explore Air 2 has a setting that allows it to cut (and write on) certain materials at twice the speed of its older sibling, the Cricut Explore Air.

Tools & Accessories

Cutting Blades

While the Cricut Joy works with an all-purpose fine-point blade, the Explore Air 2 can use three specialty blades to suit your crafting needs.

Fine-Point Blade

This is the Standard Cricut blade you will use most of the time. It's made from German carbide steel, which is probably the best there is. You can cut a variety of materials, including vinyl, Iron-On, poster board, and cardstock. This blade and its housing are gold. When you buy an Explore Air 2, it comes with a pre-installed fine-point blade.

Deep-Point Blade

This is technically also a fine-point Blade, but it has a steeper angle and is made from a harder steel than the regular fine-point blade. You'd be right if you've guessed it must be for thicker materials. You'll install the deep-point blade instead of the fine-point blade whenever you work with materials like magnet strips, felt, foam, stamp material, and cardboard. The blade and its housing are black. If you're just starting out with crafting and you're not sure what you'll cut with it yet, the fine-point blade will be enough to get you started. However, when you're ready to experiment with medium-weight materials, it will be time to invest in a deep-point blade.

Bonded-Fabric Blade

If you're into fabric, you'll love using the Explore Air to bring your sewing creations to life. Since fabric can take its toll on blades, Cricut has designed one specifically for that use. It has a longer life span and can stay sharp for many fabric projects before it needs a replacement. This blade and its housing are pink, which matches nicely with the pink *FabricGrip* cutting mat. Cricut certainly makes crafting a breeze with their use of color to help you distinguish between different tools. Unless you are into sewing or have plans to cut fabric regularly with your machine, you won't need to get this blade.

Other Specialty Tools and Accessories

Foil Transfer Tool

As with the Cricut Joy, you can create wonderful and professional-looking foil effects with the Foil Transfer Tool.

Scoring Stylus

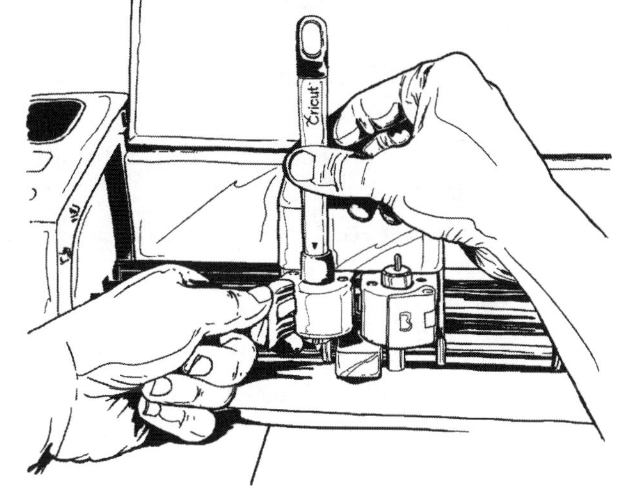

This handy tool makes subtle indented lines in everything that needs folding. Think of greeting cards, envelopes, and tiny shopping bags (because who doesn't love shopping bags and cute tiny things?)

For projects that require the scoring stylus, you'll be happy to know your machine can do both the cutting and scoring in one go, as the stylus will go into tool holder A (on your left) while the blade will go into tool holder B (on your right).

Cutting Mats

The Explore Air 2 works with all the Cricut mats we discussed in Chapter 2 (apart from the smaller Cricut Joy mats).

Handheld Tools

Whether you buy a Cricut Joy or any of the Explore or Maker series machines, your life will be easier with the same handheld tools we talked about in the Cricut Joy chapter:

- Scraper (these come in different sizes)
- Spatula
- Weeder

Cricut Pens and Markers

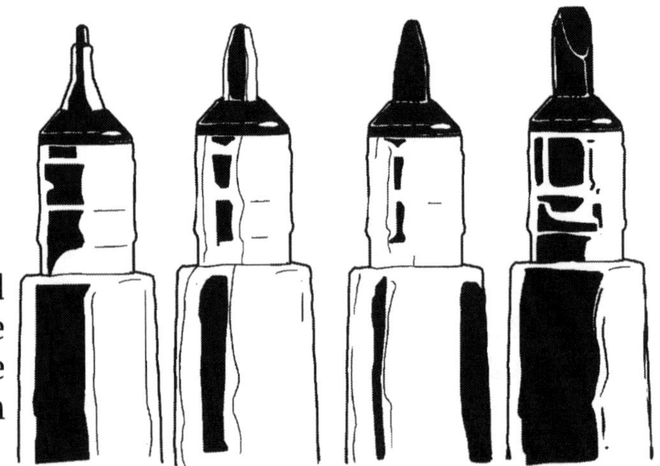

Cricut has a large variety of pens and markers to help you create unique illustrations and artful words. Because the Explore Air 2 has two tool holders, it can draw (or write) and cut in one go.

Note that there are other tools, such as a brayer, tweezers, scissors, and a trimmer. All tools are useful and can make your crafting projects run smoother and quicker, but by no means are *all of them* crucial to your crafting journey when you're just getting started. Get them if you can, but don't let their potential absence stop you from buying your Cricut machine.

Who Needs the Cricut Explore Air 2?

The Cricut Explore series is the perfect match for Newbies who are into DIY but also want to stretch their creativity to the next level. What makes the Explore Air 2 so special is the fact that it puts professional and awesome-looking results in the hands of those who have little to no crafting experience, and it doesn't come with a gigantic learning curve that can discourage you from pursuing your passion.

I cannot begin to explain the boost of confidence, motivation, and the sheer pat-on-your-own-shoulder good feeling you'll get when you see your first completed project. A huge bonus with the Explore Air 2 is that it's reliable and robust enough to help you start a crafting business. Once you're confident with your machine, there is no reason you can't put yourself out there and offer custom-made items like greeting cards, personalized mugs, t-shirts, home and office decals, or whatever you want to offer.

If you're a seasoned crafter looking for an additional tool to expand your business, you can't go wrong with this machine. That said, you might want to check out the Maker series before making your decision.

Meet the Cricut Explore 3

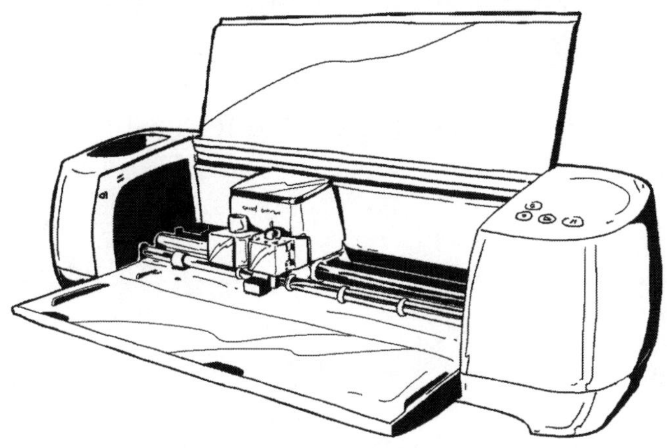

The Cricut Explore 3 is the newest sibling among the Explore series machines. It's the same size as its older sibling, the Explore Air 2, works with the same tools, and cuts the same materials. That said, there are three major differences between the Explore 3 and the Explore Air 2:

1. The Explore 3's design is slightly different.

2. The Explore 3 works with Cricut *Smart Materials*, whereas the Explore Air 2 only works with cutting mats.

3. The Explore 3 cuts twice as fast as the Explore Air 2.

Features

Design Changes

This is the first machine in the Explore series without the *Smart Set Dial*. As with the Cricut Joy, Maker, and Maker 3, you will only use Design Space to tell your machine which material it's going to cut.

The *Go* button, which you press to start the cutting process, no longer features the Cricut logo but instead has a "play" sign on it. This is probably to make the machine even more user-friendly, as the "play" sign is universal and understood by most to represent "start" or "go."

The top storage compartment (to your left when looking at the machine from the front) is bigger than on the Explore Air 2, as the new machine no longer caters for the old Cricut cartridges.

Matless Cutting

The Cricut Explore 3, like the Cricut Joy, has the capability of cutting projects without the traditional cutting mats. The best part about matless cutting is that you can let your machine cut *Smart Materials* that are up to 12 feet in one go. Note that you should only use the Cricut brand of *Smart Materials* with your Explore 3. Although there are similar materials for digital die-cut machines out there that don't require cutting mats, Cricut has not tested them with their machines. So, they are best avoided if you want to save your machine from technical issues or from producing substandard results.

Speed

The Explore 3 cuts even faster than the Explore Air 2's Fast Mode setting, especially with the new *Smart Materials.*

Shortened Name

Back when Cricut released the Explore Air and Explore Air 2, the use of Bluetooth to connect devices was still a new thing, and most devices needed special Bluetooth adapters to work. The Cricut Explore Air and Explore Air 2 had the "Air" in their names to advertise their then state-of-the-art built-in Bluetooth capabilities. These days, built-in Bluetooth is a given in most devices, so the company dropped the "Air" in the latest Explore machine's name.

Apart from updated technology and the above changes, the rest of the Explore 3's features are identical to the Explore Air 2. It even works with the same tools and is capable of cutting the same variety of materials as the Explore Air 2.

Who Needs the Cricut Explore 3?

The Explore 3 is just as beginner-friendly as the Explore Air 2 and will serve you well if you are serious about crafting for fun or developing your skills so you can start a crafting business. But if you inherited or received an Explore Air 2 as a gift, you need not be concerned about upgrading your machine just yet. The older model is still very much relevant and will give you many years of service and fun.

However, if you're still contemplating which machine to buy, I think the Explore 3 should be a stronger consideration than the Explore Air 2—if you can afford it—simply because it is a newer machine. That said, even if you have the money and you don't see yourself needing to work with Smart Materials, there's nothing wrong with choosing the Explore Air 2.

Cricut Explore Must-Have Tools, Accessories & Materials

Whether you have (or will get) the Explore Air 2 or Explore 3, the extra supplies you need remain the same, apart from some Smart Materials for the Explore 3, which I'll point out below:

Tools

- Replacement fine-point Blades.
- Cricut Essential Tool Set. (You'll learn more about this tool set in Chapter 8.)
- Bonded-Fabric Blade (if your main craft is working with fabrics).

Accessories

- An extra set of *LightGrip*, *StandardGrip*, and *StrongGrip* cutting mats in all sizes.
- At least one black Cricut pen and one black Cricut marker (but get sets of colored pens and markers if you can; you might need them sooner than you think).

Materials

- Adhesive vinyl
- Iron-on or Heat Transfer (HTV) Vinyl
- Transfer Tape
- Cardstock
- Removable Smart Vinyl (if you have the Explore 3).
- Smart Iron-On (if you have the Explore 3).

As with the Cricut Joy, I recommend that you *don't* stockpile on your first materials; it's good enough to buy one roll of each or (at most) three different colors of each. If you have an Explore 3, I suggest you get normal adhesive vinyl and Smart Vinyl to see the difference between cutting with a cutting mat and without one.

Materials You Can Cut with the Cricut Explore Series Machines

There are over 100 materials you can cut with the Cricut Explore machines. These include everything you can cut with the Cricut Joy, plus:

- Adhesive Foil
- Aluminum Foil

- Birch Wood
- Canvas
- Adhesive-backed Cork
- Different Fabrics
- Craft Foam
- Wool-Bonded and Wool Fabric Felt
- Genuine Leather
- Light Chipboard
- And more! (Check out the Cricut website for information on all the materials you can cut with your Explore Air 2.)

Note: You can't cut Smart Materials with the Cricut Explore Air 2.

Let's check out the Cricut Maker series next.

Chapter 4 Notes

Use this space to jot down the best take-aways you learned from Chapter 4. Use these notes as your personal quick-reference guide whenever you want to refresh your memory ons something specific.

CHAPTER 5

MEET THE CRICUT MAKER SERIES

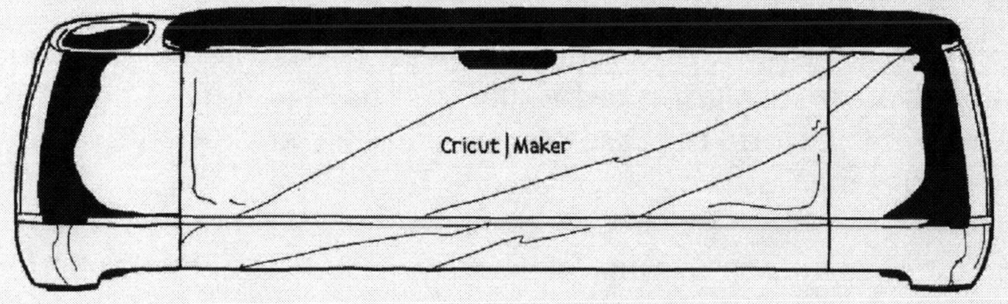

Cricut's Maker series is just as easy to operate as the Cricut Joy and the Explore series. So, really, if you're a new crafter and received the Maker or Maker 3 as a gift, there's absolutely nothing to worry about. This chapter will help eliminate any overwhelm that may be stopping you from starting your first project. If you're still shopping around and haven't quite fallen head over hills for the Cricut Joy or the Cricut Explore series, the Maker series is sure to win your heart.

Meet the Cricut Maker

Since the Explore 3 no longer features the *Smart Dial Set*, it's easy to miss the difference between it and the Cricut Maker if you give the two a quick glance. They may look similar, but, like any siblings, they've got their differences.

Features

Physical Traits

The Cricut Maker is no smaller than the Explore Air 2 at face value; but, if you really, really wish the Explore Air 2 was just 0.99 inches shorter, you'll be happy to know the Maker offers just that. At 21.18'' by 6.99'', the Maker offers a slightly more streamlined design.

The Maker has a USB port on the lower end of its right side that allows you to charge your tablet or cell phone while working in Design Space. There is also a space on top of the machine where your tablet or cell phone can rest while you create designs or wait for the machine to finish a cut.

Another small but significant difference between the Explore series and the Maker series is a teeny bit more storage space for tools on the Maker machines. Yes, this makes all the difference in the world because your Maker can work with twice as many tools as the Explore series machines.

The Cricut Maker does not feature an *Open* button like the Explore machines. Although this might have been done with more practicality in mind, I really would have loved to press a button and watch it open all by itself in the same mesmerizing way as my Cricut Explore Air 2. With the Maker, when you pull on the top panel ever so slightly, the machine will still open up automatically. But the real magic, of course, lies inside, where your machine can cut over 300 materials.

Close your eyes and let that sink in ...

Is your inner creative bug jumping up and down yet?

The easiest way to tell the Maker apart from the Explore 3 is by looking at the machine's top panel. With the Explore 3, you can always see the right-side buttons on top of the machine, whereas the Maker's top panel covers the buttons when the machine is closed.

Being the most robust of the Cricut machines, the Maker series is so much more than a DIY buddy—it's a reliable business partner with a fun and magical side (who just so happens to be a DIY expert, too!).

Tools and Accessories

Cutting Blades and Specialty Tools

The Maker works with all the blades and specialty tools the Cricut Explore Air 2 and Explore 3 work with, but it has even more to offer. By the way, the Explore series and Maker series tools are interchangeable, apart from the ones we'll chat about below, which you can only use with the Cricut Maker and Maker 3:

Rotary Blade

This blade looks kind of like a tiny pizza cutter. It spins as it cuts and can move in any direction, which makes it super precise. It's especially useful for cutting fabric. While the Cricut Explore series can also cut fabric, the results are honestly so much better with the Cricut Maker's revolutionary rotary blade. Also, while you need special backing or a stabilizer when cutting fabric with the Explore series, there is no need for it with the Maker series. So, if you're a crafter who works with fabric a lot, the Maker series will serve you better. There are other soft materials you can cut really well with the rotary blade, including felt and even tissue paper.

Knife Blade

Sturdy materials call for a sturdy blade, and that's where the Cricut knife blade has your back. It can cut deeper than the other blades and is perfect for strong and thicker materials like acetate, mat boards, and wood. The blade also features adjustable star wheels that can adapt based on the thickness of the material it cuts, which is brilliant because you don't want marks on your precious projects.

QuickSwap Tools

These are the tools that really set the Maker series apart from its siblings. *QuickSwap* tools are basically end bits that fit on a specialized housing, called the *QuickSwap* housing. With these bits at your disposal, the possibilities of what you can achieve with your Cricut are literally endless. And the best part? As time goes by, you'll see more and more tools being added to this collection, and you won't need to replace your machine to use them. So, the Cricut Maker series was made to grow with you on your crafting journey.

Currently, *QuickSwap* Tools include:

- Wavy Blade (To give more interesting edges to cardstock, leather, vinyl, and other projects—because straight edges can get kind of boring, right?)

- Perforation Blade (To make it easy to tear materials apart once cut. Think of coupons, tear-out cards, and similar projects.)
- Engraving Tip (To inscribe text and shapes onto materials like metal, leather, and acrylic.)
- Debossing Tip (To create cool imprints on materials like cardstock.)
- Scoring Wheel and Double Scoring Wheel (To create precise and crisp fold lines for various projects.)

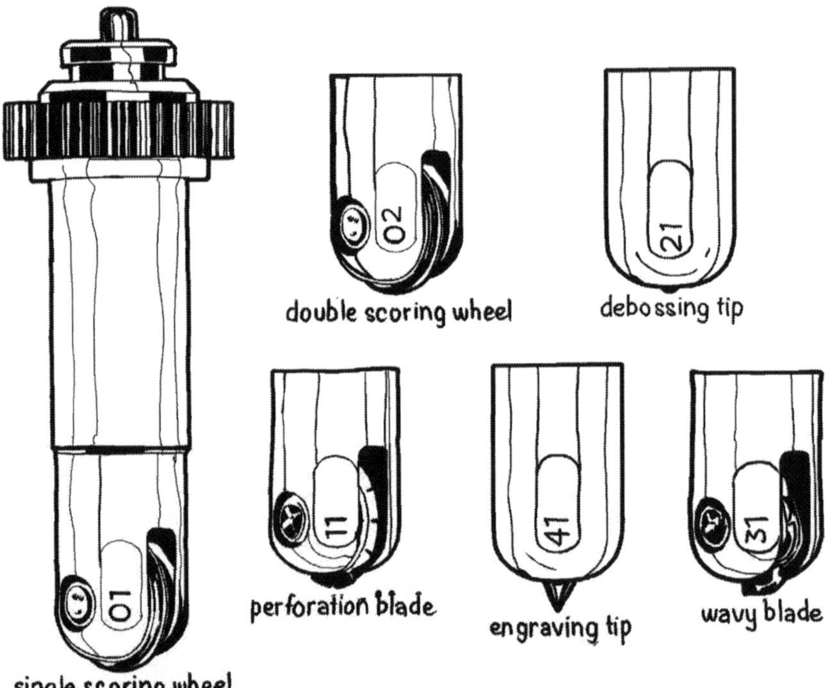

How to Change *QuickSwap* Tools

The QuickSwap housing looks almost like the regular blade housings, but the top looks like a golden-colored gear. On top of the "gear" is a little nib. When you push the nib, it releases the tool tip currently attached to the housing. While pressing the nib down, remove the attached tool tip by gently pulling it away from the housing. To attach the new tool, press down on the housing nib and fit the tool to the other end. Once the tool slides on, release the nib and tug on the tool tip at the other end of the housing to make sure it's secure. You'll know it's secure if it doesn't come loose when you tug on it.

That's it; easier than pie!

Note: If you received a Cricut Maker or Maker 3 as a gift and it included the Scoring Wheel or Double Scoring wheel, you already have the QuickSwap housing and won't need to buy a new one when shopping for other QuickSwap tools. However, if your gift did not include any of the scoring wheels, you'll need to get the QuickSwap housing if you want to use its tools.

When it comes to cutting mats, pens and markers, and handheld tools, the Cricut Maker series works with the same ones as the Explore series.

Who Needs the Cricut Maker?

You and the Maker are meant for each other if you are an established crafter looking to upgrade to a machine with more capabilities, or if you want to expand your current collection to create more specialized projects.

If the above describes you and you can afford the Maker, I think you should get it instead of an Explore machine. While the Explore machines certainly need not stand back for the Maker machines in terms of professional results, it cannot cut all the materials the Maker can, and it's not compatible with the QuickSwap tools.

Consider yourself very, very lucky if you received this amazing machine as a gift because you will have no need to replace it for a long time.

Meet the Cricut Maker 3

Features

Design Changes

The Maker 3 features minor design updates:

The *Go* button is no longer represented by the Cricut logo, but a more universal play sign.

The material tray now features raised material guides, which help you insert your *Smart Materials* or cutting mats into the machine with more precision. As insignificant as this may sound, it's really a time-saver and yet another proof of how Cricut strives to make crafters' lives as easy as possible.

Matless Cutting with Smart Materials

As with the Explore Air 2 and Explore 3, the biggest difference between the Maker and Maker 3 is the Maker 3's ability to cut Cricut *Smart Materials.*

Speed

The Maker 3 can cut twice as fast as its older sibling.

Who Needs the Cricut Maker 3?

At the start of 2023, the Maker 3 is still "the latest and greatest" of all Cricut machines. The only reason I would recommend it over the Maker is if you believe you will often cut Smart Materials. Also, if you want the fastest machine, this is the one. Other than that, the original Maker is the best option. It costs less and will take care of all your crafting needs as your business grows.

Cricut Maker Must-Have Tools, Accessories & Materials

As with the Explore Air 2 or Explore 3, the extra supplies you need remain the same for the Cricut Maker or Maker 3 machines.

Tools

- Replacement fine-point blades.
- Replacement rotary blade.
- The *QuickSwap* Housing and its different tool tips (only if you plan on doing specialized projects from the get-go).
- Cricut Essential Tool Set. (You'll learn more about this tool set in Chapter 8).

Accessories

- An extra set of *LightGrip*, *StandardGrip*, and *StrongGrip* cutting mats in all sizes.
- At least one black Cricut pen and one black Cricut marker (as with the Explore series, consider getting sets of colored pens and markers if you can).

Materials

- Adhesive Vinyl
- Iron-on or Heat Transfer (HTV) Vinyl
- Transfer Tape
- Cardstock
- Removable Smart Vinyl (if you have the Maker 3)
- Smart Iron-On (if you have the Maker 3)

As with the Cricut Explore Series, don't buy too much material at first. Get to know your machine before venturing into more and other (more specialized) materials. However, if you are a seasoned crafter, you should, of course, choose the materials with which you want to work.

Materials You Can Cut with the Cricut Maker Series Machines

In addition to everything you can cut with the Explore series, you can use your Cricut Maker to create projects with the following:

- Acetate
- Balsa Wood
- Basswood
- Carbon Fiber
- Flex Foam
- Fleece
- Mesh
- Nylon
- Oxford
- Tooling Leather
- And so, so much more! (Consult the Cricut website for a list of all the materials you can cut with the Cricut Maker and Maker 3.)

Note: You can't Cut S*mart Materials* with the Cricut Maker.

Honestly, all Cricut machines are awesome and are worthy of a spot in your home. But, as they say, there can only be one winner. Which one takes the number one spot is unique to each person. Whichever machine you get in the end, it is a huge investment. So I understand that you want to be absolutely sure you pick the right one. If you're still not 100% sure of your future Cricut, head over to the next chapter, where I'll help you ask the right questions and weigh up different criteria to make the best choice. Otherwise, skip to Chapter 7, where I'll guide you through your new machine's setup (yes, you may yell, "Finally!" and make a fist pump now).

Chapter 5 Notes

Use this space to jot down the best take-aways you learned from Chapter 5. Use these notes as your personal quick-reference guide whenever you want to refresh your memory ons something specific.

CHAPTER 6

HOW TO CHOOSE YOUR CRICUT MACHINE

One day you will wake up and there won't be any more time to do the things you've always wanted. Do it now.
—Paulo Coelho

Now that you know what each Cricut Machine offers, it's time to choose which one will become your crafting companion. This chapter will give you some factors to consider before making your purchase.

Why Do You Want a Cricut?

Consider your own needs before anything else, as a clear understanding of this will lead to the best choice. When you think about it, all of us use this approach in almost every choice we make. For example, when you get dressed, you do it according to the occasion. Likewise, what you plan on doing with your machine should determine which one you'll buy. Grab a pen and notepad, then find a quiet spot and jot down the reasons you want a Cricut. Afterward, compare your reasons with the table below to see which machine will be your best choice:

POSSIBLE REASONS YOU MAY WANT A CRICUT	BEST MACHINE
I've recently decided to start crafting and read about Cricut in my research.	Cricut Joy
I'm an avid DIY crafter and want a faster way to complete my projects.	Cricut Joy or Cricut Explore Air 2.
I'm an avid DIY crafter, and someone close to me has encouraged me to sell some of my crafts. I did some research and came across the Cricut brand.	Cricut Explore Air 2 or Explore 3.
I need new equipment to expand my growing crafting business.	Cricut Maker or Maker 3.
I sew in my free time and have heard Cricut machines can cut fabric, so I'm thinking of getting one to work a little faster.	Cricut Maker
I'm not a crafter, but I love making handmade gifts for friends and family.	Cricut Joy or Cricut Explore Air 2
I want to craft for fun, but I don't have time to do everything manually.	Cricut Joy or Explore Air 2
I want to sell mugs and t-shirts with my designs on them.	Cricut Explore 3, Maker, or Maker 3

POSSIBLE REASONS YOU MAY WANT A CRICUT	BEST MACHINE
I want to use Cricut for my scrapbooking hobby.	Cricut Joy

Budget

Crafting is not the cheapest hobby, but there's nothing better than the satisfaction of creating your own stuff and seeing how others appreciate it. What I love about Cricut is the fact that their machines are so accessible to most of us. Even so, with their latest model selling for just under 400 USD, pricing is definitely a consideration when choosing your machine. Sales and bundles that include extra tools and materials are not uncommon, so be sure to shop around for the best bargain before buying your machine.

How Often Do You Craft?

If you've only started crafting recently or have recently discovered crafting as a possible creative venture, the Cricut Joy is perfect to get you started. If you've been crafting for a while but don't spend time on your hobby at least once a week, the Cricut Joy is still the best option, as you might not take on projects that require more complex materials any time soon. But if you're a total craft addict who spends every free second crafting, you'll love having the Explore Air 2 or Explore 3 by your side. Finally, if you're a craft addict who spends every free second crafting and have a million ideas dancing around in your head (and another million in queue), the Maker or Maker 3 will help you realize them.

Ask Yourself about the Future

This one is hard, I know! Creative people live in the moment, and let's just say we have many talents, but planning ahead is not the best of them. I'm not suggesting you sit down and come up with a solid, day-to-day outline with goals and deadlines. Instead, close your eyes and imagine where you'll be with this crafting aspiration a year from now. Do you see yourself sticking to casual DIY projects, or do you feel kind of excited at the thought of turning it into a business?

Keep in mind that the Cricut Maker and Maker 3 models can do everything the other models can, plus a whole lot more. If you have the slightest feeling that you might use your machine for more than DIY in the next 12 months, and if you have the money, I recommend you get one of those models. In Chapter 5, I mentioned that a Cricut Maker or Maker 3 can grow with you, and that's all thanks to the *Adaptive Tool System* the company introduced when it released the Cricut Maker. If you can see yourself turning your hobby into a business but money is an issue, buy the Cricut Joy or one of the Explore series machines, because you can still make it work for now and upgrade later.

Whatever you do, don't deprive yourself of getting your first Cricut machine, because there's so much magic, happiness, and fulfillment it can bring into your life.

Features Comparison Table

If you're more of an analytical decision maker, the table on the next page will help you compare each Cricut machine side-by-side.

CRICUT MODEL	JOY	EXPLORE AIR 2	EXPLORE 3	MAKER	MAKER 3
WORKS WITH SMART MATERIALS	Yes	No	Yes	No	Yes
MAXIMUM CUTTING SIZE (INCHES)	4.5 x 6.5 4.5 x 12 4.4 x 6.25 (card mat)	12 x 12 12 x 24	12 x 12 12 x 24	12 x 12 12 x 24	12 x 12 12 x 24
CONNECTIVITY	Bluetooth	Bluetooth USB	Bluetooth USB	Bluetooth USB	Bluetooth USB
MATERIAL COMPATIBILITY	50+	100+	100+	300+	300+
TOOLS	3	6	6	13+	13+
WORKS WITH QUICKSWAP HOUSING	No	No	No	Yes	Yes

Chapter 6 Notes

Use this space to jot down the best take-aways you learned from Chapter 6. Use these notes as your personal quick-reference guide whenever you want to refresh your memory ons something specific.

CHAPTER 7

HOW TO SET UP YOUR NEW CRICUT MACHINE

The desire to create is one of the deepest yearnings of the human soul.
—Dieter F. Uchtdorf

The basic setup of each Cricut Machine is the same. Whether you have a Joy, Explore series, or Maker series machine, you have to connect it to Design Space to use it. Below, I'll walk you through a new machine's setup. Afterward, I'll tell you all about the surprises you can expect in the box when your Cricut arrives.

First-Time Setup

Download Design Space

Computer or Laptop Instructions

Before you plug in your machine, head over to https://design.cricut.com/ to download the desktop version of Design Space.

Whether you use a Windows or Apple computer, you'll find the downloaded file in your *Downloads* folder. Double-click on it. Your computer may ask if you trust the application, in which case you can confirm that it is safe to install. After confirming, the installation should complete automatically.

Run the Software on Your Windows Computer

After the installation is complete, Windows will launch Design Space. Unless you have already created a Cricut ID in the past, your next step is to click on *Create a Cricut ID* when the program prompts you to sign in. Follow the on-screen instructions to create your new Cricut account. After the sign-up process, you should see the Cricut Icon appear on your Windows desktop screen. Whenever you want to use Design Space, simply double click on that icon to open the program.

Run the Software on Your Apple Computer

To complete the installation, your computer will open a new finder window that shows the Cricut icon and your Applications folder. Click on the Cricut Icon and drag it to the Applications folder. Next, go to your Launchpad or Applications folder and look for *Cricut Design Space*. Once you have it, double-click on the icon. Apple may notify you that the application has been downloaded from the Internet and ask whether you still want to open it, in which case you can confirm by clicking on *Open*. When the application opens, it will prompt you to sign in with your Cricut ID. Click on *Create a Cricut ID* and follow the on-screen instructions to complete the process.

Android and iOS Instructions

Go to your mobile device's App Store and search for *Cricut Design Space*. The app icon has Cricut's official logo, which is a green "C" with little bug antennas. When the download is complete, follow the on-screen instructions to register a new Cricut account.

Switch On and Connect Your Cricut to Design Space

After creating your Design Space ID, you'll see an option for *New Machine Setup* in the app's drop-down menu. First, connect your machine to its power adapter and plug it in. The Cricut Joy has no buttons and will switch on the moment it's plugged in. If you have one of the other machines, press the power button.

Note that the Cricut Joy is the only machine that does not come with a USB cord, so you have to enable your computer or mobile device's Bluetooth to connect with your machine. With the other models, you can either connect them via Bluetooth or their USB cords. If you're not sure which device name represents your Cricut when trying to connect via Bluetooth, you can find it at the bottom of your machine, next to the little Bluetooth icon.

In the Design Space drop-down menu, select your machine. Once the machine connects, Design Space may prompt you to do a firmware update on the machine. Let the update run before you do anything else. It's usually quick and should only make you wait a few minutes before you can test out your machine.

Delayed gratification is worth it, I promise.

Your Test Project

Once your machine and computer or mobile device are connected, Design Space will guide you through a test project. This step is very important for the machine's calibration and also for you to familiarize yourself with the project creation process, so please take your time here. For the test project, you will use the sample material you received with your machine in the box.

With the Explore Air 2 and Maker, you'll use the supplied sample material together with the supplied cutting mat.

With the Joy, Explore 3, and Maker 3, you'll use the supplied *Smart Material* sample.

First, the software will give you a few options of images to choose from; pick the one you like most. Next, Design Space will ask you to double-check that the blade is set in place and that the clamp is closed. Since your machine comes with the blade pre-installed, everything should be fine. You can gently press against the clamp to make sure it is closed properly. Click on the *Next* arrow to go to the next step.

On the next screen, the software will tell you to either insert your cutting mat with the sample material attached to it (if you have the Explore Air 2 or Maker), or to insert the Smart Material directly (if you have the Joy, Explore 3, or Maker 3).

It's impossible to insert Smart Materials or your cutting mats with the incorrect orientation, as it won't fit in your machine if you accidentally try to insert it the wrong way. When you insert a cutting mat, the hole in the mat can be at the top or bottom; that's a little secret few people know. Give the mat or *Smart Material* a gentle push until the machine responds by gripping and sliding it through. Every time you insert a *Smart Material* or cutting mat, the machine will measure it before cutting to make sure there is enough material for the project.

If you have a Cricut Joy, your next step will be to click the *Go* button on your Design Space app. If you have any of the other machines, the *Go* button on the machine itself will flash, which means it's time to press on it.

When the machine is done cutting, Design Space will say *Test Cut Complete*. Now, with the Cricut Joy, you'll use Design Space to click on *Next* and then on *Unload* on the next screen to unload the material. With the other machines, you will see the up/down arrow button flashing. Press the button to make your machine release the *Smart Material* or cutting mat. Never try to pull out material from your machine without clicking the *Unload* button on your app (for the Joy) or machine (for the other models). If you try to force out material, it may damage your machine.

Finally, peel away the excess material from the cut project. Then go ahead and apply your first design to any surface as a reminder of what you had just accomplished, even if it's in your journal or diary.

After the test cut, you can start using your machine for all kinds of DIY or other projects. If you're not sure where to start, check out Chapter 10 for cool follow-along, step-by-step Cricut projects.

Cricut Arrival: What's in the Box?

You can buy any Cricut machine as is or as part of a bundle. If you buy it as is, you'll receive sample materials in the box to help get you familiar with using your machine. However, to start crafting, you'll have to buy additional materials. You can consider buying a bundle instead, as there are typically good deals available that include tools, accessories, and materials. There are different bundles for each machine, and which bundle you choose will depend on your needs and budget.

Below, I'll share what you can expect inside the box when you order your machine as is. If you order a bundle, you will still get everything in the main box as described below. The extra goodies that are part of the bundle will be in a separate box when the package arrives at your door.

Cricut Joy

- Your Cricut Joy Cutting Machine (it's so cute!).
- A pre-installed Cricut Joy Blade (with its housing).
- A black fine-point pen.
- One 4.5" by 6.5" *StandardGrip* cutting mat (the green one).
- A power adapter.
- Sample Material (usually Smart Vinyl and a piece of cardstock for the cutting mat).
- A welcome card with setup instructions.

Cricut Explore Air 2

- Your Explore Air 2 cutting machine.
- A pre-installed premium fine-point blade (with its housing).
- A black fine-point pen.
- One 12" by 12" *LightGrip* cutting mat (the blue one; some crafters have actually received the green *StandardGrip* mat instead, so don't be surprised if that happens to you).
- A power adapter.
- A USB cable.
  Some sample materials for your first practice project.
- A welcome envelope with setup instructions.

Cricut Explore 3

- Your Explore 3 cutting machine.
- One pre-installed premium fine-point blade (plus its housing).
- A power adapter.
- A USB cable.

- A variety of sample *Smart Materials* to get you started with your first projects.
- A welcome envelope with setup instructions inside.

Unlike the Explore Air 2, your Explore 3 does not include a cutting mat inside the box. So, if you're planning on cutting materials other than vinyl, iron-on, and other *Smart Materials*, you'll definitely want to invest in cutting mats. You can save some money by purchasing a machine bundle as opposed to buying the machine and additional materials separately.

Cricut Maker

- Your Cricut Maker cutting machine.
- A pre-installed premium Fine-Point cutting blade (with its housing).
- One rotary blade (with its housing).
- A black fine-point pen.
  One 12" by 12" *FabricGrip* cutting mat (the pink one; this is the mat with the most adhesive power, so don't stick lightweight materials like paper to it by accident ... it will ruin your project because the stickiness is too much for those materials).
- One 12" by 12" *LightGrip* cutting mat (the blue one).
- Power adapter.
- USB cable.
- Sample materials.
- A welcome box with setup instructions and other documents (this is also where you'll find your rotary blade).

Cricut Maker 3

- Your Cricut Maker 3 cutting machine.
- A pre-installed premium Fine-Point cutting blade (with its housing).
- A power adapter.
- A USB cable.
- Sample Materials.
- A welcome envelope with setup instructions and other documents.

Like the Explore 3, the Maker 3 does not include a cutting mat, so bear in mind that it might be better to buy a machine bundle with extra materials instead of the standalone machine.

Good to Know

None of the Cricut machines have Bluetooth connectivity buttons. The moment you switch on your machine, it activates the built-in Bluetooth. All you have to do is to go to your computer or mobile device's Bluetooth settings to do the pairing. If you are prompted to insert a password, it is 0000.

Each Cricut machine comes with a free trial subscription to Cricut Access for new subscribers. Cricut Access is a subscription service that gives you access to premium design content on Design Space. But, for those who don't need premium content, there are more than enough free resources. We'll talk more about this service when we deal with Design Space in Chapter 9.

If you felt overwhelmed when you first met your Cricut, I really hope Chapters 3 TO 6 have helped you realize Cricut is not difficult to set up or use. Hopefully, the creative fire inside you has been rekindled and you're ready to create to your heart's content. And if you have not bought your Cricut yet, I hope you now have enough information to make an informed decision about which one to get.

Next, I'd like to tell you how you can best prepare yourself for your first Cricut projects. Grab your favorite cuppa! I've got so much to tell you.

Chapters 7 Notes

Use this space to jot down the best take-aways you learned from Chapters 6. Use these notes as your personal quick-reference guide whenever you want to refresh your memory ons something specific.

CHAPTER 8

IMPORTANT TIPS BEFORE YOU START CRAFTING

You can't use up creativity. The more you use, the more you have.
—Maya Angelou

I'm all for unbridled creativity, and while I can't wait for you to start your first project, there are things you need to know first. Trust me, if the information in this chapter was all I had when I started with my first projects, I would have leaped for joy, saved a lot of money, and avoided some seriously frustrating moments.

Of course, we learn through our mistakes, but no one said you can't learn from someone else's mistakes instead of your own. This chapter deals with everything I had to learn the hard way when I started working with my first Cricut.

Invest in the Cricut Essential Tool Set

We've all been in situations where we assumed we had everything in place, only to discover we needed something crucial to get started or complete a task. Yeah, it's a bummer, to say the least ... I would never encourage you to spend your last dime on extra Cricut tools and accessories. Strictly speaking, you can get away without them, but it *will* make your first project harder to complete and possibly discourage you from taking on the second one.

I hear from new crafters every day, and there is a common issue that stands out: **"I have had a Cricut for months now and have only used it once."**

These stories are from Cricut Newbies who got over the initial overwhelm of getting a new machine, only to be hauled into frustration with their first projects because they did not know how to complete them. So, if you have a few dollars to spare, I'm willing to go so far as to say getting the *Essential Tool Set* is non-negotiable. The included tools are not gimmicks; they're meant to help you finish your projects quickly and easily. Here's what you'll get:

- Paper trimmer (It can actually trim heavier materials like iron-on and vinyl, too, and the trim blades can be replaced.)
  Scissors
- Small scraper
- Spatula
- Tweezers
- Weeding tool
- Scoring Stylus (It is compatible with the Cricut Explore and Maker series.)

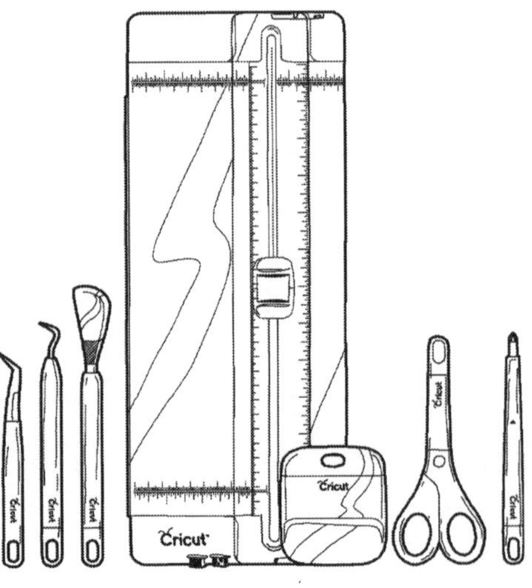

You might not need everything in the Essential Tool Set from day one, but as your crafting journey progresses and you become comfortable taking on more specialized projects, these tools will be waiting in your drawer to serve you.

Don't Ignore the Cricut Manual

Granted, books and other resources are there to help you learn everything you can about Cricut, but please read the manual that comes with your new machine. It is there for a reason, after all. Your Cricut manual may contain information you won't get elsewhere and help you troubleshoot common issues you might experience as a new Cricut owner.

Familiarize Yourself with Cricut Tools and Materials

The aim of this book is to prevent any uncertainties holding you back from using your Cricut. So, I've dedicated many sections to explaining the tools, accessories, and materials you'll likely work with in your projects. That said, I want to encourage you to learn as much as you can about them from various sources like blogs and videos.

By educating yourself as much as possible, the fear of not knowing what certain tools or accessories do, or how to work with common materials like cardstock, vinyl, or fabric, will disappear. In the end, you will feel more comfortable trying out your machine.

Familiarize Yourself with Cricut Design Space

Your crafting life will be so much easier if you spend a little time every day getting to know the software that works with your Cricut. You cannot cut a project without Design Space, so you have to know how it works. I don't want you to overwhelm yourself by trying to understand every single feature in one day, though.

This is supposed to be fun, remember?

When you work through the chapter on Design Space, don't try to absorb everything in one sitting. If you have your machine already, treat Chapter 9 as a practical exercise. Work through each section of the chapter at your own pace, maybe one or two sections a day, by opening your desktop or mobile version of Design Space and using it to familiarize yourself with the interface and software functions. This will help you move forward little by little; and, before you know it, you'll be a pro!

A word of caution to experienced graphic designers, illustrators, or anyone familiar with design programs: while you may have a head start over someone who has never worked with such a program, you still have a few things to learn that are unique to Design Space. Don't ignore the program, thinking you'll figure it out later. Jump in as soon as possible to learn how to work with the software; doing so will save you a lot of time and unnecessary stress when "later" arrives.

Perfect the Art of Double-Checking

Before you press the *Go* button to cut out a new project, check that your settings in Design Space are correct, and then check again. I've been crafting for many years, and I still do this. Materials are expensive, so you want to prevent wastage as much as you can. Make sure your material selection in Design Space matches the actual material you want to cut, and make sure you stick your material to the appropriate mat (Design Space will tell you which mat to use based on your material selection).

You can render your cutting mats useless and end up throwing away tons of material when your settings aren't right because each material requires your Cricut to apply a specific pressure. Too little pressure, and it will fail to cut through the material or even tear it. A combination of the wrong cutting mat and too much pressure from the machine can cut straight through the mat, forcing you to invest in a new mat way sooner than necessary. Not to mention the possibility of damaging your precious cutting blade in the process ...

This is one area in life where it pays to be a pain in the neck. Don't waste your sanity owing to an "I know what I'm doing" attitude.

You can also benefit from doing test cuts. Later, when you're more familiar with different materials, test cuts won't be necessary. Eventually, you'll only need to do test cuts on new and unfamiliar materials. Test cuts are especially important for large projects, as those are where you risk wasting the most material. To do a test cut, make a small design in Design Space and select the exact settings you want for the actual project. Next, attach the same material you will use for your project to the cutting mat and let your Cricut do the cut. Once the cut is complete, unload the cutting mat and examine the material to see if it came out the way you had in mind. This simple step will help you make necessary adjustments and perfect your design before you do the real project.

By the way, there is no need to use your cutting mat's entire surface with cutting projects. If you have a 12" by 12" cutting mat, but the design you want to cut is just 5" by 5", then stick a piece of material that is a little over 5" by 5" on your cutting mat. You need not be concerned that you'll stick the material on the wrong spot because you'll have a chance to tell Design Space exactly where you want your Cricut to cut on the mat in advance. That said, it's common practice to stick material in the upper left-hand corner of your cutting mat (inside the grid like we talked about in an earlier chapter). This is also the default area where a design will show up on the preview screen before you press the *Go* button.

Subscribe to Cricut's YouTube Channel

Cricut is as passionate about seeing you use their products to their full potential as you are about crafting. Apart from articles and product guides on their website, they have a lot of useful how-to videos on their YouTube channel.

Most creative people are visual learners, so I have no doubt that you'll master your Cricut even faster if you spend some time watching Cricut's videos. Apart from tutorials, you'll find a ton of inspiration for your first projects from Cricut.

Go to https://www.youtube.com/c/OfficialCricut to subscribe.

Have Your Own Crafting Corner

You don't need a dedicated crafting room, but you do need enough space for your Cricut machine and all your craft supplies and accessories. The Cricut machines aren't huge, but they need enough space all around to work at their best. Each Cricut has an opening at the back through which cutting mats and Smart Materials must be able to move without obstructions. Ideally, you need at least 10 inches of open space in front, behind, and above your Cricut. Apart from that, it's best if you can finalize your projects after the cutting process on the same surface where your machine stands. This is important for productivity. Like it or not, we humans are kind of apathetic, and if things aren't comfortable or easy to do, we tend to shy away from doing them at all—especially when we've just discovered a new hobby.

No matter how exciting something new is, if you perceive it as too much work, you will probably avoid it. To solve this issue, you need a dedicated workspace where supplies and tools are within reach of each other. Also, remember that your crafting corner is your creative space, so set it up in your favorite colors, organize it in a way that makes sense to you, and do whatever you can to put your stamp on it and make it a place you *want* to spend time in.

When setting up your crafting corner, keep these practical considerations in mind:

- You need storage space for your Cricut cutting mats and extra tools and accessories.
- You need storage space for your materials and will probably want to separate opened and unopened materials.
- Have a dedicated area for works in progress.
- Have a dedicated area for finished projects.
- You'll use your crafting corner to brainstorm new ideas.
- Apart from your cutting machine, you'll need enough room for a desktop computer or a laptop (unless you'll only be using your tablet or smartphone to operate Design Space).
- Think practically in terms of keeping your crafting corner clean (lots of nooks, crannies, and exposed supplies means you'll spend more time cleaning than necessary).

- If your space is especially small, try a minimalistic approach to avoid that cramped feeling when working.

Embrace Mistakes and Manage Your Expectations

Cricut crafting is exciting, mesmerizing, and relatively easy to master, but I want you to have realistic expectations as a beginner. When I say "relatively easy," I mean that anything new in life is intimidating and comes with a learning curve. Cricut's learning curve is not that steep, but it can feel like a mountain if you approach it with unrealistic expectations and think you're going to do everything well from the start. You're not. Even with help from this book and whatever other resources you gather, you're going to make mistakes. Sometimes, you're going to face situations in which you don't know what to do. This is a normal part of the journey. So, please, have an open mind and a can-do attitude. When you face uncertainties and make mistakes, embrace them as opportunities to learn and grow as a Cricut crafter.

Ready to tackle Design Space? Let's do this!

Chapters 8 Notes

Use this space to jot down the best take-aways you learned from Chapter 8. Use these notes as your personal quick-reference guide whenever you want to refresh your memory ons something specific.

CHAPTER 9

YOUR MEGA GUIDE TO DESIGN SPACE BASICS

The creative adult is the child who survived
—Ursula Leguin

Design Space is Cricut's proprietary software program that works in perfect harmony with your Cricut machine to make magic. The software allows you to create your own designs and access thousands of ready-made designs for your projects. You can also access the Cricut Community via Design Space, where you can share your designs and see what your fellow crafters are creating.

You can think of your Cricut machine and Design Space as inseparable companions. You can't have one without the other. While you can use other programs like Adobe Photoshop or Illustrator to create designs and import them into Design Space, there's no way to instruct your Cricut machine to cut a project without Design Space.

The best way to learn how to use Design Space is by using the software as you read through this chapter. If you haven't completed your Cricut's setup yet, head back to Chapter 7 and follow the guidelines before returning here to explore the Design Space interface.

If you're kind of terrified because you've never worked with a design program, that's totally normal. Design Space *can* be tricky without help, but you've got all the help you need right here, so take a deep breath and tell yourself you've got this. If you want to reread sections over and over, then go ahead. Please don't put yourself under any pressure or feel discouraged if some things don't make sense just yet. Take as much time as you need with this chapter.

If you're reading this book, I'm assuming you've either never owned a Cricut or the one you have has been tucked away so long, its only companions right now are a few abandoned cobwebs. So, I'm not going to tell you *everything* there is to know about Design Space and how to use it, but I am going to share everything you *need* to know to start designing with confidence.

Understand the Difference Between Features on Different Devices

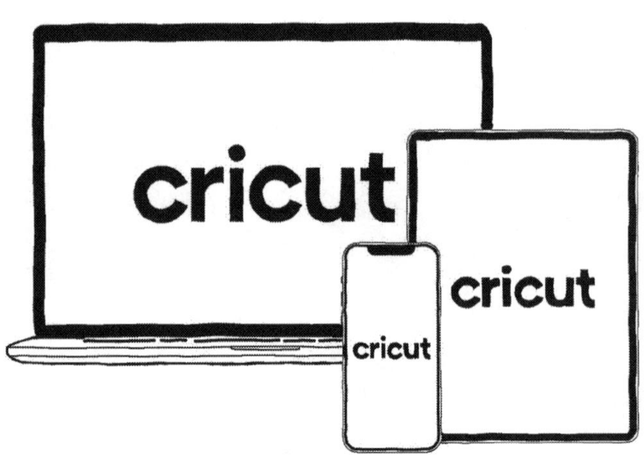

The Design Space features you have access to vary depending on the device you use. You'll be able to use most features on any device, but the desktop version and iOS version offer more advanced features. That said, some features differ between the desktop and iOS versions, too.

If you only have the mobile version, there are still a ton of cool things you can achieve, and (more likely than not) you'll have no need for advanced features for a while. Regardless if you have a laptop or computer, I encourage you to download the desktop version of Design Space in addition to the mobile version.

The table below illustrates what you can do with each version of Design Space. Please note, however, that Cricut is constantly adding updates to all versions of the Design Space app, so while the below table is accurate at the time of writing this book, things can change within the next few months.

FEATURES	DESKTOP APP	iOS APP	ANDROID APP
Attach	•	•	•
Contour	•	•	•
Cut and Write in One Step	•	•	•
Flatten to Print	•	•	•
Writing Style Fonts	•	•	•
Machine Setup	•	•	•
Print Then Cut	•	•	
Slice and Weld	•	•	•
Use System Fonts	•	•	•
Works Offline	•	•	
Photo Canvas		•	
3D Layer Visualization		•	
Smart Guides		•	•
SnapMat		•	
Pattern Fills	•		
Templates	•		
Image Upload	•	•	•

FEATURES	DESKTOP APP	iOS APP	ANDROID APP
Link Physical Cartridges	•		
Curve Text	•	•	
Knife Blade Cutting	•		
Cricut Community (share profile and projects)	•	•	
Offset	•	•	
Project Collections	•		

The Home Page

Whenever you open Cricut, you'll automatically be taken to the *Home* page. This is where you'll see an overview of Cricut's latest updates, featured images, your current projects, video tutorials, and more.

What It Looks Like on the Desktop App

At the very top of the screen is the header, also known as the menu bar. In the middle of the header, you'll see *Welcome, Your Name.* To the left of the welcome message are three stacked lines, with *Home* written next to them. When you click on the three stacked lines, called a hamburger menu (think of two buns with a succulent patty in the middle), you'll see additional menu items.

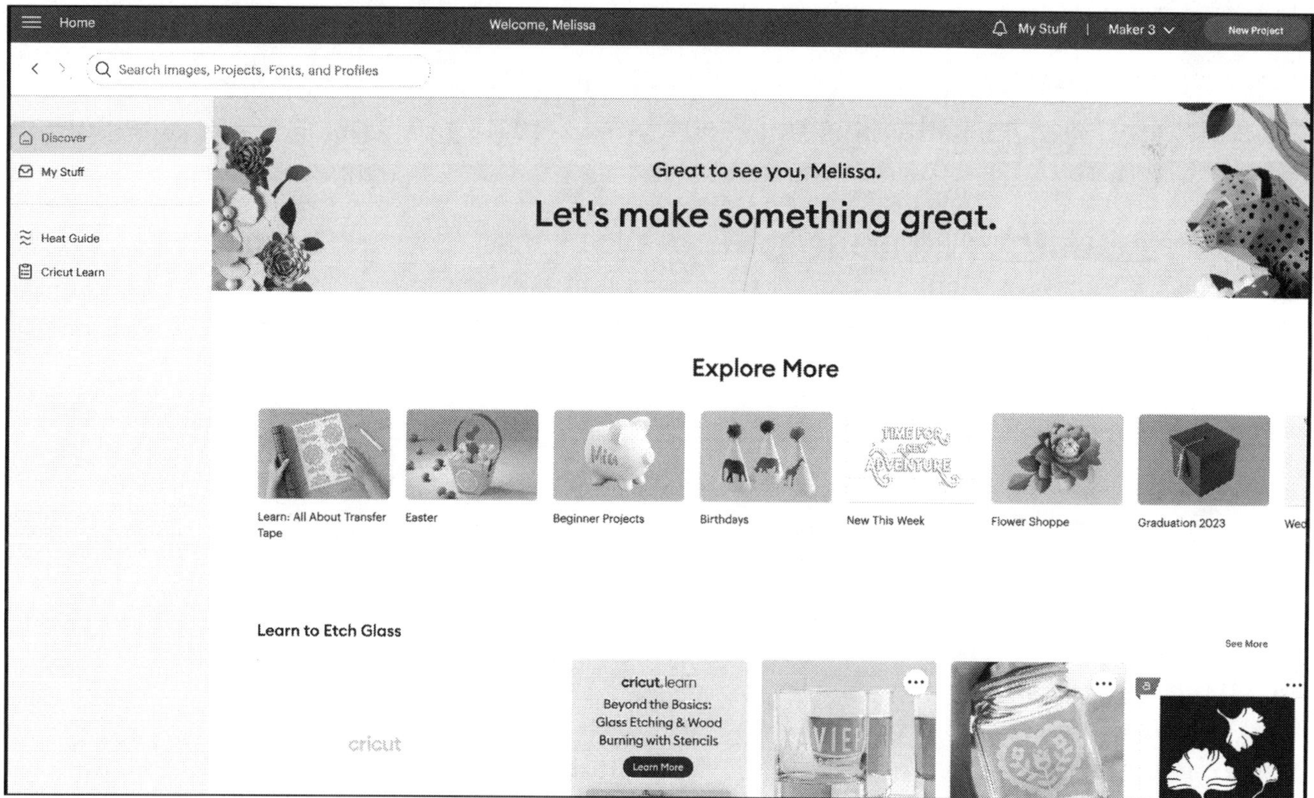

From top to bottom, here is what you'll see when you open the hamburger menu:

Your Name

Follow this link to edit your Cricut profile. You can also see how many people are following you and how many you are following. There is also an option to share your profile via Facebook, Pinterest, or a personal link.

Home

If you ever get lost in Design Space and you're not quite sure how to find your way to a certain screen, you can always go back to the Home page to readjust your bearings by clicking on this helpful link.

Canvas

This link will take you to the design interface where you can create your project ideas. You'll spend most of your time here when working in Design Space.

New Product Setup

Here, you can add additional Cricut machines (or other Cricut products like the Mug Press or EasyPress) to your Design Space account. Unless you haven't set up your machine yet, you'll probably not visit this part of Design Space any time soon.

Calibration

Calibrate your Cricut machine for Print Then Cut projects. We'll talk about Print Then Cut a bit later, but, basically, it's for when you will print out a design before feeding it to your Cricut to cut.

Manage Custom Materials

This is an advanced feature that lets you add and specify settings for materials not available in Cricut's library of pre-programmed material settings.

Update Firmware

Firmware is basic built-in software your Cricut comes out with. From time to time, Design Space may prompt you to run an update on this software. However, if you're curious whether there are updates available, you can always click on this link.

Account Details

Not to be confused with your profile, the account details link will take you to a special Cricut URL in your web browser where you can update your address and payment information, manage your Cricut Access subscription, and view your order history.

Link Cartridges

Earlier, we talked about how Cricut used to have cartridges you had to plug into their machines to cut out designs. Although the technology is obsolete, Cricut has given an opportunity to people who had the older machines to upload the designs that were on their cartridges to Design Space, allowing them to still use the designs. Unless you inherited a legacy (or older generation) machine and some cartridges, you can ignore this link. However, if you're curious to see what's on your cartridges, this is where you can go to link them to your Design Space account.

Cricut Access

This link will give you the opportunity to join Cricut Access. We'll chat about this subscription later.

Settings

See options to change the software's language, save files online or offline, the canvas grid settings, and measurement units.

Legal

This link will open a URL in your web browser where you can access the contract between you and Cricut that specifies the terms on which you can use their services.

What's New

See detailed information on recent changes in Design Space.

Country

Allows you to choose your country of residence, which is important for Cricut to show you relevant content related to your region.

Help

A useful link that takes you straight to Cricut's resource library where you can follow quick start guides for Design Space, Cricut machines, materials, tools, and more. You can also use the search bar on top of the resources page to query specific issues you may be experiencing.

Report Issue

Use this link to share feedback with Cricut about your experience with Design Space. If you're having an issue that persists, this is where you can go to report it.

Sign Out

This option will log you out of your Cricut account. If you want to use Design Space after signing out, you'll have to sign in again.

That's everything you'll see when you click on the hamburger menu. Now, If you look to the right of the welcome message (the middle part where Design Space shows your name), you'll see three more links:

My Stuff

This link will take you to a new screen and show an overview of all your Cricut projects. As a newbie who has never created a project, you'll see a message that says, *"Looks like you don't have any projects. Begin creating one now."* Soon, though, you'll fill up your project library.

Machine Selection

Many crafters have more than one Cricut machine. If you plan on turning your hobby into a business, you'll most likely invest in an additional one, too. When that day comes, this menu item is a convenient way to switch between your different models. If you click on the downward arrow next to the machine's name, a list of the other models will appear. From there, you can select the one you want to use.

New Project

A quick way to go straight to the Canvas (or design interface).

***

What you see directly below the header will change periodically. Sometimes, you'll see a welcome message and at other times, you'll see Cricut's latest updates and deals.

Just above the header image, you'll see a search bar. You can use it to look up images, projects, or other Cricut profiles. This feature is a convenient time-saver when you're in a hurry. To the left of the screen is a panel with quick links to helpful resources like *Cricut Learn* and the *Cricut Heat Guide.*

Moving further down the screen, you'll see thumbnails with links to projects and ideas related to themes like holidays, weddings, cardmaking, and so on. You can use your home page to find inspiration for your unique ideas or to create ready-to-make projects. As you browse through projects on the home page, you'll notice that each thumbnail has a little green label with a white "a". These labels indicate that those projects are accessible through Cricut Access, a subscription-based service that lets you download premium designs for your own use. You don't have to join Cricut Access to open designs you like, as you can purchase them at an affordable, one time fee.

The home page is constantly changing, so the project ideas you see today may change next week. If the current ideas disappear, you can still find them elsewhere in Design Space by either navigating to the relevant category or searching for them using the search bar.

What It Looks Like on the Mobile App

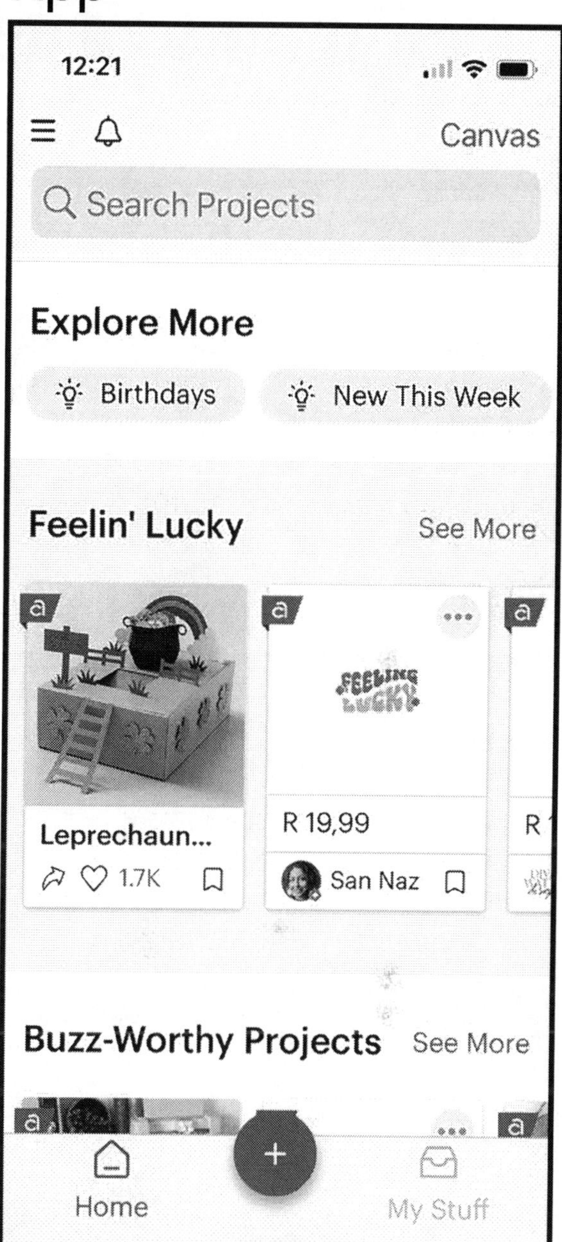

There might be slight differences between what you see on an Android device compared to what you see on an iOS device, but, for the most part, it's all the same. For that reason, I'll share screenshots from my iOS (Apple phone) app throughout the book. However, if there's a big difference between the iOS and Android app, I'll be sure to tell you about it.

Note 1: If you're using a tablet for Design Space, what you see will look more like the mobile app as opposed to the desktop app. There might be slight differences since your screen is larger than a phone, but the functions remain the same.

Note 2: Your phone's physical width might influence what you see. If things look a little different on your phone than what you see in the screenshots in this book, it might be because you have a bigger or smaller phone than me. That said, the functions are exactly the same. For example, in the first screenshot below, my search bar is underneath my app menu. If your phone is bigger than mine, you'll see a search bar icon in your menu bar. Be sure to look out for little nuances like these as you work through the chapter.

Let's get started.

There is a menu bar at the very top of the screen. From left to right, you'll see a hamburger menu icon, a notification bell, and a link that says *Canvas*.

The hamburger menu contains useful links, similar to those we talked about in the desktop app section. The mobile menu contains less items than the desktop app, but everything you need is there. We'll chat about these in a bit.

If there are new updates from Cricut or the Cricut Community, you'll find them when tapping on the notification bell next to the hamburger menu.

The *Canvas* link will take you to the design interface to start a new project.

Below the menu bar is the search bar and below that, you have a section that says *Explore*

More, which gives you quick links to project ideas people search for almost every day. As you scroll down the rest of the home screen, you'll see thumbnails similar to what we talked about in the desktop app section.

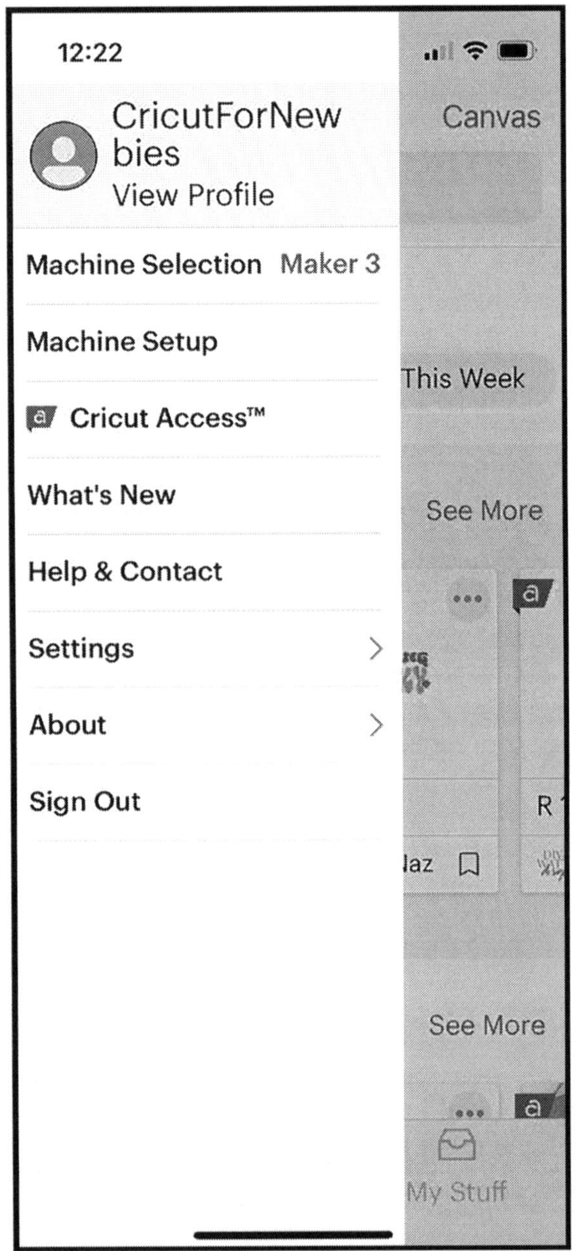

Tap on the hamburger menu icon to activate the menu. There are less menu items in the mobile version than in the desktop version, but everything you need is there. Here's what you'll see:

Your profile name. Tap on it to edit your profile and update your information.

Machine Selection (where you can choose your Cricut model if you have more than one).

Cricut Access (to subscribe to Cricut's premium subscription)

What's New (where you can see the latest software updates)

Help & Contact (to access Cricut resources like setup and project tutorials)

Settings (where you can change some software settings and access your Cricut account details).

About (you'll find information here like the version of the app you're using, legal policies, and an option to give feedback to Cricut about using their app).

Sign Out

At the bottom of your screen, you'll see bar. From left to right, the bar contains three links: *Home*, a plus icon, and *My Stuff*. At the moment, *Home* should be green, indicating that you are currently viewing the home page. If you tap on *My Stuff*, the app will take you to your personal projects library, where you can view and access all the Cricut projects you have made. The plus icon in the big green dot in between *Home* and *My Stuff* will open a new Canvas where you can start a new design.

The Design Interface (Canvas)

The *Canvas* is where you will spend most of your time when working in Design Space. You can think of it as your creative hub where you can tweak existing designs or create your own from scratch.

What It Looks Like on the Desktop App

From the home page, you can access the *Canvas* by clicking on *New Project* in the menu bar or by clicking on *Canvas* when you open the hamburger menu.

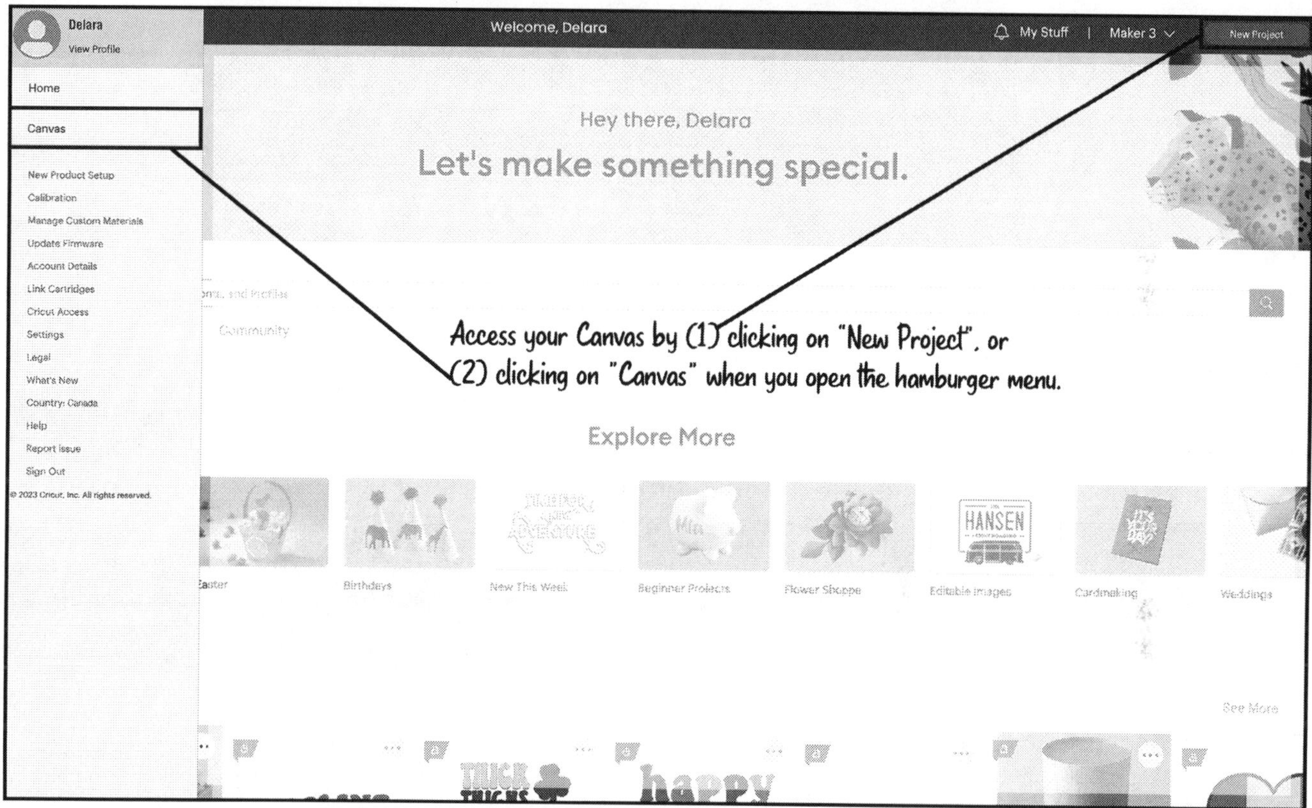

When you click on a project on display from the Featured or any other carousel, you'll have the option to customize that design in the Canvas, too. The difference between starting a new project and selecting a project to customize is that your *Canvas* will be blank with a new project, whereas it will display an existing design when you decide to customize an existing project.

Let's open a blank *Canvas* using any of the two methods you just learned.

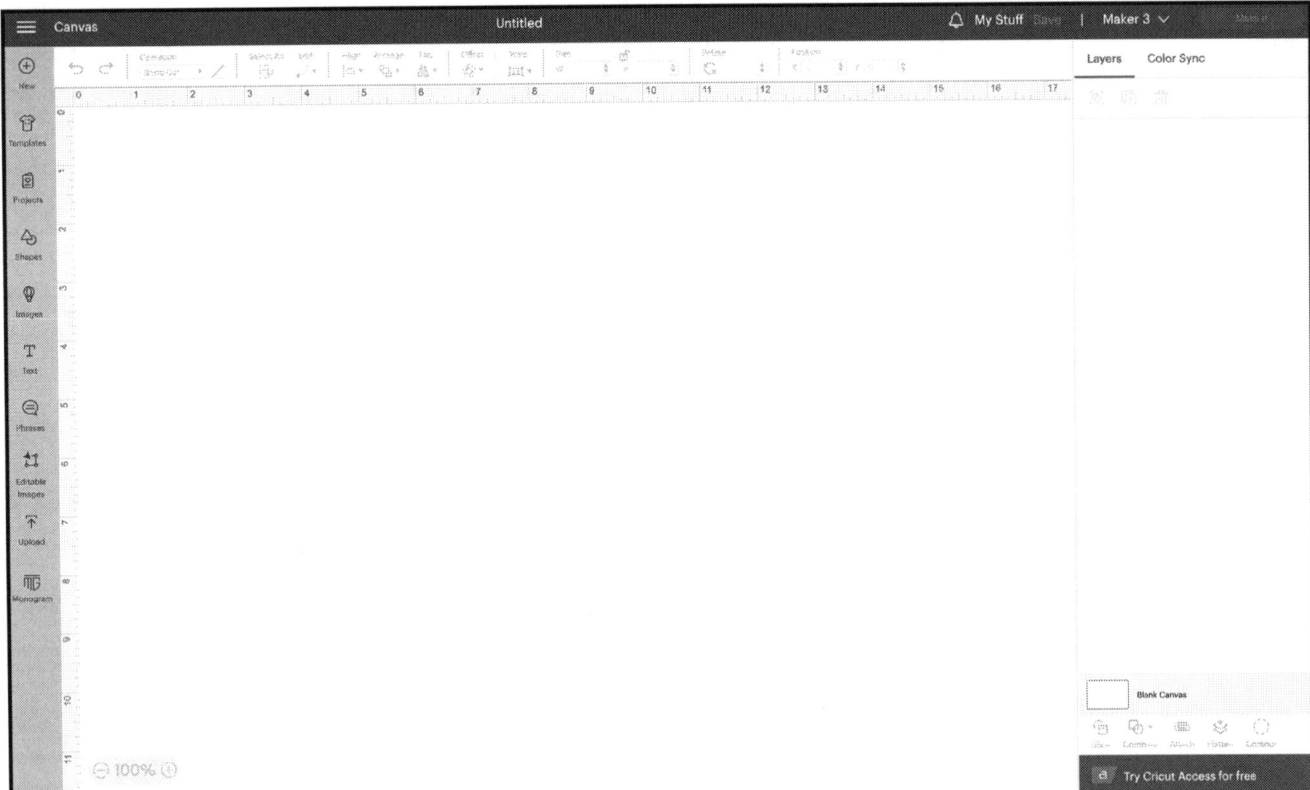

The first thing you'll notice when opening your *Canvas* is that it's not blank like mine—yours has a grid:

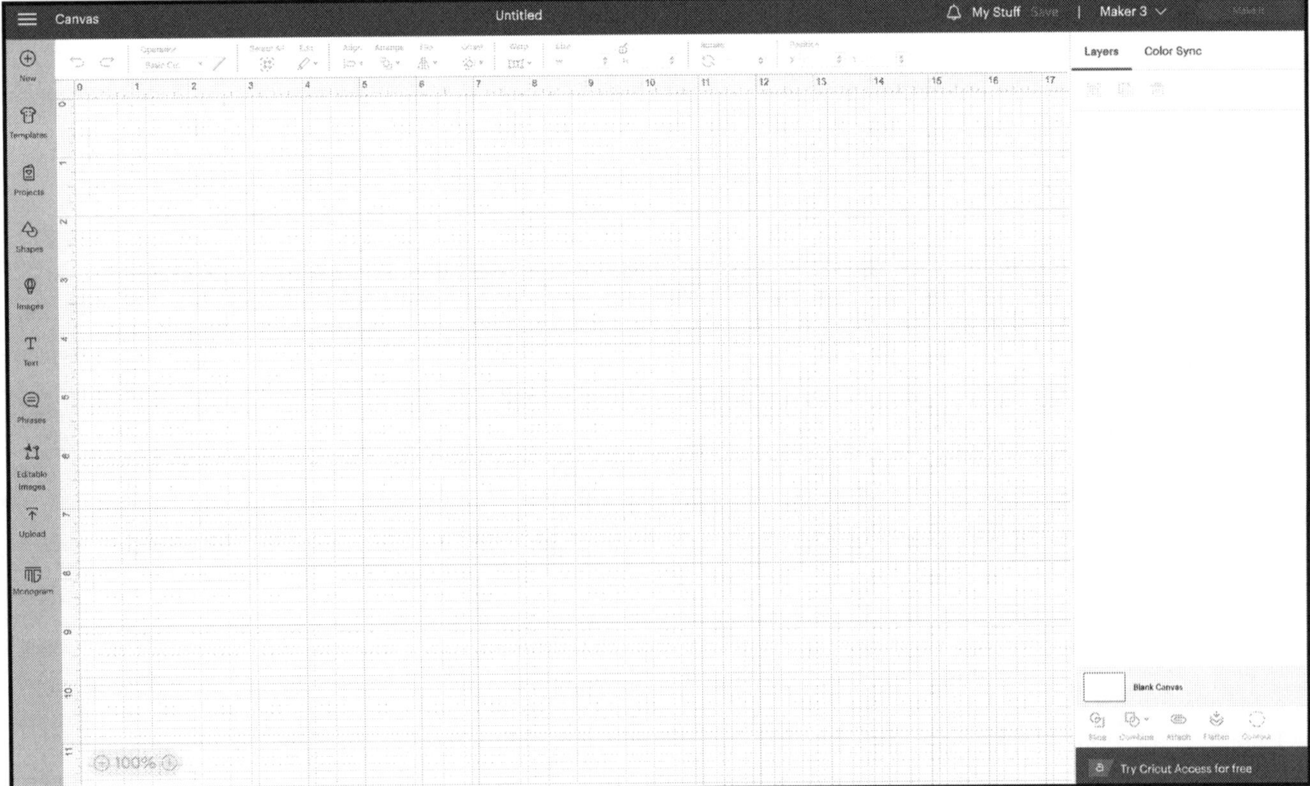

You can turn the grid on or off in your program settings. While I recommend you keep your grid turned on while learning to use the program, I'll let you decide what's best for you. So, if you want to turn your grid off, follow these steps:

1. Open the hamburger menu.
2. Click on *Settings.*
3. Choose *Canvas* (next to *General*) in the horizontal menu above the solid line.
4. The first option reads *Canvas grid.* Choose *No Grid* and then click on the *Done* button. (Note: you can even choose *Partial Grid*, which will give you bigger blocks than the standard Full Grid.)

The grid's rulers on top and to the left represent inches, but you can change them to centimeters in the same window where you can change the grid settings. If your grid is turned on, the more prominent lines are spaced one inch apart. The reason it's better to have the grid switched on while you're still learning is that it makes it easier for you to visualize the size of your designs.

At the very top of the screen is the Canvas header (or menu bar). From left to right, you'll see:

- The hamburger menu
- Canvas (It's an indication of where in the program you are; when we were on the home page, it said Home next to the hamburger menu.)
- The current file's name is in the middle (It will read *Untitled* whenever you start a new project.)
- *My Stuff*
- *Save*
- *Machine Selection* (This tells you which machine you'll use to cut out your project if you have more than one machine.)
- *Make It* (This is where you'll click when you're ready to cut your design.)

To better understand the design interface easier, you can divide it into four chunks that make up the whole:

1. The *Design Panel* to the left, just beneath the hamburger menu.
2. The *Edit Bar,* which stretches horizontally right underneath the header.

3. The *Layers Panel* to the right, just beneath *Machine Selection* and the *Make It* button.

4. The grid, which is in the middle of everything and takes up the most space.

In the following sections, we'll tackle the design interface in the above four chunks, starting with the *Design Panel*. But first, let's have a quick look at what the design interface (or *Canvas*) looks like on your mobile app.

What It Looks Like on the Mobile App

To open the *Canvas* on your mobile app from the home page, you have two options. You can either tap on *Canvas* in the menu bar or tap on the plus icon at the bottom of the screen. The mobile design interface only has the grid area, taking up most of your screen, and an *Edit Bar* at the bottom of the screen, where you'll find all the functions you need to create and tweak designs.

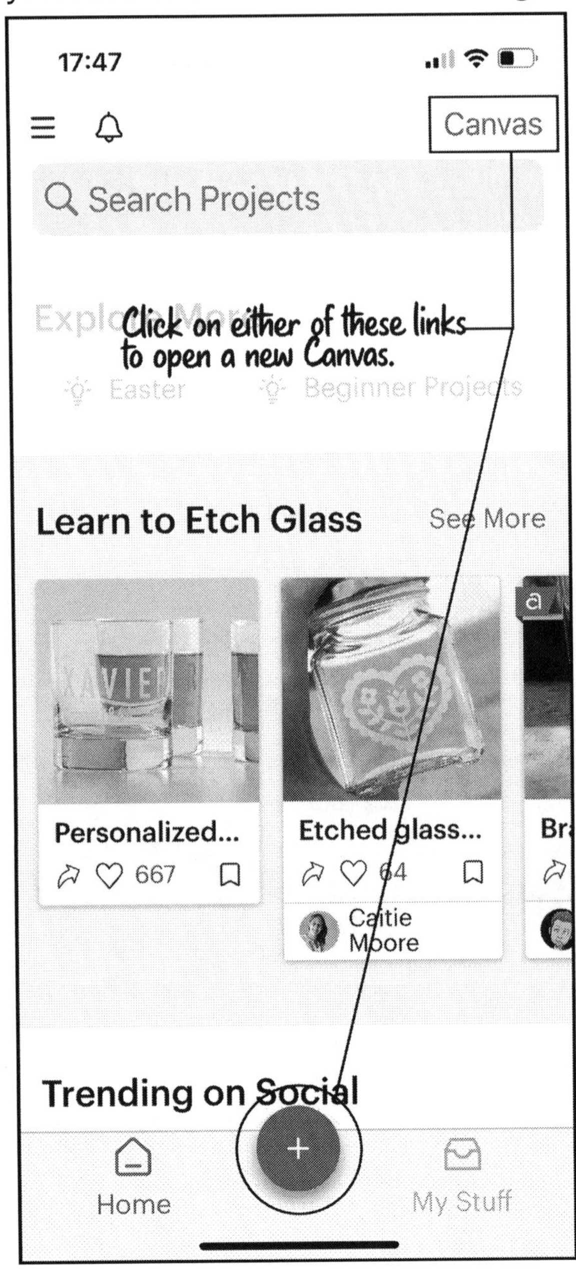

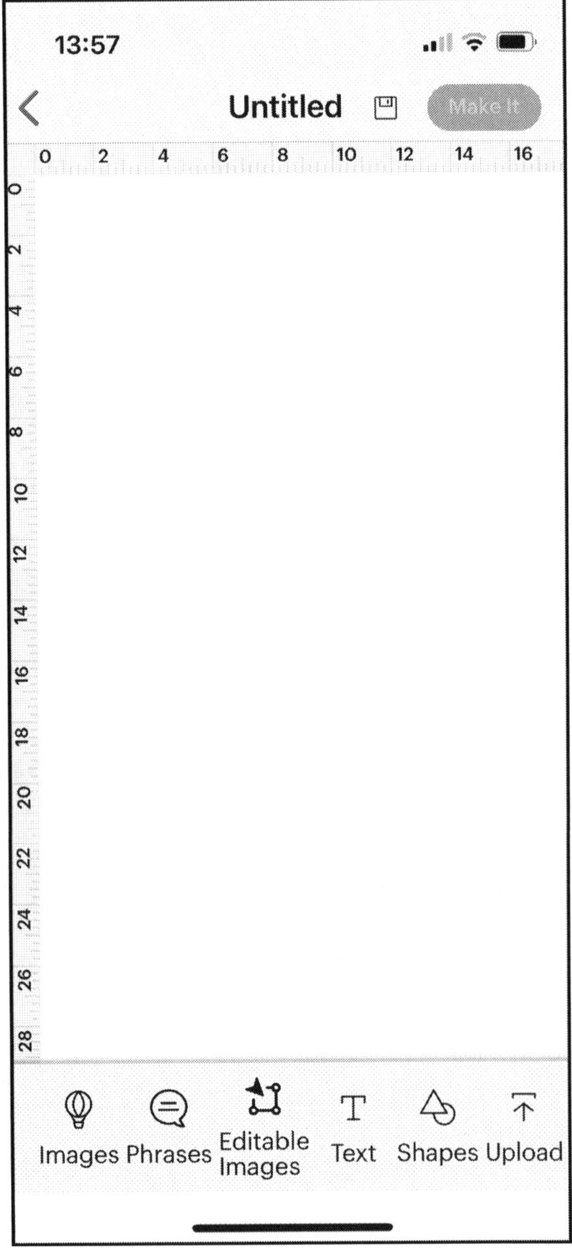

Since we can't divide the mobile app into the four distinct chunks I mentioned in the desktop app section, I'll just tell you how to activate the same function on your mobile app as we work through the desktop app functions. The most important thing to remember is that all the design functions for the mobile app are in that bar at the bottom of the screen. If I mention a function and you can't see it on your mobile app, swipe the bottom bar from right to left with your finger until you see it.

Feeling a bit overwhelmed? Take a deep breath and maybe take a break, too. You're not in a race, so take your time with this chapter. When you're ready, go ahead and jump in. Be sure to have your Design Space open and please follow along—it's the best way the information will stick.

Ready? Here we go ...

The Design Panel

This is the gray, vertical box under the hamburger menu.

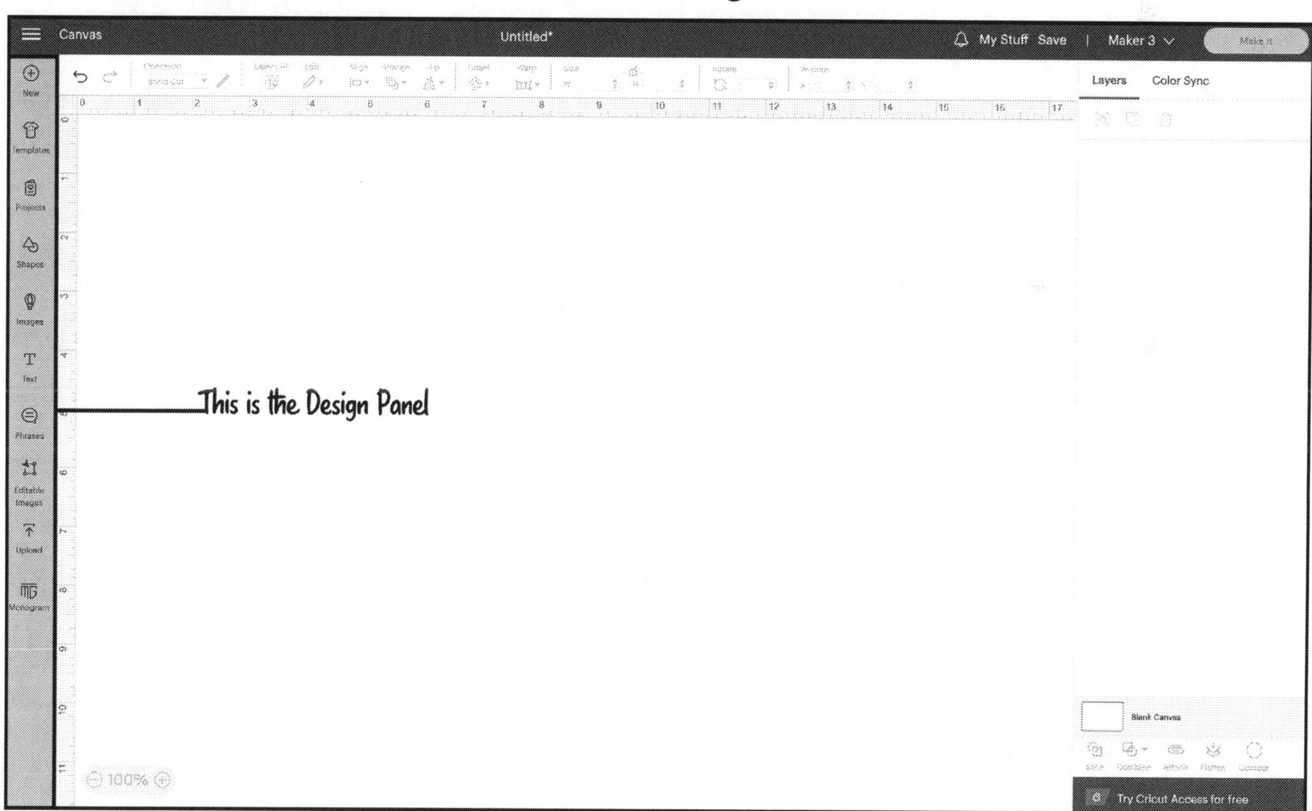

From top to bottom, here's what you can do in the Design Panel:

New

Start a new project from scratch.

Templates

Templates are illustrations of real-life objects on which you plan to apply your designs.

Templates can help you visualize what the design will look like on the item.

Once you add a template to the *Canvas*, you'll see an outline on the grid of the item you chose. The outline is not actually a part of your design, so you need not be concerned about its presence when you're ready to move on to the cutting process.

When you click on *Templates*, a window with various options will appear. They're arranged alphabetically to help you find what you're looking for with ease. That said, you can filter the results using the drop-down menu in the top-right side of the window. If you know exactly what you're looking for, go ahead and type it into the search bar and press the enter key on your keyboard. For example, you might like to see your design on a "Smart Phone" or "Mug" template. When you choose a template, Design Space will take you back to the *Canvas* and display the template on the grid area.

Once you have selected a template, you can make minor adjustments to it, which helps to get your design as close as possible to what it will look like once applied to the item you have in mind. To make changes to the template, select it from the bottom of the Layers Panel (the panel way at the right side of the screen). The moment you click on it, the bar at the top of the screen will give you a few options to play with, including *Type* and *Size*. For example, if you're using a backpack template, you might want to use the *Type* option to specify whether you're creating a design for a school backpack or a drawstring bag.

Projects

This option takes you to a page where you can select ready-to-make projects from the Cricut Community to add to your *Canvas*.

You can cut ready-to-make projects as is or use them as bases for your own designs.

Like the *Templates* page, the *Projects* page will open to show you all the categories of available projects. If you want to refine the options to better suit your needs, choose a relevant category from the drop-down menu in the top-right side of the page. Alternatively, you can use the search bar next to the drop-down menu to look for something specific.

Note that some projects are free, but you'll need a Cricut Access subscription to use most of the projects (or you can buy them at a one-time fee). However, you can open any project in your Canvas, as you'll only be prompted to pay the moment you want to cut it with your Cricut.

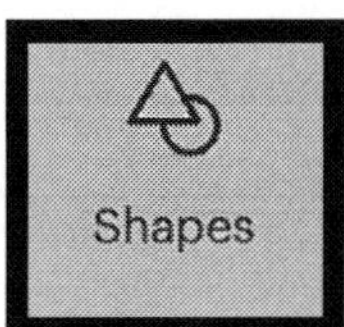

Shapes

The *Shapes* library gives you access to basic geometric shapes that you can use for your designs.

Images

The Images library contains over 300,000 standalone vector images, from bunnies to flowers, to complex shapes and everything in between.

Most of these image's colors cam be changed and the individual shapes they consist of can be tweaked one at a time (You probably won't be playing around with existing images that much as a Newbie, but it's good to make a mental note of this for when you become more comfortable with Design Space.)

The difference between projects and images is that projects are already optimized for use on specific items and come with instructions, whereas images have no predefined settings or instructions. As with ready-to-make projects, you can get some images for free and buy others through Cricut Access.

Text

Most designs comprise graphics and text, so you'll probably use this tool a lot.

The text tool lets you type whatever words you want to add to your design. You can make the text unique by changing the font and size, increasing or decreasing the space between letters, and changing the color. More advanced tweaks include curving the text or separating each letter so you can edit them individually.

Phrases

The *Phrases* library contains a ton of sayings and may or may not incorporate some other design elements like lines and shapes.

All sayings used to be a part of the *Images* library, so you might find some overlap when viewing the *Images* and *Phrases* libraries. For the most part, you can't edit the text of the designs available in the *Phrases* library, but you can make tweaks like changing the color and exaggerating the width and length of the design.

Editable Images

It used to be impossible to change the text of existing designs that contained words or sayings.

However, in late 2022, Cricut introduced *Editable Images*, allowing crafters much more freedom. Now, if you see a really cool design that says "World's Best Dad" but you wish it could say "World's Best Mom", you can just go ahead and change it (as long as you're working with an *Editable Image*).

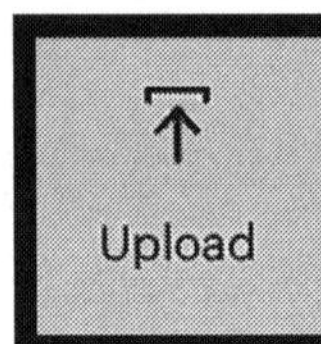

Upload

Here, you can import images or patterns that you have downloaded elsewhere or created with a different design software.

Once uploaded, you can use that image for your current and future projects.

Monogram

A cool feature that lets you design professional logo-type designs.

You can access most of the above features on your mobile app, too. However, you may experience some limitations, especially with your Android app. For now, the *Templates* and *Monogram* features are not yet available on either the iOS or Android apps.

To access the above features on your mobile app, simply look for the same icons in the bar at the bottom of your *Canvas* page.

Let's move on to the Edit Bar.

The Edit Bar

The horizontal box underneath the menu bar is the Edit Bar. This bar contains specialized features that allow you to tweak images, shapes, text, and other elements. If there are no elements on the Canvas, the entire *Edit Bar* will be grayed out.

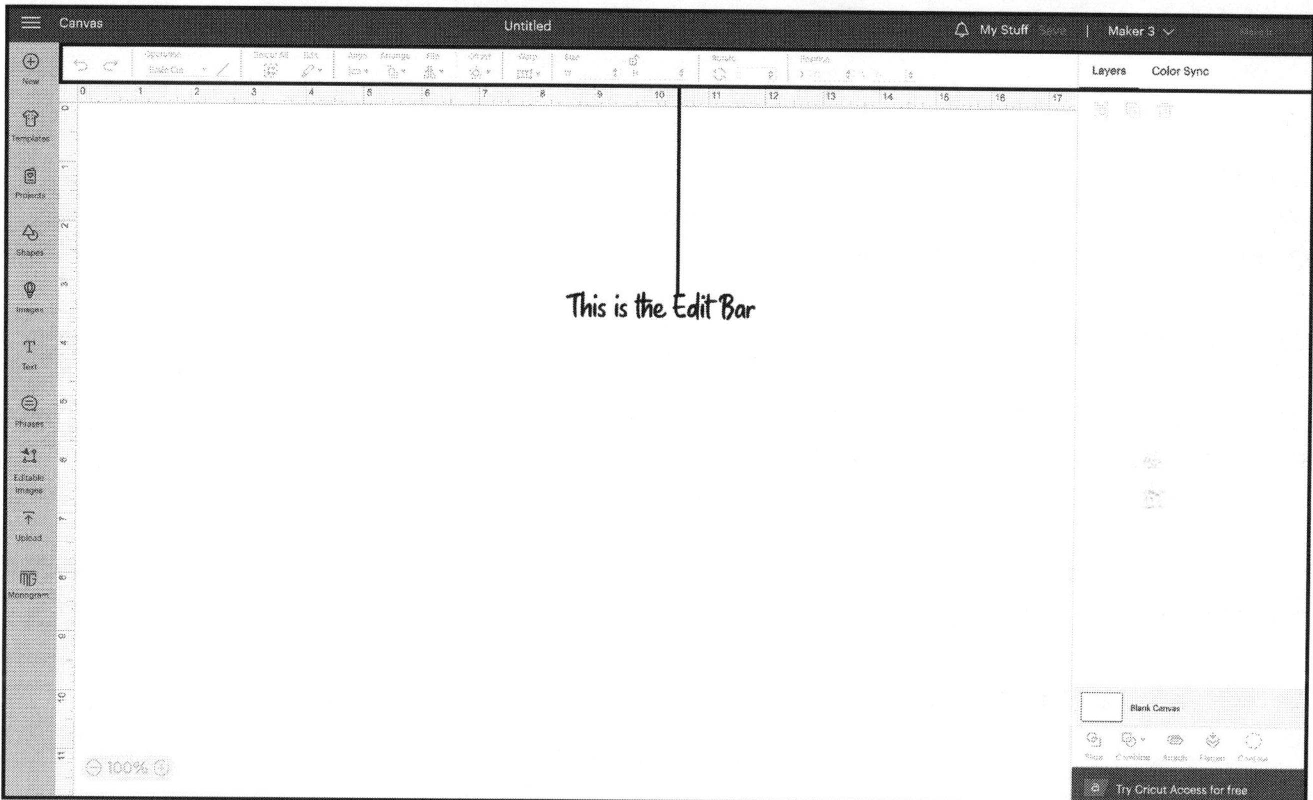

From left to right, here's what you can do in the *Edit Bar*:

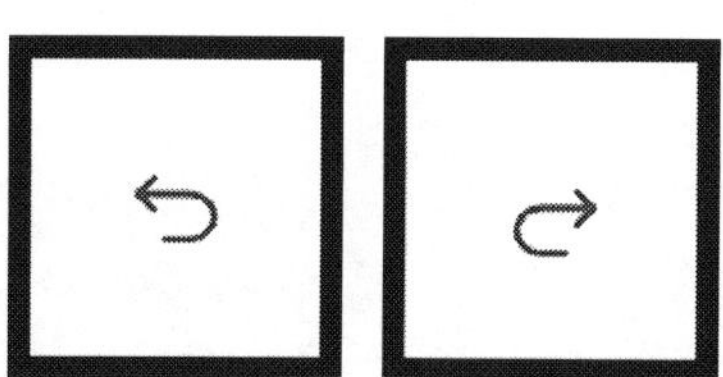

Undo/Redo

If you don't like the last change you made, you go back to the previous state by clicking on the *Undo* button (the arrow pointing to the left).

For example, if you made your text pink but liked it better when it was black, you can make it black again in a single click.

If you use the *Undo* button but change your mind again, you can reapply the change by clicking on the *Redo* button (the arrow pointing to the right).

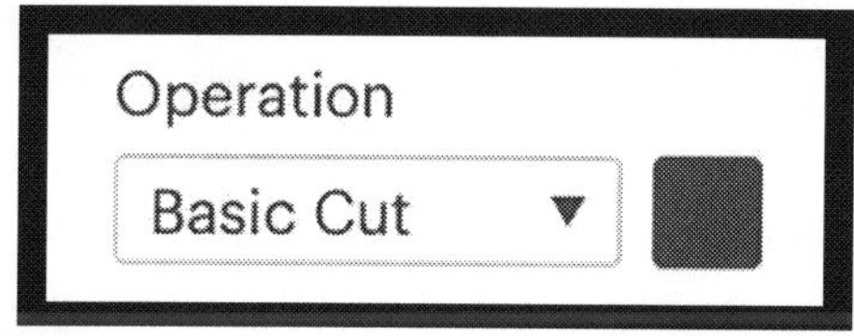

Operation

This function used to be known as *Linetype.*

So, if you come across blogs, tutorials, or videos that talk about *Linetype*, it is referring to the same thing.

Operation tells Design Space what you want your Cricut machine to do the material once you place it on the cutting mat and feed it into your the machine. Your *Machine Selection* (the Cricut model you're using) determines the options you see here. Let's see what you can do with each model.

Cricut Joy

- Cut: Basic
- Draw: Pen or Foil

Cricut Explore Air 2 or Explore 3

- Cut: Basic
- Draw: Pen, Foil, or Score
- Print Then Cut

(Note that the Explore Air 2 is not listed in the *Machine Selection* menu. If you have this model, you should choose *Cricut Explore Family.*)

Cricut Maker or Maker 3

- Cut: Basic, Wavy, or Perforate
- Draw: Pen, Foil, Score, Deboss, or Engrave
- Print Then Cut

You'll notice *Guide* as another *Operation* menu item at the bottom of the drop-down menu. This features allows you to turn any design element into a template of sorts, allowing you to visualize concepts and create designs perfectly on size. Similar to templates, Design Space won't recognize *Guides* as part of your actual design and will ignore it for the cutting process.

Next to the *Operation* drop-down options is a little color box, better known as the *Operation Swatch*; click on it to change the color of the image, shape, or text currently selected.

When you click on the color box, you'll see a range of predefined colors to choose from, but if you have something specific in mind, you can click on *Advanced*, which will allow you to refine your color selection. If you're wondering what color your image, shape, or text is currently, look at the first color option (the one that's separate from the rest), which has a check mark in the middle. Note that the swatch attributes can change based on the type of operation you choose. For example, when you have a shape and you choose *Draw* instead of *Cut*, the color will no longer fill the shape, but instead look like an outline.

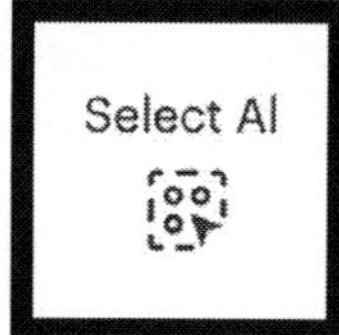

Select All

The *Select All* function allows you to grab everything on the *Canvas* at once.

This is useful if you have more than one element on your Canvas and want to change something on all of them, like the size or color, or if you perhaps want to combine them into a single element.

Understanding the Selection Box

When we talk about selections in design, it refers to the design element (or layer) you are currently working on. Open a shape on your *Canvas* (using the *Shapes* option in the *Design Panel*) and then click on it; you'll see a gray box form around it.

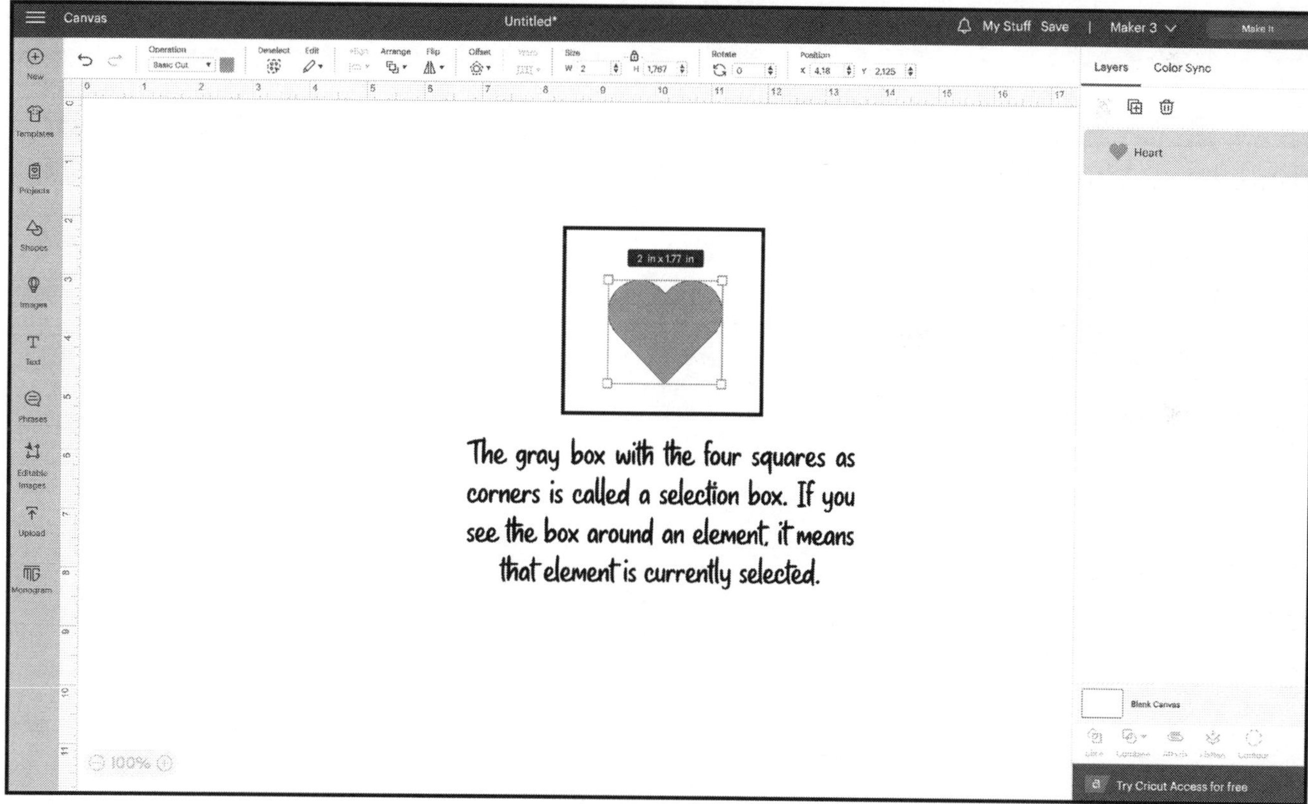

The box tells you that you are now working with that element and whatever changes you make will affect that specific element. To get a better idea of how this works, open another shape, click on it, and change its color. Notice how the other shape's color (the one that was not selected) doesn't change along with the one you just changed.

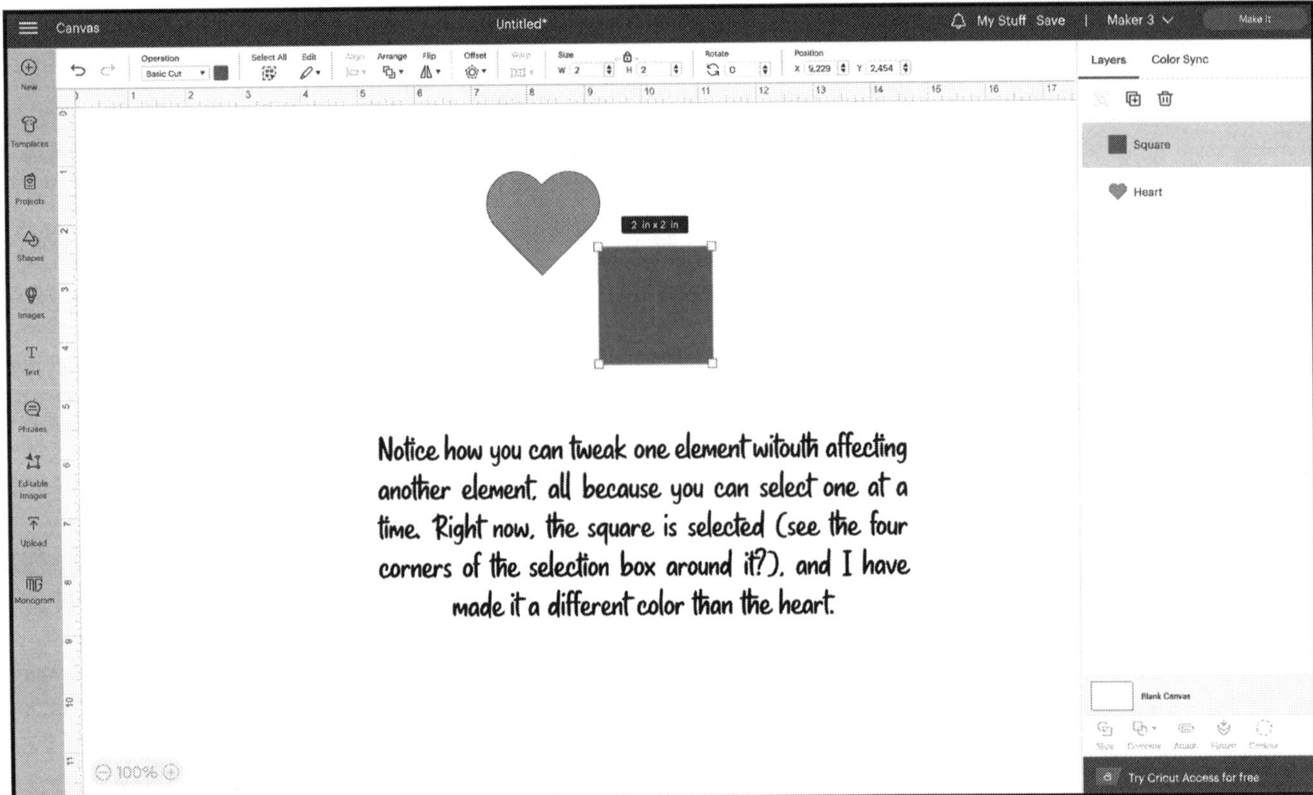

However, if you use the *Select All* feature and then go to change the color, you will see both shapes' colors change. Note that if an element or multiple elements are selected, the *Select All* option changes *Deselect*. As the name suggests, *Deselect* is there to unselect whatever is currently selected.

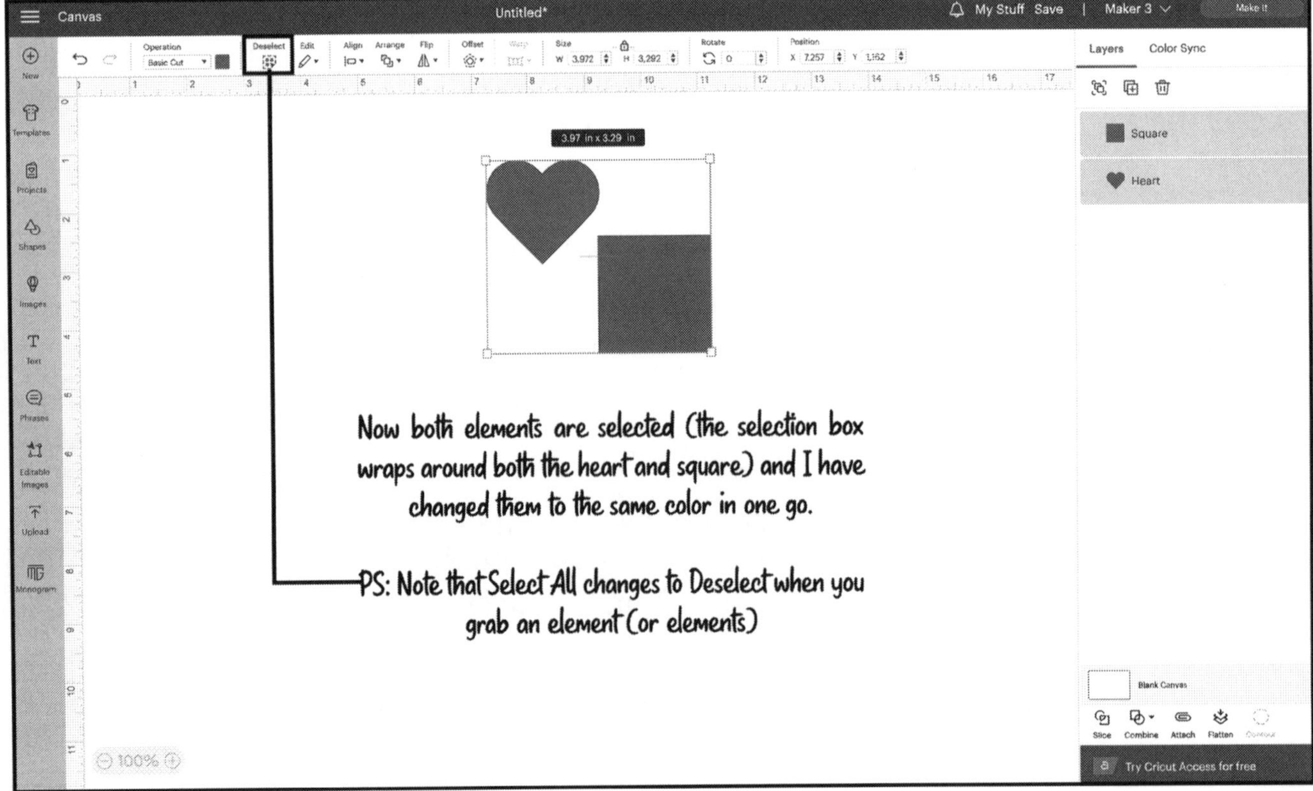

The selection box also allows you to perform a few basic functions with selected elements. By grabbing one of the corners (typically the lower-right corner), you can resize an element. Click the corner, hold it, and drag the element. Drag away from the element to enlarge it and push toward the element to shrink it.

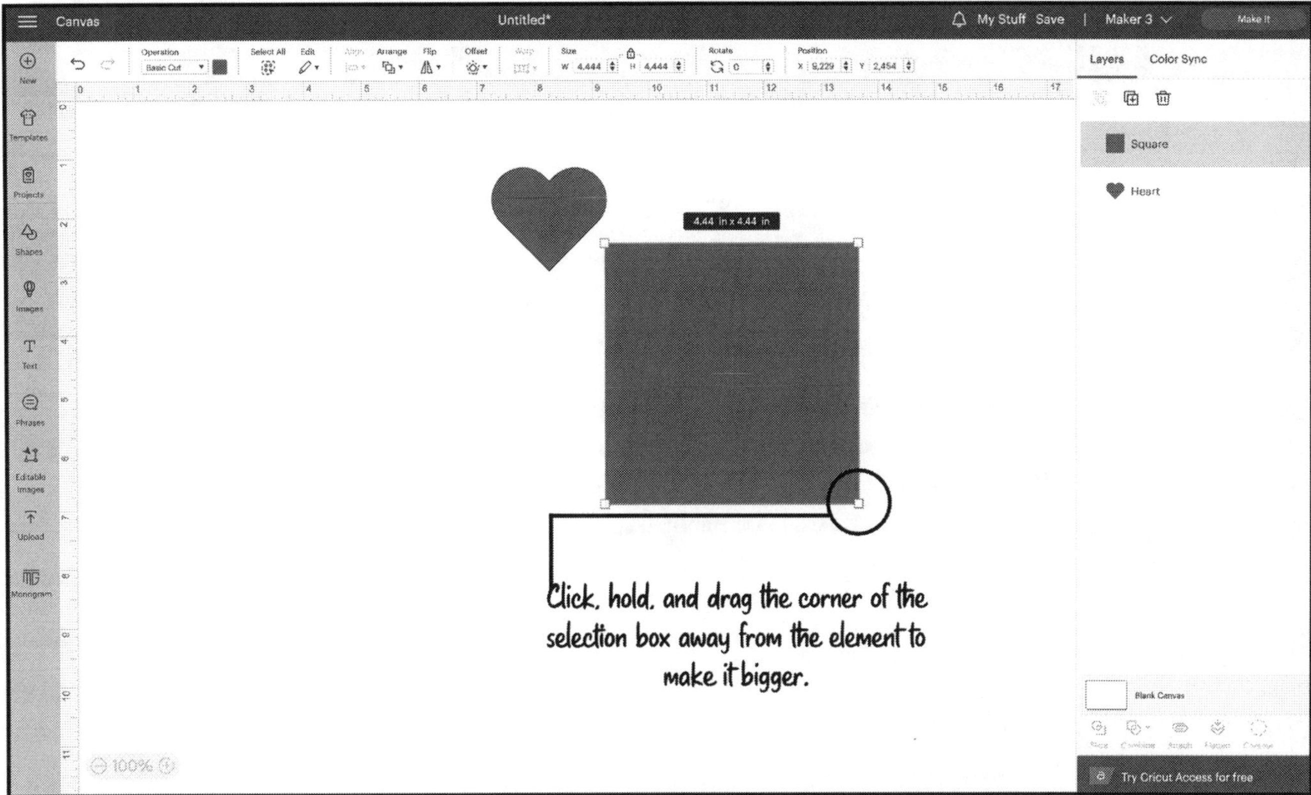

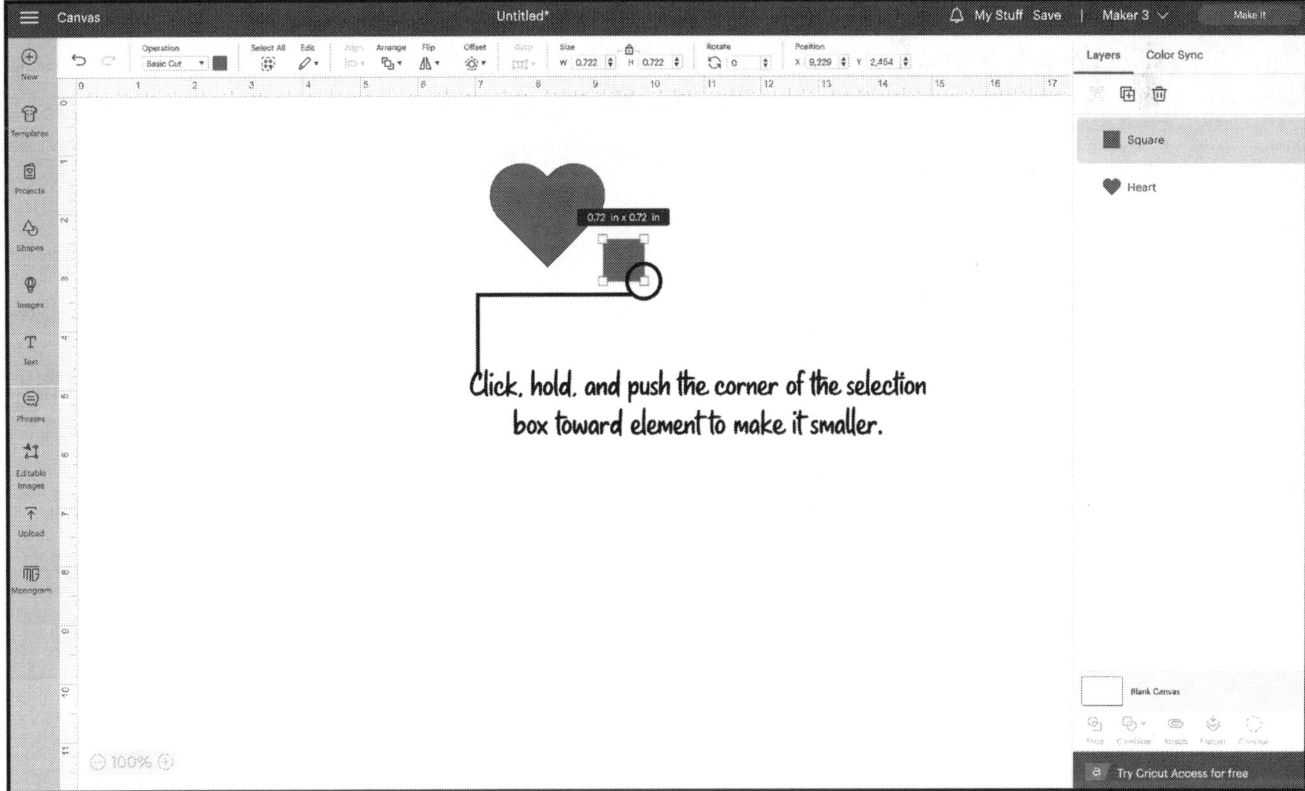

By holding your mouse cursor a little further away from one of the corners of the selection box, you can rotate selected elements in any direction. Slowly move around one of the corners (not on top of it) until you see a curved arrow. The moment you see it, click, hold, and move your mouse to the left or right to rotate the element.

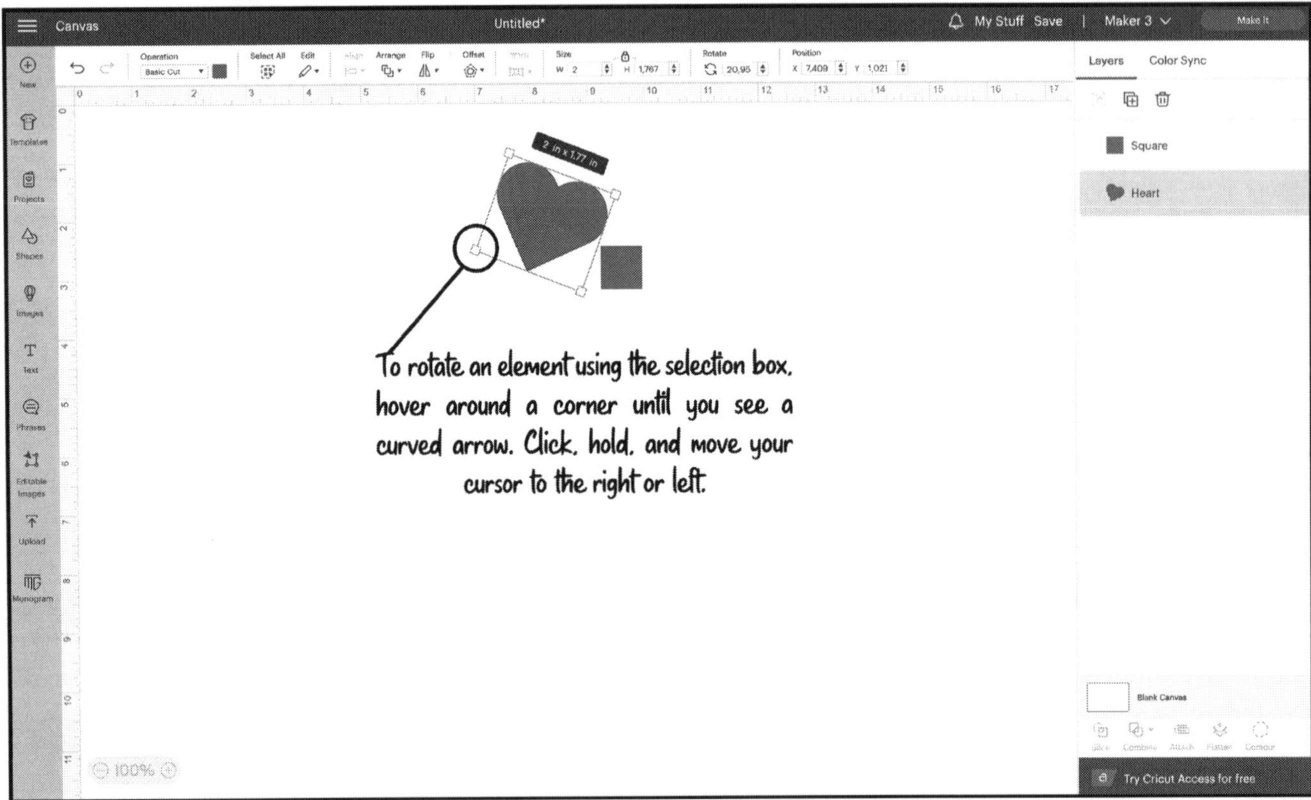

You can also stretch and squash elements using the selection box. Click, hold, and drag or push any of the four sides of an element's selection box to exaggerate its proportions.

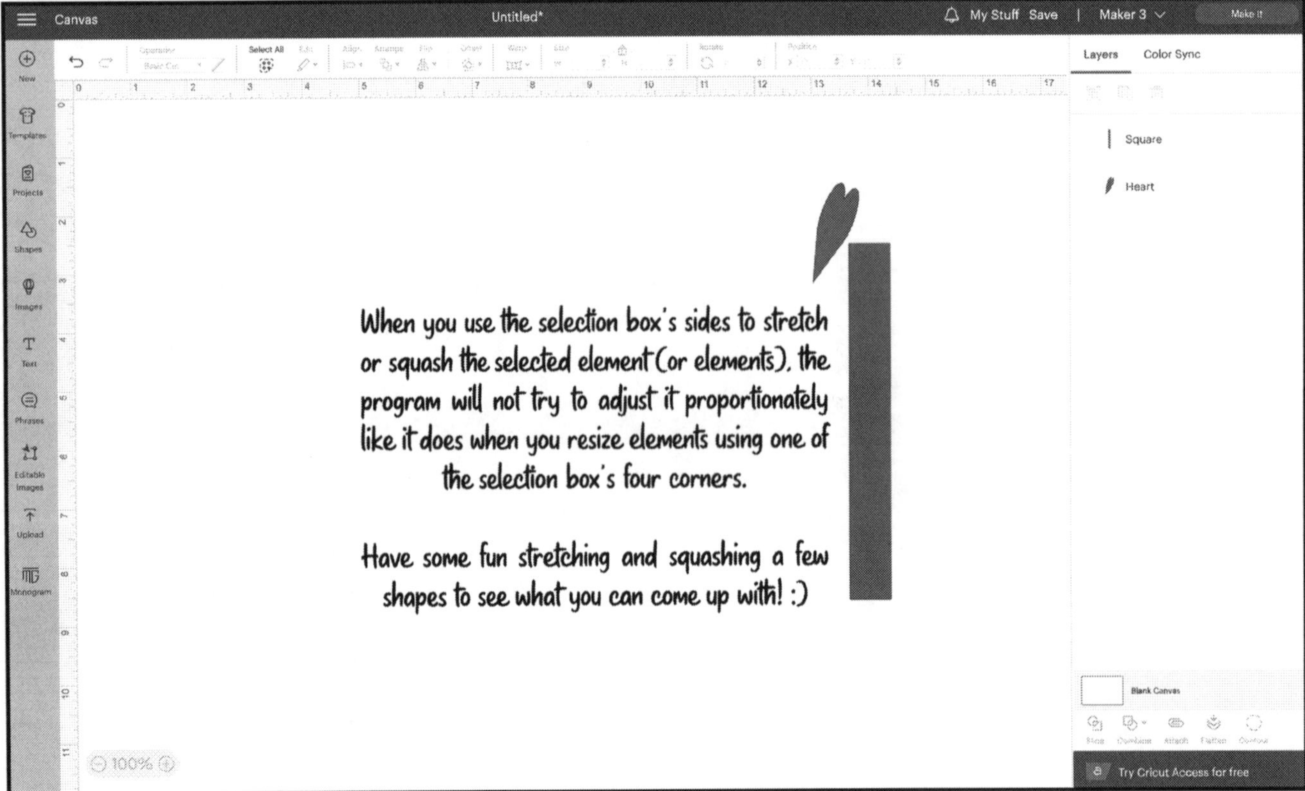

Finally, you can move elements around on the grid (*Canvas* area). With the element (or elements) selected, click in the middle of the box (more or less where you see the cross), hold, and drag the element to a new spot on the grid.

How to use the selection box on your mobile app

To select a single element on you mobile app, tap on it. You'll know you have it selected when the selection box appears around it. To select multiple elements, put your finger a little ways away from the elements and drag toward them. You'll see an outline of a box form as you drag. Expand the outline until it covers all the elements you want as part of your selection and then lift your finger. You'll now see the selection box around all the elements.

Pro Tip: If there's an element nearby the ones you intend to select, but you don't want that particular one to be a part of the selection, tap on it first and move it away from the other elements. If you're working on your phone and space is an issue, zoom out of the Canvas by placing two fingers on the screen and moving them toward each other.

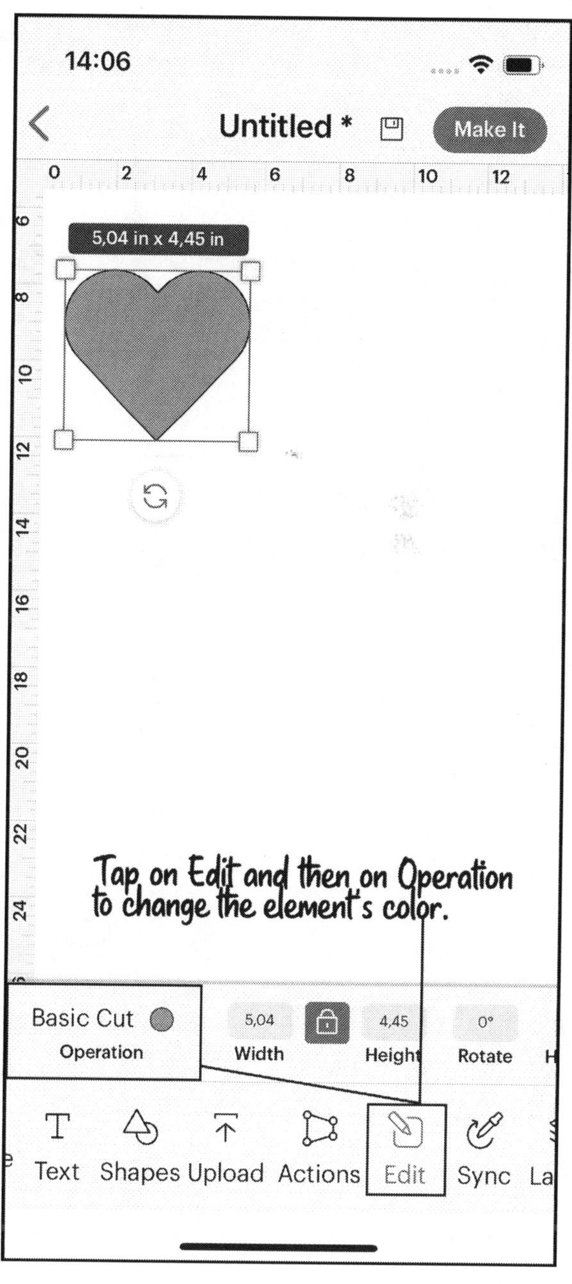

With the mobile app, you can only move, resize, and rotate elements using the selection box. If you want to squash and stretch elements, you'll have to do it by adjusting the size settings, which we'll get to in the *Size* section further down.

Let's add a heart to the *Canvas* and change its color.

1. Tap on *Shapes* in the bar at the bottom of your screen.
2. Scroll until you see the heart and select it.
3. If you don't see a selection box around your heart, tap on it.
4. With the heart selected, find the *Edit* function in the bar at the bottom of your screen and tap on it.
5. A secondary bar will appear on top of the regular bar.

6. Tap on the option that says *Basic Cut.* (This option is equivalent to the *Operation* function in the desktop app.)

7. Tap on *Material Color.*

8. Choose any color you like. If the app doesn't take you back to the *Canvas* automatically, simply tap the back button until you're back on the *Canvas.*

9. Your selected shape should now be the color you chose.

Next, let's enlarge the heart. Tap on any of the selection box's four corners, hold, and drag away from the heart. After enlarging it, shrink it by doing the same, but this time, push toward the heart. Finally, rotate the heart by placing your finger on the icon below the selection box and them swinging your finger to the left or right.

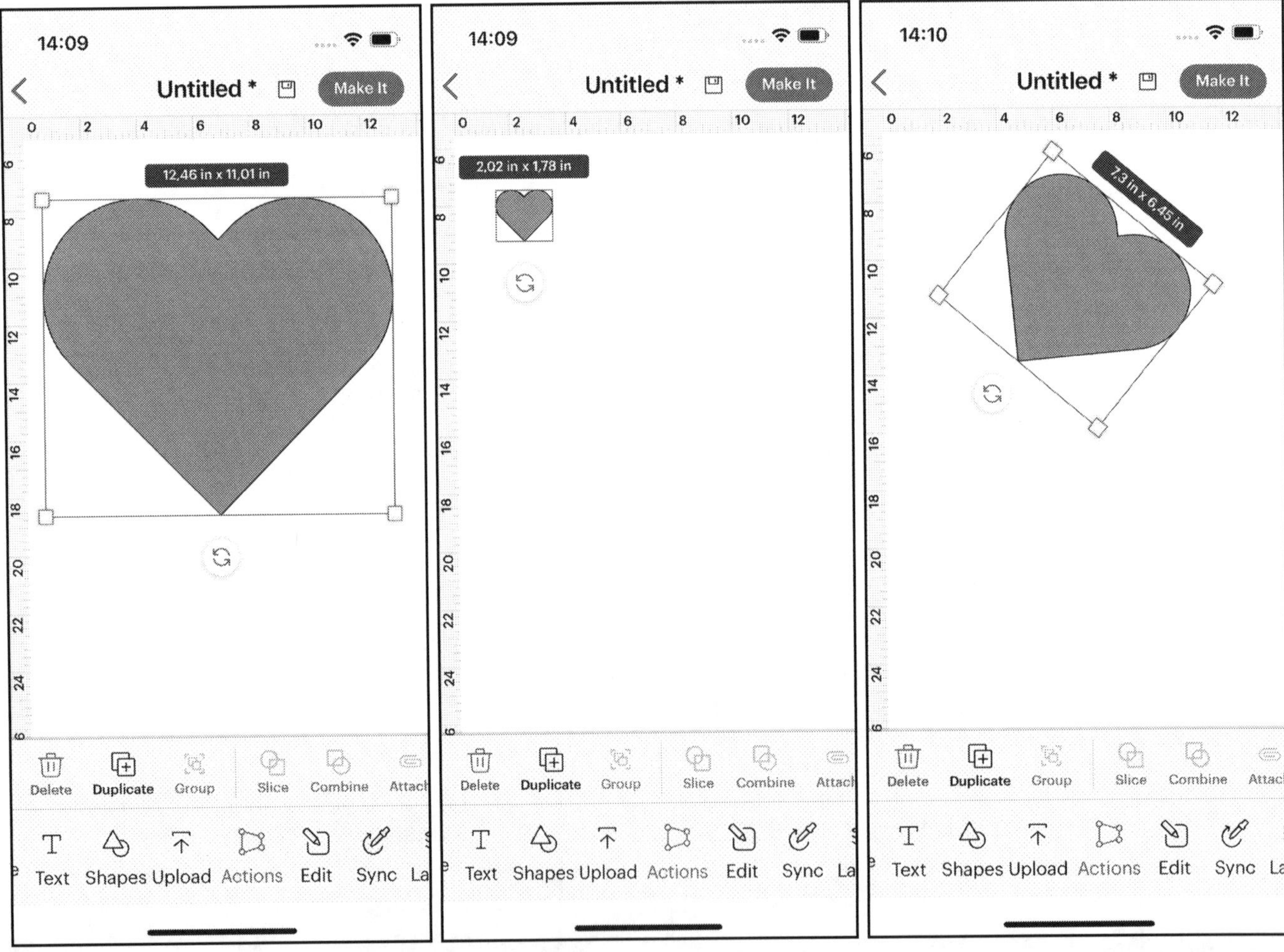

Before we move on, select all the shapes on your Canvas and delete them by pressing the backspace key on your keyboard. On the desktop app, select the shapes and press the Backspace key on your keyboard. On the mobile app, first deselect the heart by tapping anywhere on the Canvas away from it, then tap on it again. You'll now see a red dustbin in the secondary bar at the bottom of the screen. Tap on it to get rid of the shape.

Edit

With this function, you can achieve five things:

1. Cut the selected element, which copies it to the clipboard but removes it from the *Canvas.*
2. Copy the selected element, which copies it to the clipboard but keeps the original on the *Canvas.*
3. Paste a cut or copied element onto the *Canvas.*
4. Duplicate the selected element, which acts like an instant 'copy paste' function.
5. Delete the selected element.

Pro Tip: All devices, from computers to smartphones, have clipboards.

A clipboard is a memory of sorts that can store information you have cut or copied, enabling you to use it again. However, whatever you cut or copy overrides whatever was cut or copied before it, so you can't access things from before the last cut or copy action. Also, the memory is short-lived. You can't copy something now, turn off your device, and then paste it, as the information will be lost.

You'll use the cut/copy/paste functions for different reasons while creating your designs, but you'll use the copy/paste function much more than the cut function. Yet still, if you want to make a design with a repeating shape, it's much easier and quicker to just duplicate the same shape and skipping the copy, paste, copy paste, copy paste ... sequence

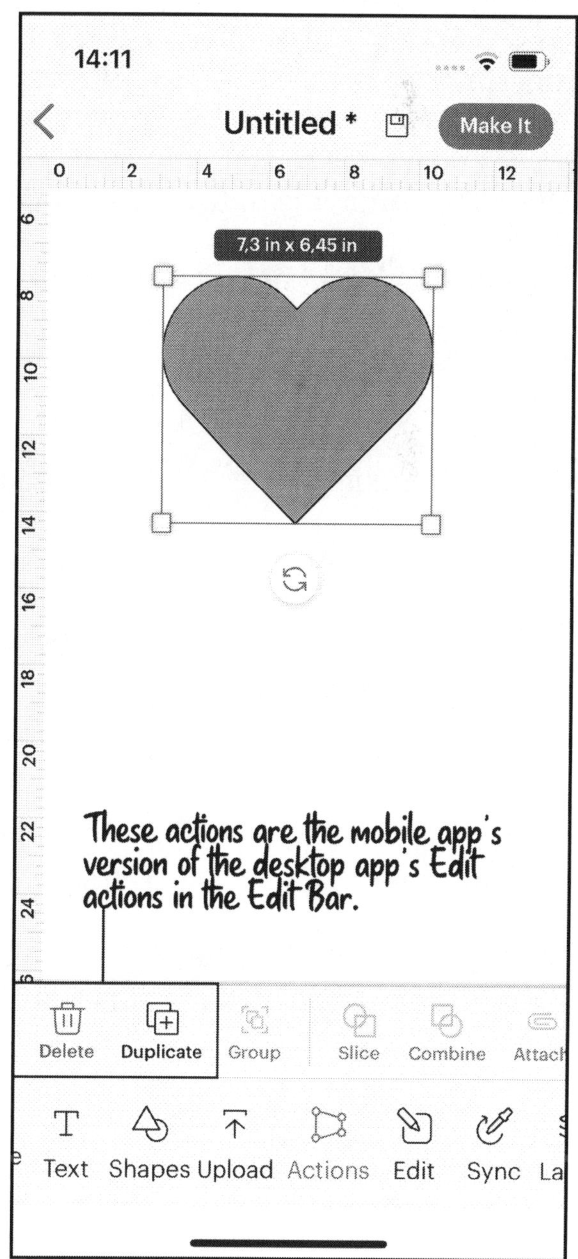

How to use the *Edit* functions on your mobile app

The mobile app does not feature the copy, paste, or cut functions at all. But if you think about it, with the duplicate function, you really don't need the other three. So, your mobile app only gives you the ability to duplicate and delete selected elements. When you tap on a shape or any other element, the *Actions* function should activate automatically and show you options in a secondary bar right above the regular Edit Bar at the bottom of your screen. If not, tap on *Actions* in the bottom bar to activate the secondary bar. The first two options, *Delete* and *Duplicate*, are equivalent to the Edit functions you have on the desktop app.

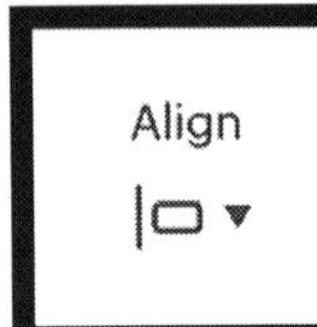

Align

The Align function only works when you have two or more elements selected at the same time.

Alignment offers a quick way to get everything lined up perfectly. If it weren't for this simple feature, you would waste hours trying to get everything right (and lose a fair amount of sanity in the process).

To see how it works, add a heart to the *Canvas* and duplicate it twice, using the *Edit* function.

Move the hearts to separate spots on the grid area. Now select them all and click on *Align*. The following options will appear:

- *Align Left* (pushes all the elements to the left side of the selection box).
- *Align Horizontally* (lines up all the elements down an invisible vertical line inside the selection box).
- *Align Right* (pushes all the elements to the right side of the selection box).
- *Align Top* (pushes all the elements against the top side of the selection box).
- *Center Vertically* (lines up all the elements across an invisible horizontal line inside the selection box).
- *Align Bottom* (pushes all the elements against the bottom side of the selection box).
- *Center* (lines up all the elements square in the middle of invisible vertical and horizontal lines inside the selection box).

Be mindful with the *Center Horizontally* and *Center Vertically* options, as they actually do the opposite of what the functions say. Look at the below illustration of my hearts.

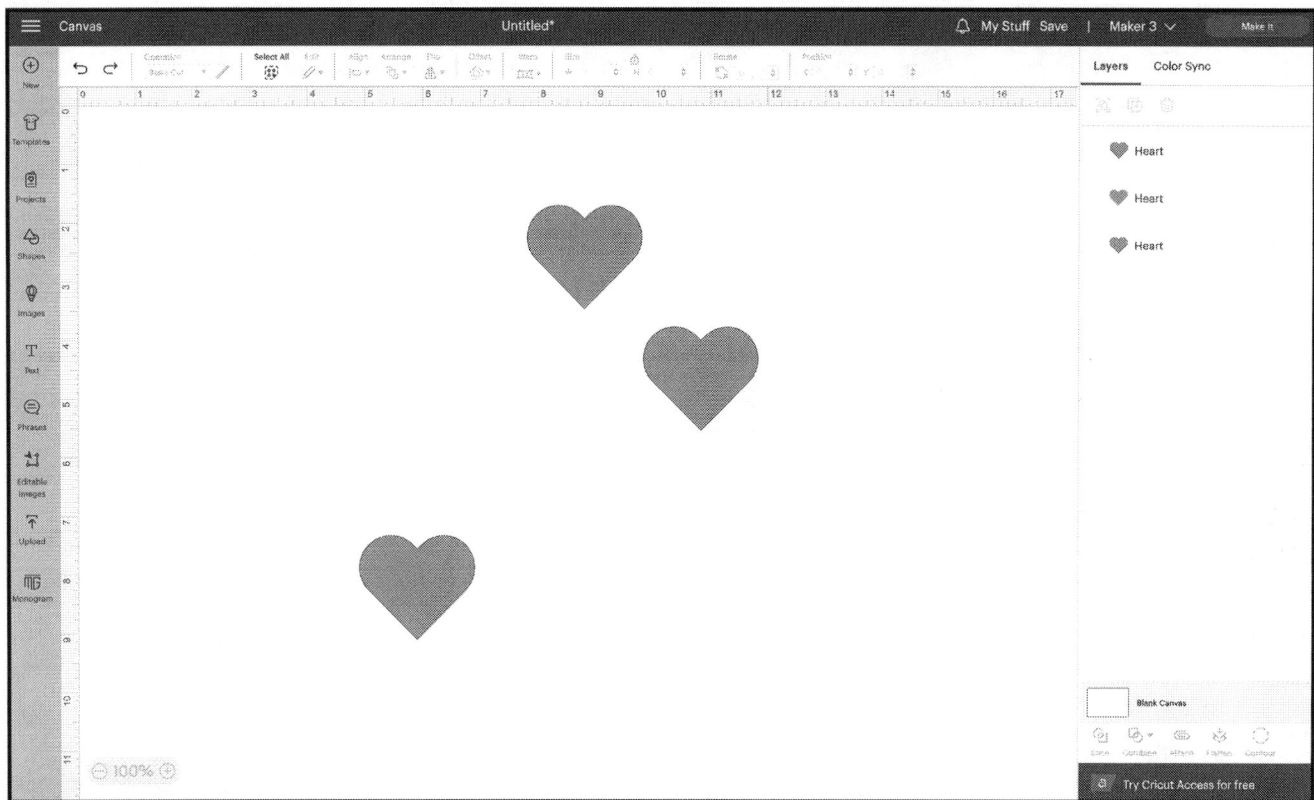

If I choose *Center Horizontally*, the program will arrange the hearts down a vertical line.

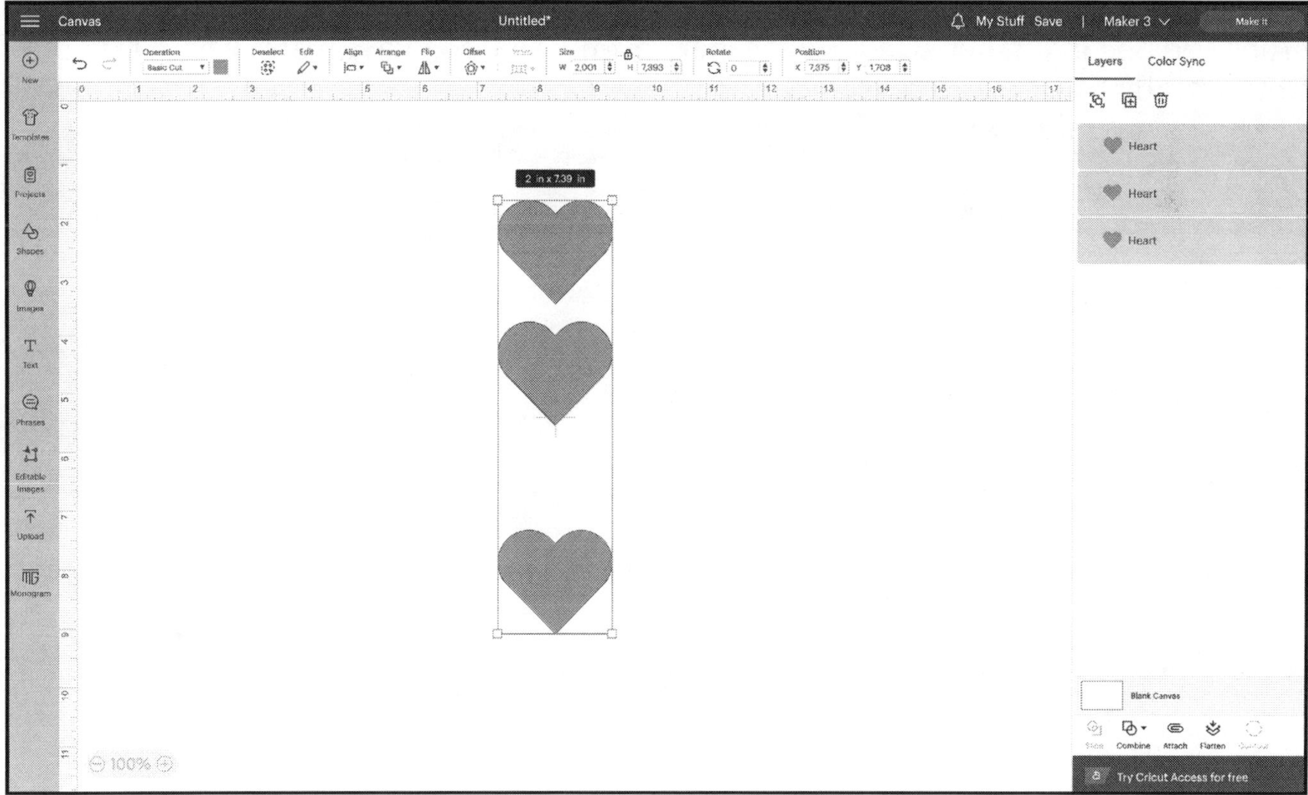

And if I choose *Center Vertically*, the program will arrange the hearts across a horizontal line.

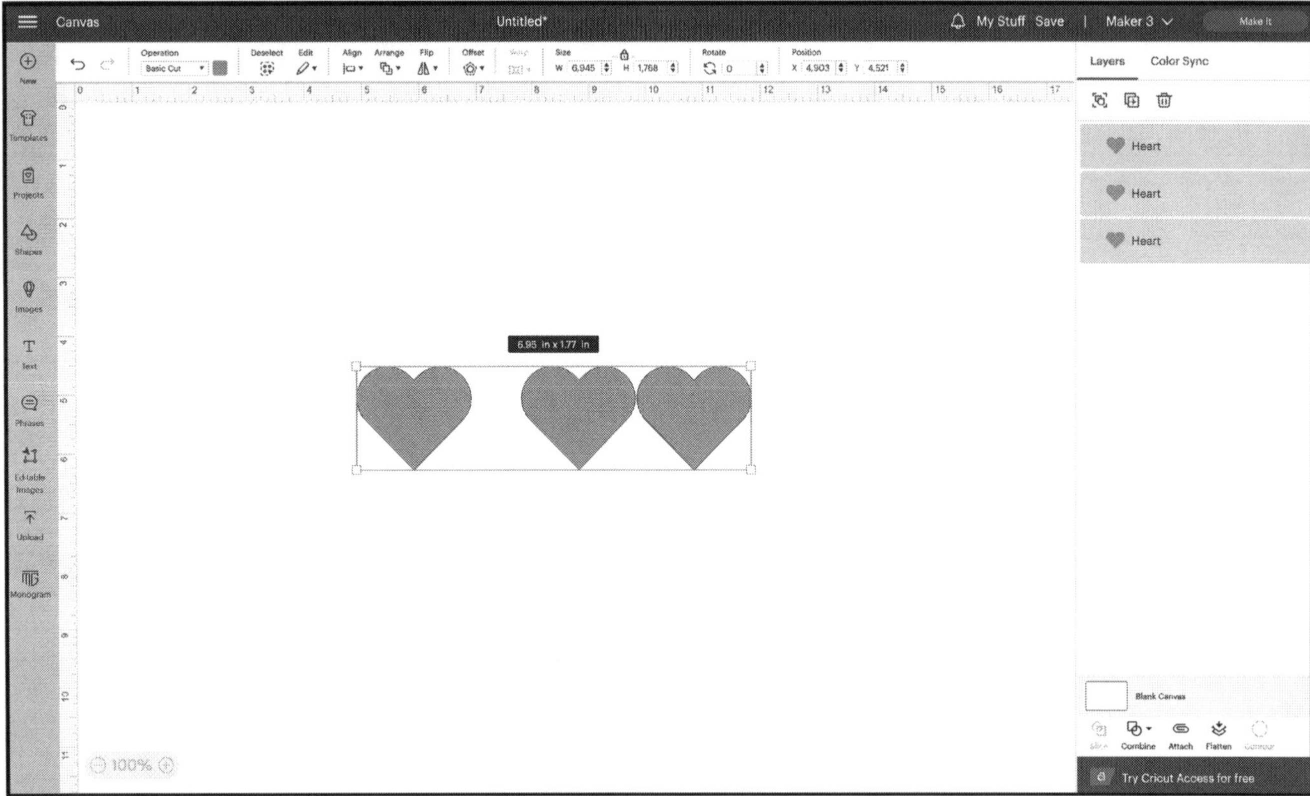

At the bottom of the *Align* menu are two *Distribute options*. These settings help you space out elements evenly. For example, in the above screenshot, two hearts are close to each other and one is further away. To get them evenly spaced, we can apply the Distribute Horizontally function. Here is the result:

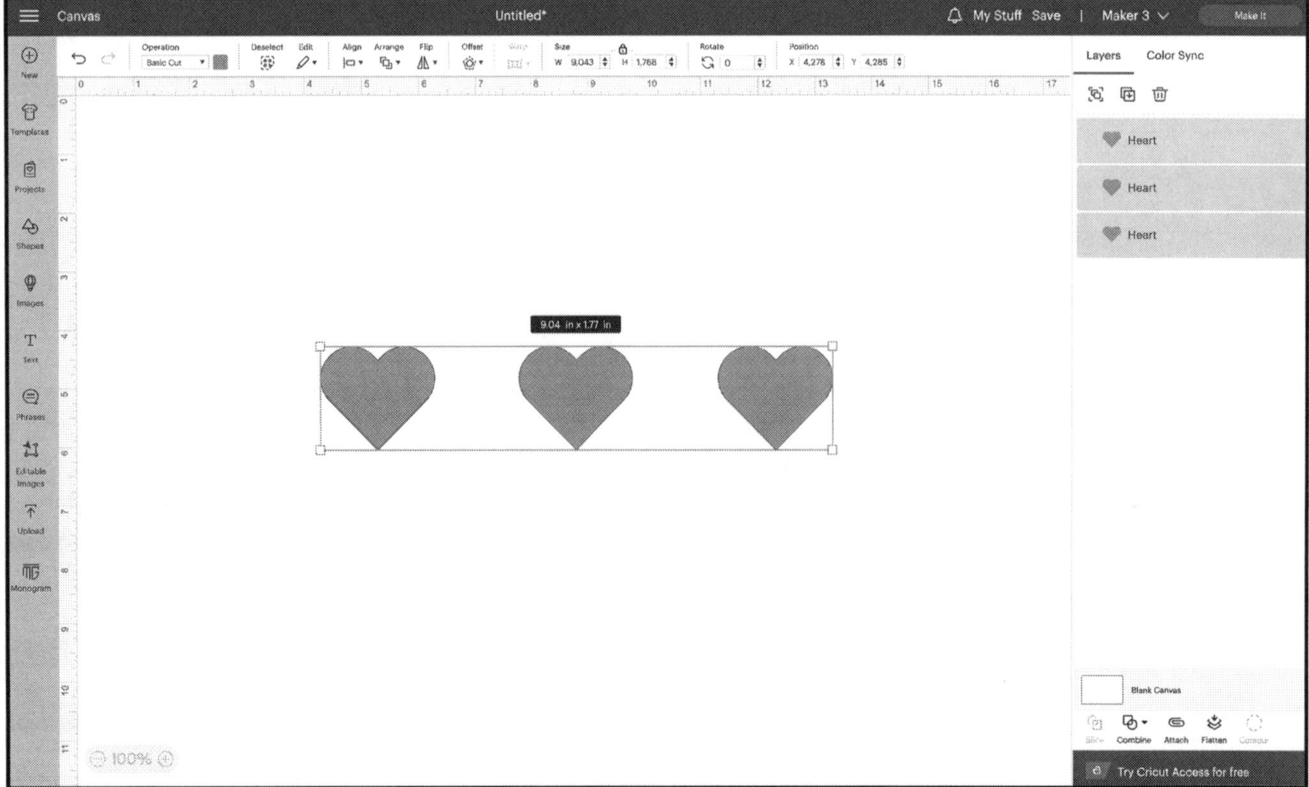

Don't be afraid to experiment and play around with all the alignment options to get a feel for how they work and influence the design elements on your *Canvas*.

Pro Tip: The way elements within your selection box are scattered will influence what you see when applying the *Align* options. For example, if two shapes are more or less on the same height and you choose *Align Left*, the two shapes will overlap each other. But if one shape is higher than the other, it will look like they're stacked on top of each other when you apply the *Align Left* option.

How to use the *Align* functions on your mobile app

Duplicate the heart on your *Canvas* twice, scatter the copies around, and then select all of them using the selection method you learned earlier. Find *Edit* in the primary bar at the bottom of the screen (not the secondary bar that pops up when you select elements, but the one underneath it). Tap on *Edit*. Now swipe the secondary (on top of the primary bar) to the right until you see *Align* and tap on it. Choose any alignment option you'd like to test out and see how it affects your shapes. Next, distribute your shapes horizontally or vertically using the *Distribute* function right next to the *Align* function.

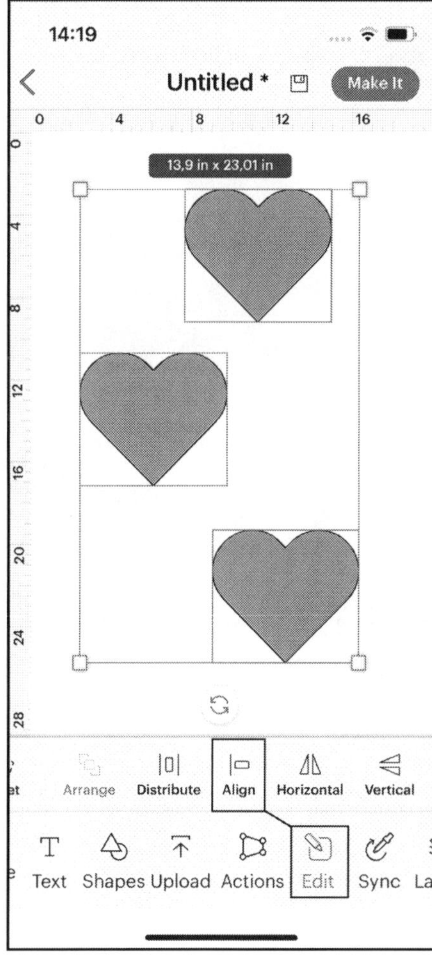

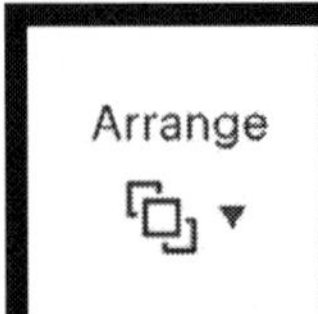

Arrange

In *Design Space* language, every element on the Canvas is also known as a layer.

For example, if there are five shapes on your *Canvas*, there are actually five layers on *Canvas*. Like an onion's layers, the layers on your Canvas each occupy a level, and no two layers can be on the same level, meaning there is a hierarchy at play. You can't really see this hierarchy when elements are all over the Canvas or next to each other, like you see below.

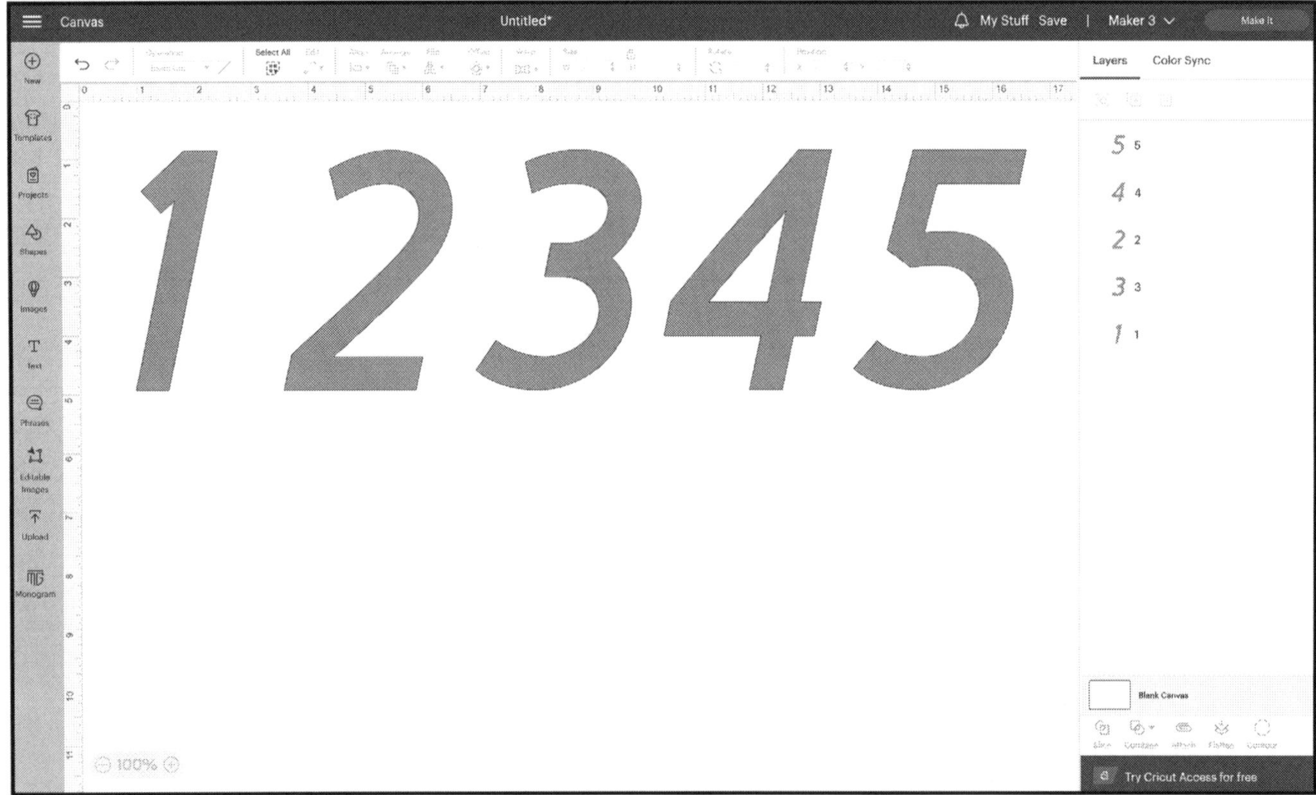

However, when we bring elements closer to each other, we can see that they overlap, and one element always lies underneath or above another element. For example, when we bring the numbers 1 to 5 together, we can now see that number 1 lies underneath numbers 2, number 2 lies underneath number 3, and so on (See the screenshot on the next page).

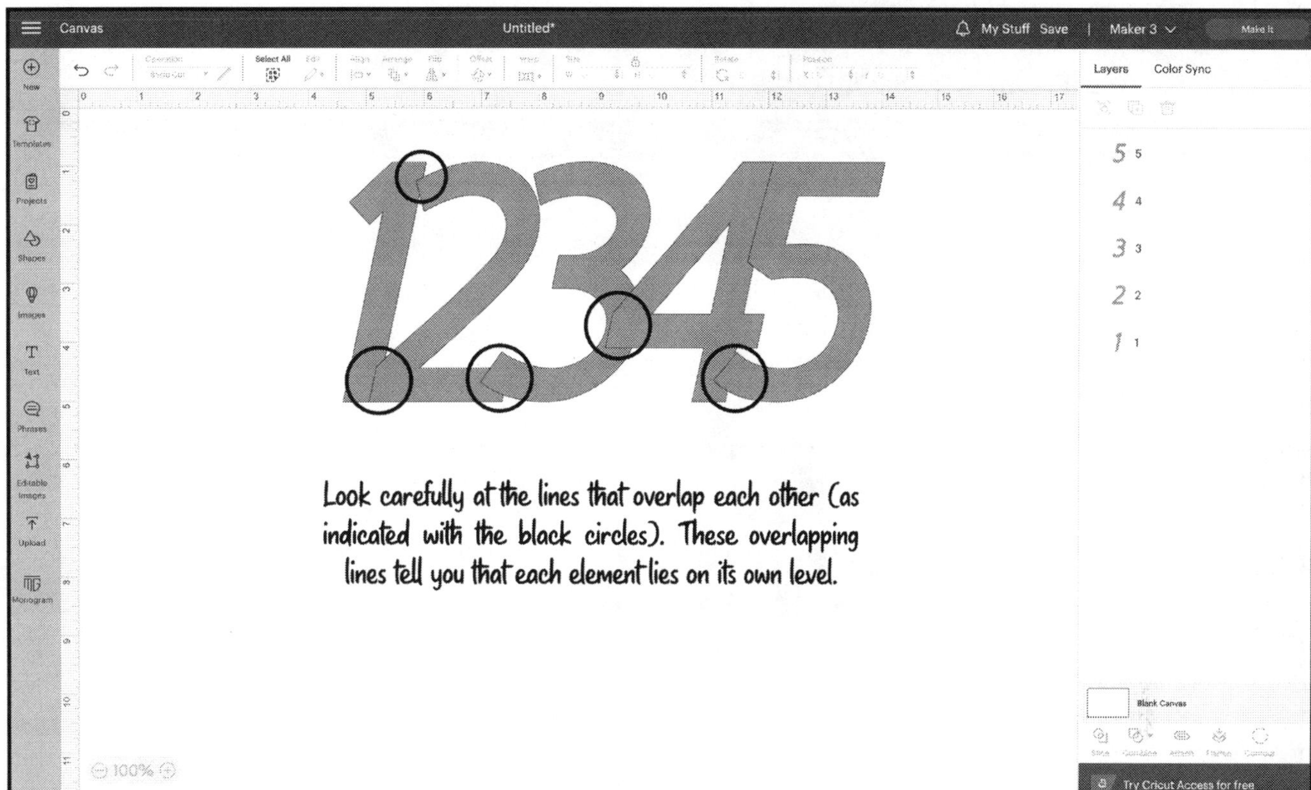

Arrange allows you to choose the hierarchy of each element on the *Canvas*. The ability to do this gives you a lot of design freedom and allows you to come up with unique elements within your design. Let's change the arrangement of the numbers in the above example. I want number 1 to be in front of number 2. To do this, we need to select the number 1, click on *Arrange*, and then choose *Bring Forward*. As you can see in the below screenshot, number 1's outline is now in front of number 2's outline, which means we have successfully moved number 1 one level up.

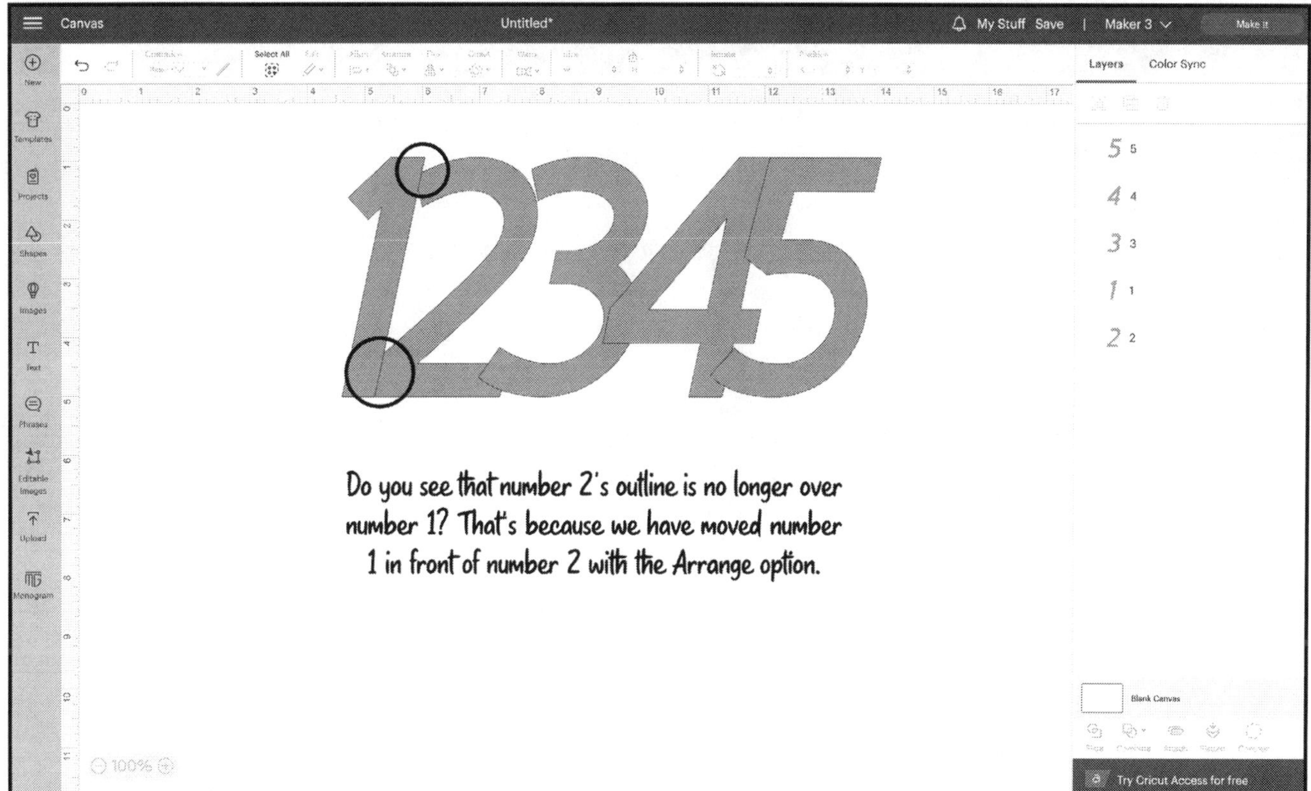

To get a better idea of what *Arrange* looks like in an actual design, have a look at the below screenshot. Can you spot the issue?

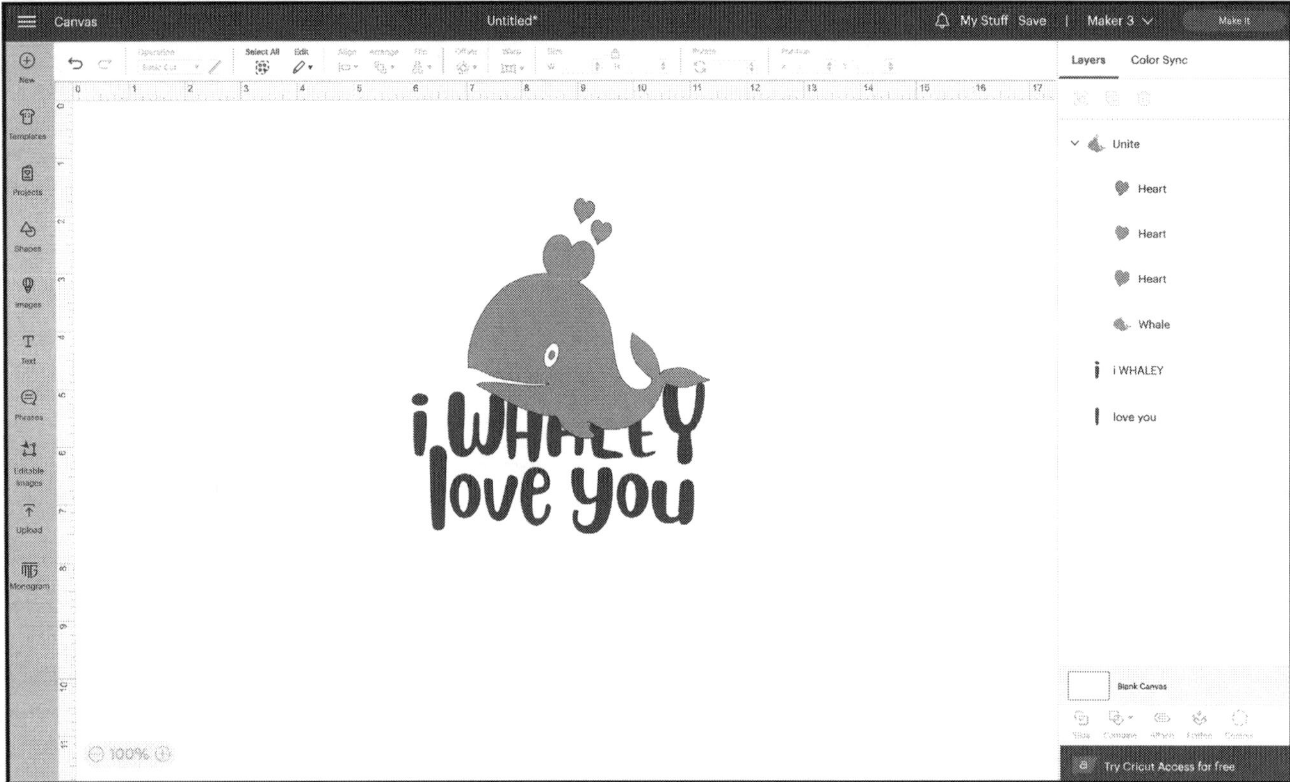

That's right! It's nearly impossible to read the text underneath the whale. To fix this, we need to either move the whale backward or move the text forward. It doesn't matter which option you choose, because both will have the same outcome. Since the whale is on top, it will be easier to select. Once selected, I'll click on *Arrange* and then choose *Send Backward*. Here's the result:

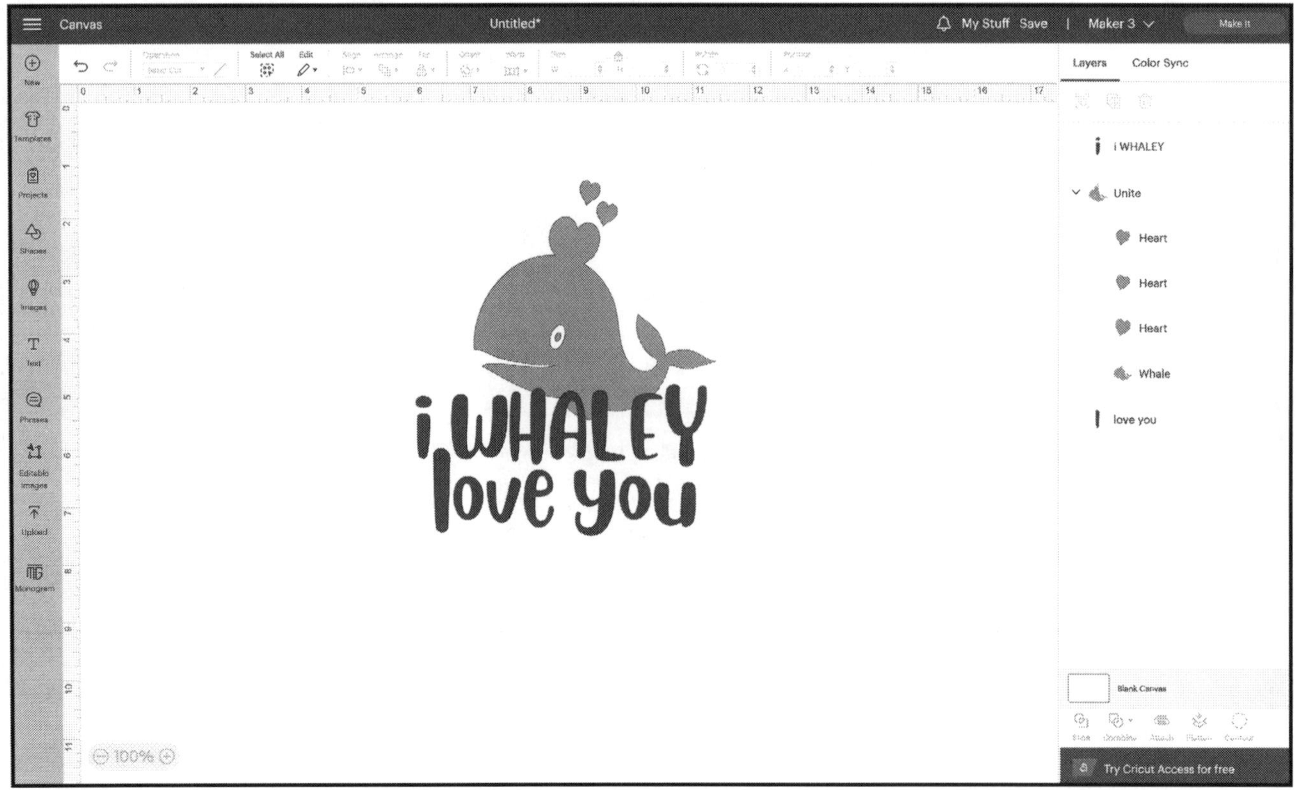

Pro Tip: When you have elements that overlap each other for design purposes, you want to be sure they're stacked properly. If not, your final project may make you shed a tear or two after you have put all that hard work into creating your design.

Simply put, the *Arrange* function helps you to define what goes on top, what goes in the middle, and what goes at the back. *Arrange* has four options:

- *Bring to Front* (sends the selected element all the way in front of the other elements on the *Canvas*).
- *Bring Forward* (sends the selected element one level forward, pushing it in front of whatever element is currently in front of *it*).
- *Send Backward* (sends the selected element one level down, pushing it underneath the element it is currently in front of).
- *Send to Back* (sends the selected element all the way behind the other elements on the *Canvas*).

How to use the *Arrange* functions on your mobile app

Tap on the element you want to move forward or backward, find and tap on *Edit* in the primary edit bar at the bottom if your screen, and then select *Arrange* from the secondary bar. From there, you can choose what you want to do with the element.

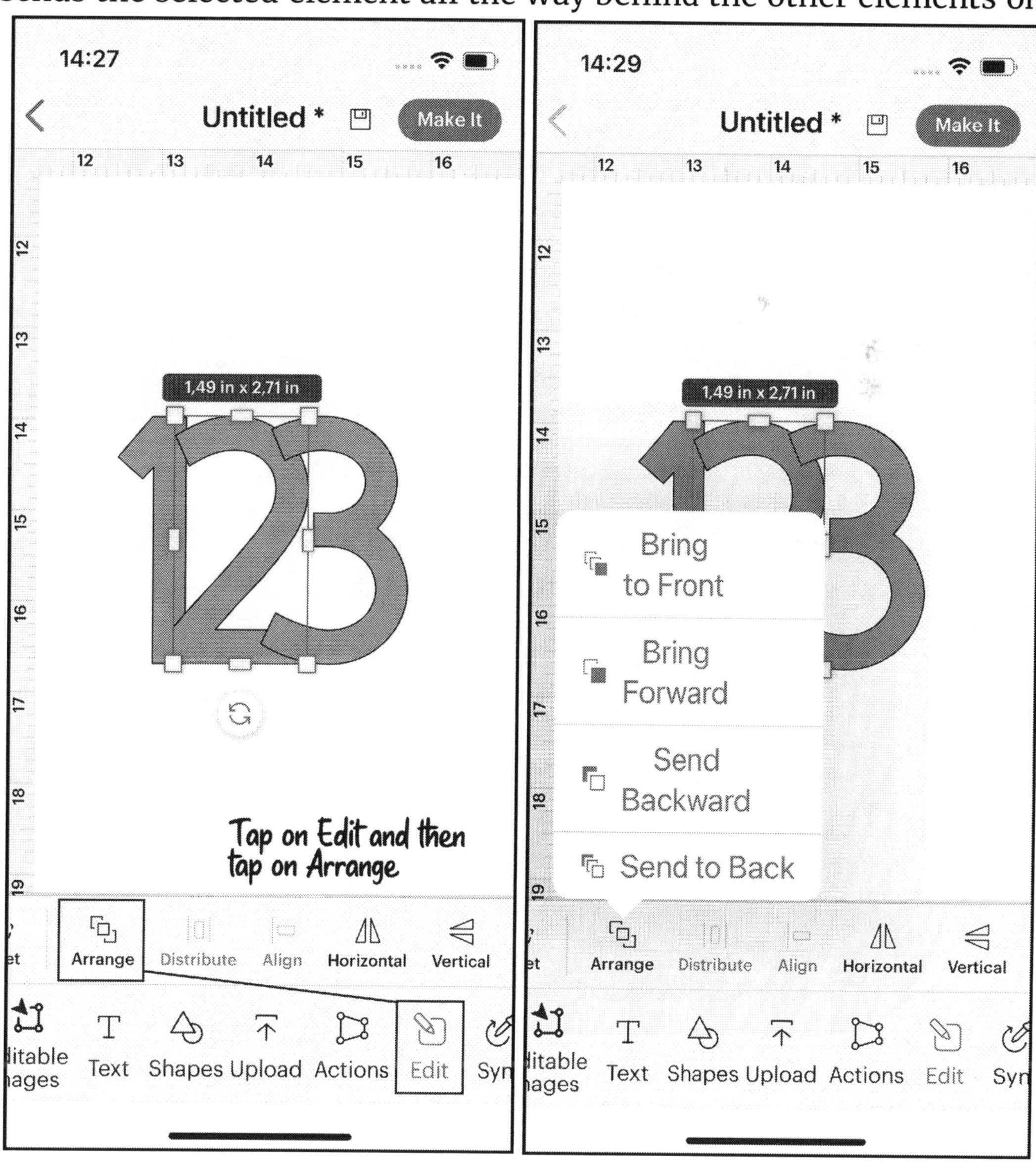

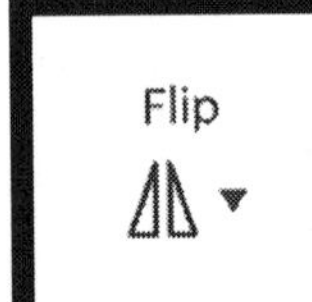

Flip

This handy feature allows you to flip the direction of an element or an entire design, essentially creating a mirror image of the original.

Flip Horizontal lets you mirror the selected element sideways, while *Flip Vertical* lets you mirror the selected element upside down.

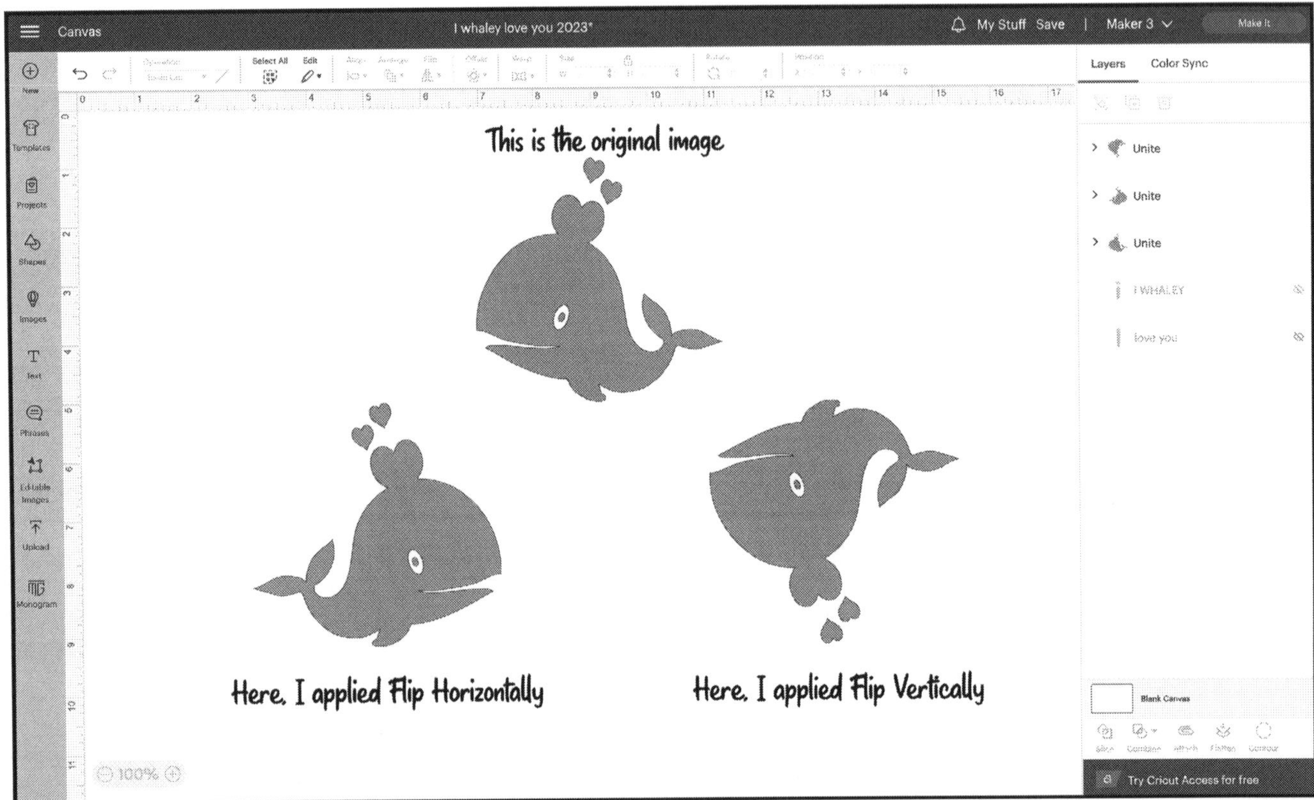

How to use the *Flip* function on your mobile app

Select the element you'd like to flip, tap on Edit in the primary bar at the bottom of your screen, and then swipe the secondary bar until you see *Horizontal* and *Vertical*. *Horizontal* will flip your element horizontally and *Vertical* will flip your element vertically.

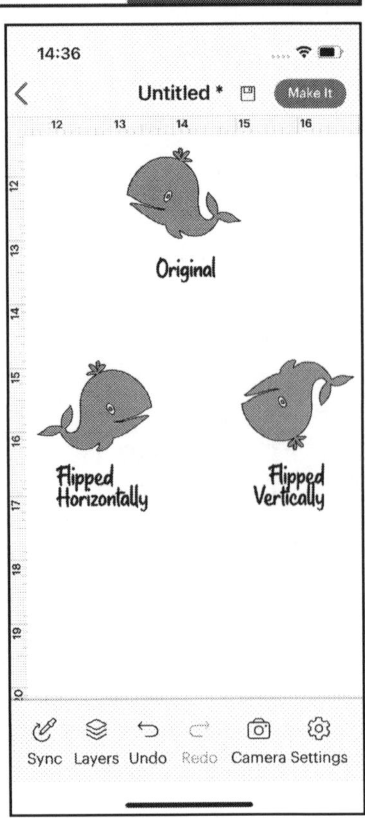

Offset

This feature creates a proportionally larger or smaller copy of the selected element.

The copy does not have the same details as the original; rather, it is like a blank silhouette. According to Cricut, this feature adds more depth and increases the visual impact of your designs.

For now, though, I don't want you to be concerned with Offset at all; you have a ton to learn and need to master the basics first.

Warp

This feature works with text elements only.

When you select text and click on the *Warp* function, you'll see various options to make the text adhere to different shapes. Essentially, this function automatically stretches and squashes letters out of proportion to create certain effects. In the past, you would have had to spend hours tweaking individual letters to get the same results. At the time of updating this book, the Warp function is not yet available on the mobile app.

Size

Use this function to manually adjust an element's size.

The Size function works the same as when you grab a selection box's corner to make an element bigger or smaller. However, this way gives you more accuracy and control over the size, as you can specify the exact inches (or centimeters if you have metric measurements enabled) you want the element to be.

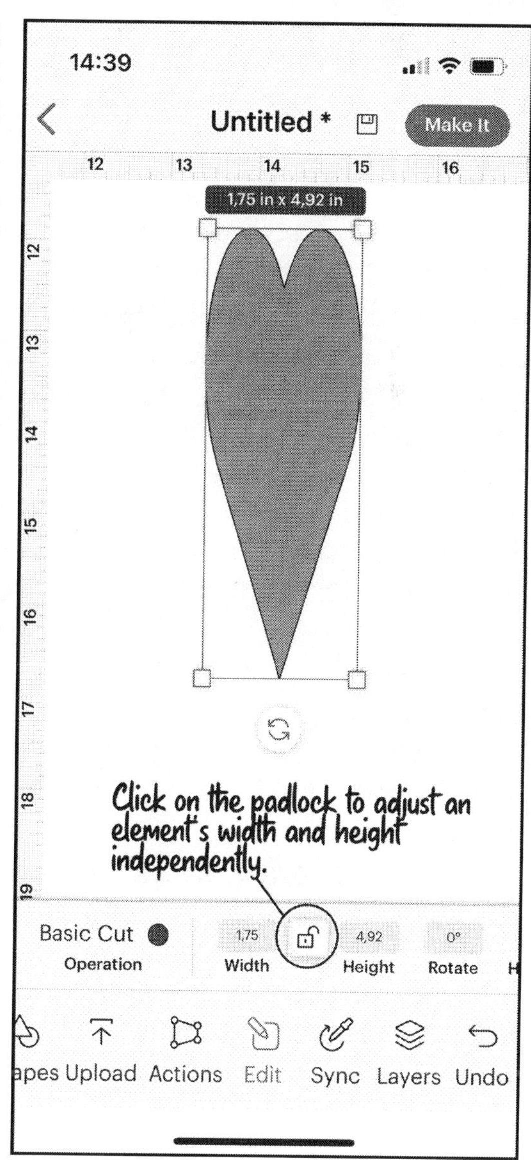

By default, an element's proportions are locked. This means that if you increase or decease the width (indicated by the "W"), the height (indicated by the "H") will automatically increase or decrease in proportion to the width, and vice versa. However, if you click on the little padlock between the height and width, you will unlock the proportions and be able to adjust the width and height independently of each other. This is the same as grabbing one of the four sides of a selection box and stretching or squashing it in the desktop app. When the padlock is closed, the proportions are locked and when it's open, the proportions are unlocked.

Remember how I said you can't stretch and squash an element using the selection box on the mobile app? Well, this is the function you'll use to do it when working on a tablet or cell phone. To activate the *Size* function on your mobile app, select the element and choose *Edit* in the primary bar at the bottom of the screen. On the secondary bar, you'll see the width and height settings with a padlock in between them. Tap on the padlock to unlock it.

Now you can go ahead and achieve the same stretch and squash results as you would when adjusting the sides of the selection box on the desktop app.

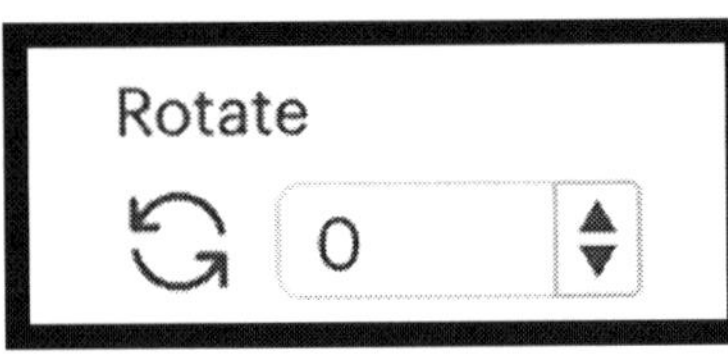

Rotate

Use this function to manually tilt an element to the left or right.

This function does the same thing as when you tilt an element using the selection box. The only reason you would use this method is if you have an exact angle, like maybe 40 degrees, in mind for your design element. On your mobile app, you can find the *Rotate* function by selecting the element, tapping on Edit in the primary bar at the bottom of the screen, and then swiping the secondary bar until you see the *Rotate* settings box. Tap on the box to specify the angle you want for your element.

Position

Use this function to manually move an element.

Since it's more convenient to just move elements around with the selection box, you'll not use this method often. It does, however, come in handy when you need to nudge an element ever so slightly up, down, left, or right to get it in the perfect spot. You can find the *Position* settings on your mobile app by selecting the element you want to move, tapping on *Edit* in the primary bar at the bottom of the screen, and swiping the secondary bar until you see the *X Position* and *Y Position* settings. Tap on those to adjust the position of your element.

The Text Edit Bar

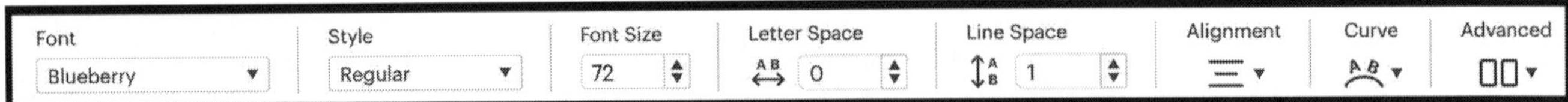

When working with text, you'll see another bar appear underneath the regular *Edit Bar* on the desktop app. This is the text edit bar, and it allows you to specify fonts, font styles, font size, line and letter spacing, and text alignment for text elements. There are also advanced features, like text curving and the ability to separate each letter in a word onto separate layers, allowing for more design freedom.

Right now, text curving is only available on the desktop app and the iOS version of the mobile app. You'll learn more about what you can do with text in Chapter 10, when we do some projects together.

The Layers Panel

Remember how I told you that each element on the Canvas is actually a layer when we talked about the *Arrange* function? Well, the box to the right of the grid is called the *Layers Panel*. Here, you have a birds-eye view of all the elements on your Canvas, as well each element's order (or arrangement).

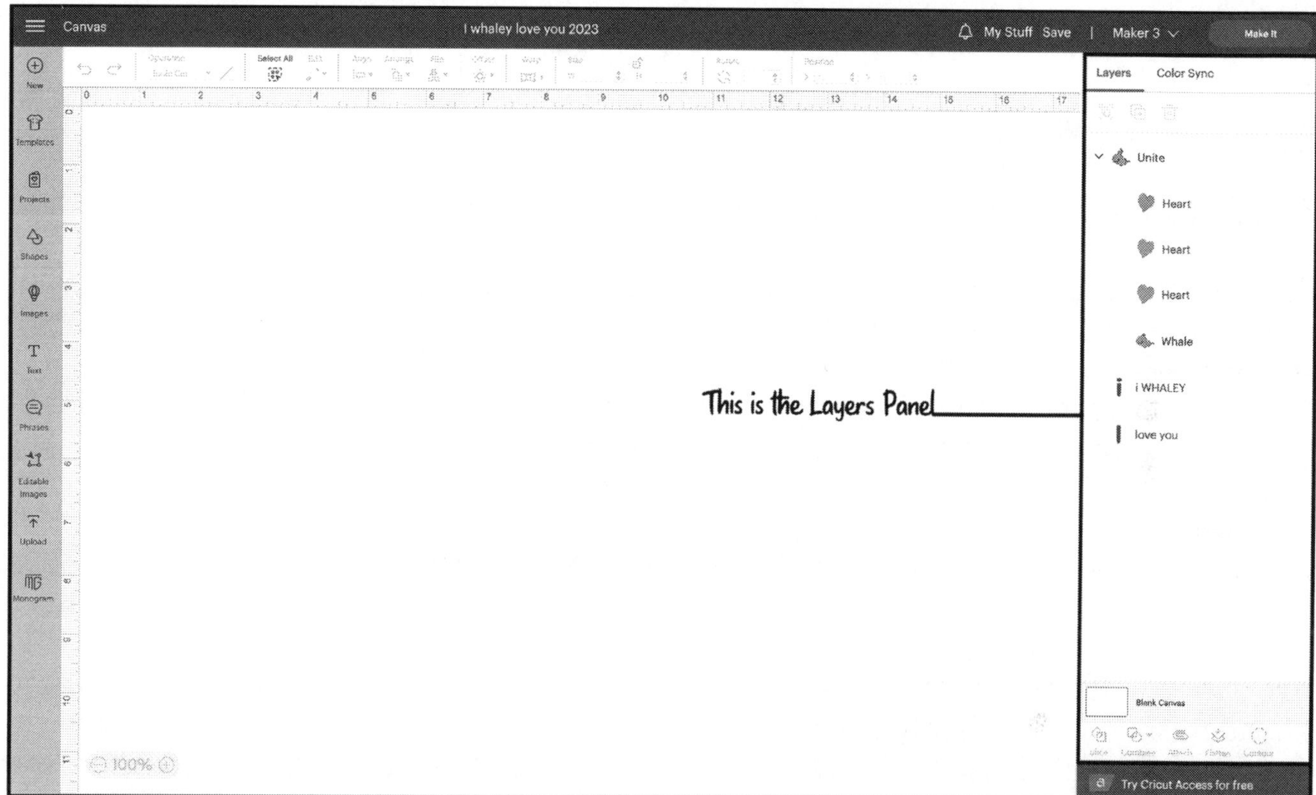

Most designs are made up of different layers built on top of each other. The beauty of layers is that each one can be edited independently, meaning a change in one will not change anything in the rest of the design. This is important, because if you make a mistake with one layer, you can simply fix that layer or delete it if things aren't working out, all while keeping the bulk of your design intact. If it weren't for layers, you'd have to start an entire design from scratch every time you made a mistake or simply wanted to change something small.

You'll gain a solid foundation on working with layers from this chapter and the upcoming projects chapter. That said, my other book, *Cricut Design Space Handbook for Newbies*, dives deeply into layers and each Design Space function. Later, when you're ready to take the plunge into becoming a Design Space ninja, it will definitely be worth your while to check out the other book.

Let's see what you can do with layers, starting at the very top of the panel.

Layers Color Sync

Toggle between the Layers Panel and the Color Sync Panel

The *Color Sync Panel* sorts every design element (or layer) into categories according to their colors. This gives you a convenient way to quickly change one design element's color to match the color of other elements in your design. For example, if you have black squares and pink text but would like to change the text to black, you can simply drag the text to the squares right there in the *Color Sync Panel* to make the change.

Group & Ungroup

This function allows you to bundle different elements together to make them function as a unit. For example, you might have a group of hearts that you want to move to a different spot, but you don't want to move them one by one. You might also want to change their color to something else without having to do it one by one.

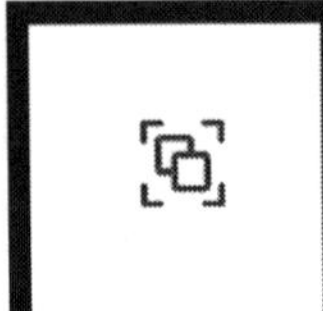

That's where the *Group* function comes in. Select all the hearts you want to bundle together and click on the *Group* icon. Now they're a unit. If you want to move them, they'll move as if you're working with a single element.

Likewise, if you want to change them from, say, gray to pink, they'll all change at once when you apply the new color.

Pro Tip: You know how to select a single element, and you know how to select all the elements on the Canvas. But there's a way to select two or more elements while leaving the others alone ... Press your keyboard's Shift key and hold it in while you click on the elements you want to select together. When you have everything you want, you can let go of the Shift key.

Once elements are grouped together, you can't tweak them individually anymore. If, for some reason, you want to tweak one element inside the group without affecting the other elements, like making it bigger or smaller than the rest, you'll have to separate the elements first.

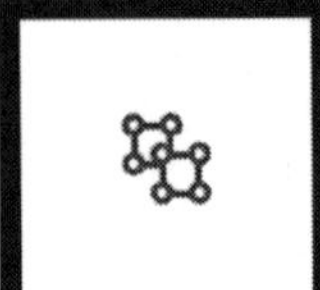

That's where the *Ungroup* function comes in. The moment you apply the *Group* function to a set of elements, the same button becomes the *Ungroup* function.

To separate grouped elements, select the group and then apply the *Ungroup* function. Now you can tweak each element on its own without affecting the others.

To group and ungroup elements on the mobile app, select the elements you want to bundle together. The *Group* function will become visible immediately in the secondary bar at the bottom of your screen. Tap on it to bundle the elements. Now that they're bundled, you'll see the *Ungroup* function (right next to the *Group* function) become active. So, if you need to separate the elements again, tap on the *Ungroup* function.

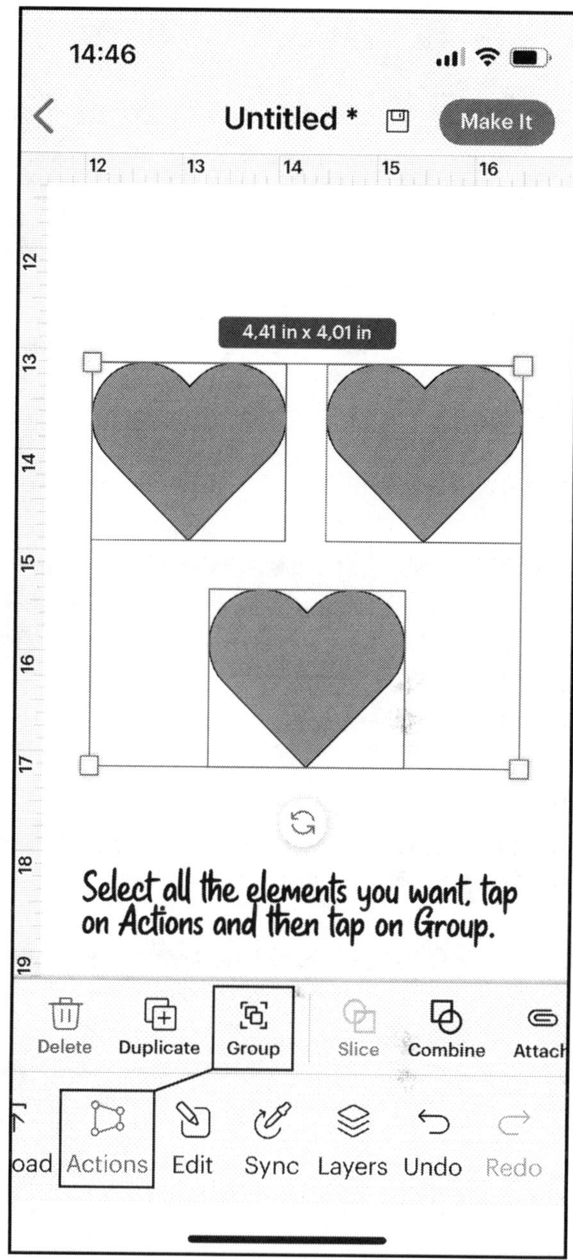

Pro Tip: To make a selection of specific elements on your mobile device, tap on one element first. With that element selected, press your finger on the next element you want to add to the selection and hold it there until you see the selection box expand to include the element you were pressing down on. Move on to the next element and do the same. Continue doing this until you have all the elements inside the selection box that you want.

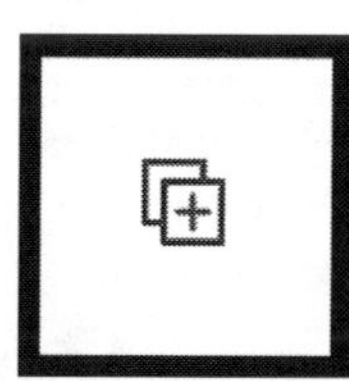

Duplicate

The *Duplicate* icon is the same *Duplicate* function from the *Edit Bar.*

Think of it as a convenient, quick-access button.

Select any layer (or element) you would like to copy and click on *Duplicate.*

You'll see a new copy of it appear on the *Canvas.* Most of the time, the duplicate will overlap with the original, but you can move it away and edit it as you would any other layer. Remember that the Duplicate icon pops up in the secondary bar at the bottom of your screen the moment you select an element when using the mobile app.

Delete

The *Delete* icon is the same *Delete* function from the *Edit Bar.* This is also a quick-access button, just like the Duplicate icon next to it.

If you want to remove an element from the Canvas, select it first and then click on the *Delete* icon. As with the Duplicate icon, the Delete icon pops up in the secondary bar at the bottom of your screen in the mobile app when you tap on (or select) an element.

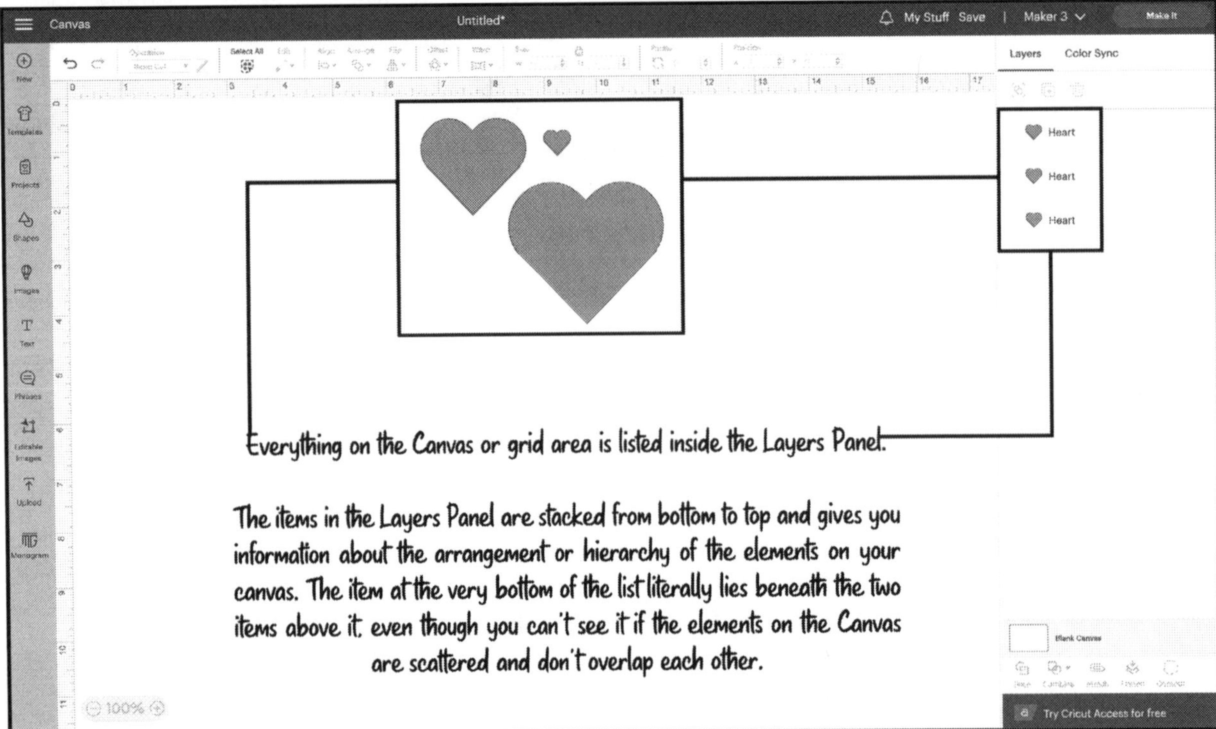

If you have design elements (or layers) on your Canvas, your Layers Panel will display all of them, in order of their arrangement or hierarchy, in the space below the functions we just discussed.

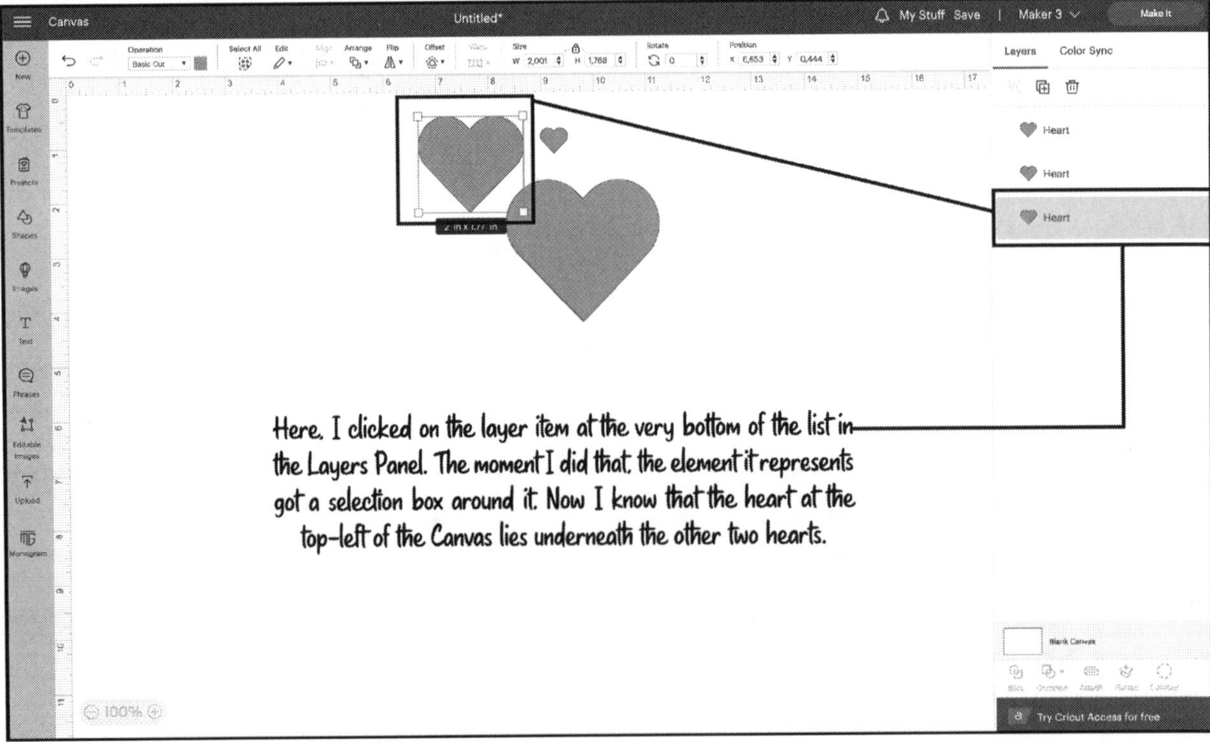

By default, Cricut names each layer according to the element it represents. If you have multiple copies of the same element, the program will simply name each layer the same. This can be a little confusing. As a Newbie, you might be wondering, "But how am I supposed to know which layer is which on the Canvas if they all have the same name?" To solve the issue, you can click on any of the layer items inside the Layers Panel. The moment you do that, a selection box will form around the corresponding element on the Canvas.

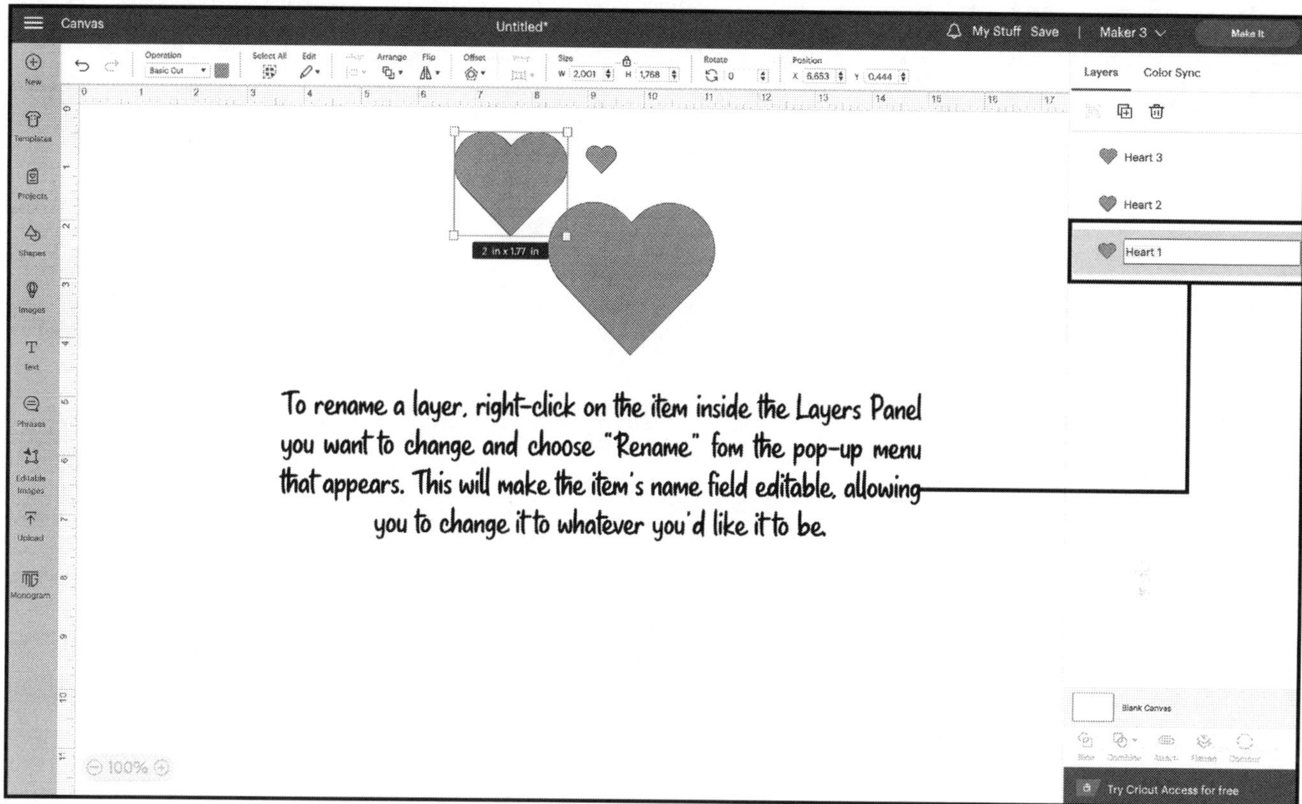

To help yourself get a better grip on the *Layers Panel*, you can rename the layers inside the panel so they make better sense to you. For example, I can name the heart at the bottom of the list in my *Layers Panel* "Heart 1", the one in the middle "Heart 2", and the one at the top "Heart 3".

When you right-click on items inside the *Layers Panel*, a pop-up menu with various options will appear. These options are no different than the functions you find in the *Edit Bar* and *Layers Panel* above and below the listed layers. You can also move list items inside the *Layers Panel* up or down. This is no different from using the *Arrange* feature in the *Edit Bar.* To move an item's order in the *Layers Panel*, click and drag it up or down. If you move an item so it sits on top of another item, you have moved it forward, and if you move it so it sits underneath another item, you have moved it backward.

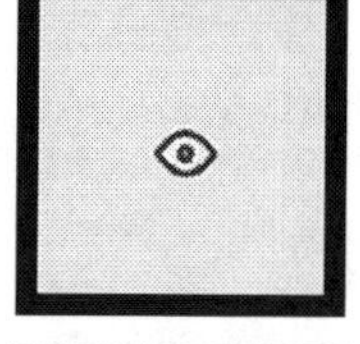

Finally, when you hover over a list item, you'll see an eye icon appear to its right. This icon tells you the item is visible on the Canvas and your Cricut will cut it out during the cutting process.

However, if you click on the eye, you can hide that layer and your machine will not cut it. Hiding elements (or layers) is not the same as deleting them, because you can make them reappear by clicking on the eye icon again. So, if you're not too in love with a layer, but you're not entirely sure you want to dump it either, it's better to just hide it instead of deleting it while you think it over.

The mobile app has a Layers Panel, and you can access it from the primary bar at the bottom of your screen, but you will rarely have use for it other than familiarizing yourself with the order of the elements on your Canvas. You can only do the following actions in the mobile app's Layers Panel:

- Duplicate the layer
- Hide/Show the layer
- Delete the layer
- Access extra information about the layer if the design element comes from Cricut

In time, you'll develop your own design rhythm and use your Canvas in a way that best suits you. There is no right or wrong way to use functions that can be accessed in different ways. Whatever works for you, that's what you should do.

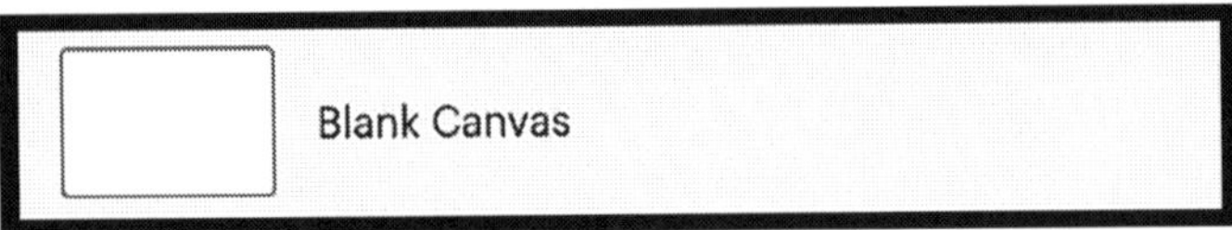

Below the list of layers in the *Layers Panel*, you'll see a little window with a description next to it.

If you're working on a project from scratch, it will say *Blank Canvas*.

However, if you're working with *Templates* from the *Design Panel*, it will indicate the one you have selected.

For example, if you have chosen a backpack template, it will say *Backpacks* next to the window. When working with a blank canvas, nothing will happen when you click on this window. However, when you're working with a template and you click on the window, a bar will appear at the top of the screen, right beneath the *Edit Bar*.

You can use it to tweak the template you're working with a bit to give you a better representation of the actual item you will apply your design to. Note that you can also hide the template with the little eye icon to the right of the description.

Further down below, under the *Canvas* description, there are more adjustment options for layers. These adjustments are a little more advanced than the others, and you may not use them right in the beginning of your crafting journey. That said, I'll give you a quick overview of them. From left to right, they are:

Slice

Slice gives you the ability to use one element to cut out a piece of another element.

This feature will cut off the parts of two layers where they overlap, as well as create a new layer that has your intended effect. For example, if I wanted to slice out a smaller heart shape out of a larger heart shape, this is what I would do:

1. Add a heart shape to the *Canvas.*

2. *Duplicate* the heart.

3. Make one of the two hearts larger.

4. Position the small heart on top of the large heart and align them using the *Center Align* option on the *Edit Bar.*

5. Select both hearts at the same time and click on the *Slice* icon.

This is what it looks like:

Of course, when following the above steps, you won't see all those hearts in the screenshot above, as you'll only be working with two. I only added so many to help you visualize the process from start to end result.

Combine

Combine is an umbrella term for a set of different actions that allow you to achieve some cool results with overlapping elements.

Before Cricut added the *Combine* feature, you could only *Slice* and *Weld* elements. *Weld* is like the opposite of *Slice* and fuses elements together instead of slicing parts of elements out of each other. Although *Weld* is still an available option, there's really no need for it anymore with the new actions, so we'll only talk about the new actions below.

Unite

This action is basically the new *Weld*.

It allows you to fuse two or more elements into a single element. Unlike with *Weld*, though, you can undo the *Unite* action.

Subtract

This action is basically the new *Slice*.

It allows you to cut parts out of elements using the other elements that overlap it. Unlike with *Slice*, though, you can undo the *Subtract* action and apply it to more than two layers at a time.

Intersect

This action gives you a cutout of the intersection where two or more elements overlap.

Exclude

This action does the opposite of *Intersect* by leaving behind the parts outside the overlapping parts of two or more elements.

It allows you to cut parts out of elements using the other elements that overlap it. Unlike with *Slice*, though, you can undo the *Subtract* action and apply it to more than two layers at a time.

The screenshot on the next page shows the effects of each of the actions on the same group of shapes.

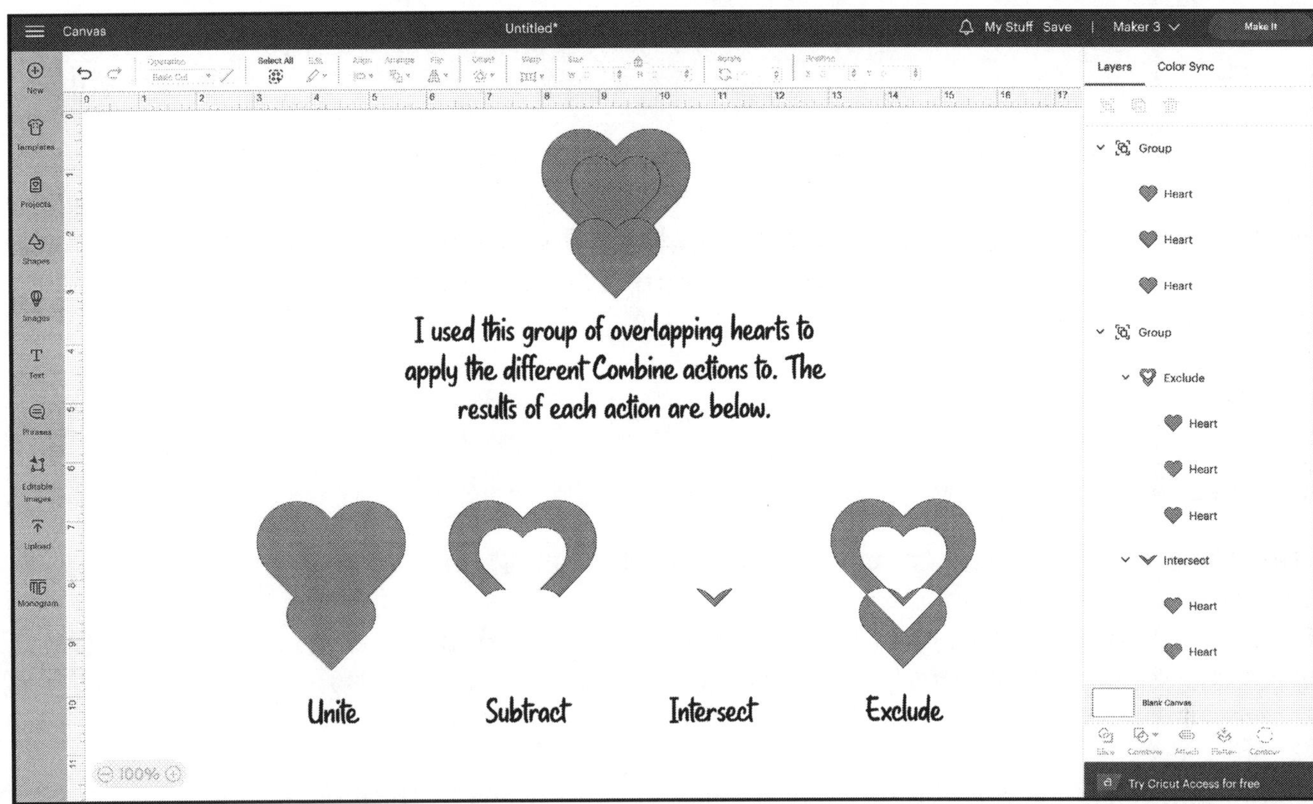

The *Combine* options are currently only available on the iOS version of the mobile app. If you have an Android device, you still have access to the older functions, *Slice* and *Weld*. To access the *Weld*, *Slice*, or *Combine* actions on your mobile app, select two or more overlapping layers. Make sure the *Actions* function is active in the primary bar at the bottom of the screen, then swipe the secondary bar until you see the *Combine* (or *Weld* and *Slice* on the Android app) actions.

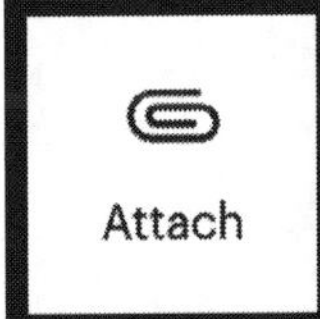

Attach/Detach

This feature can give you the impression that it's the same as the *Group* function, as it also links layers to each other.

However, *Attach* ensures that your design will be cut exactly as see it on the screen. If you don't apply the *Attach* function before moving on to the *Make It* screen, Design Space will arrange the different design elements that make up your design any way it thinks will save the most material during the cutting process. This will leave you with the mammoth task of having to bring everything back together after the cut. Sometimes, you won't need the Attach function, like when you want to cut out copies of the same shape for something like labels or stickers. But, for the most part, you'll want to remember this important action.

If you realize some part of your design still needs some tweaking after applying the *Attach* function, you'll have to separate the design elements first.

Like the *Group* icon that becomes the *Ungroup* icon, the *Attach* icon becomes the *Detach* icon, which you can use if you need to separate elements to change them.

However, keep in mind that when you *Detach* layers, they will no longer be connected to each other for the cutting process and will be treated as independent files. So, remember to apply the Attach function again when you're done tweaking things.

Flatten/Unflatten

The Flatten function merges all your layers into a single layer (kind of like an image), making it an ideal file ready for print.

You'll use this feature whenever you want to do *Print Then Cut* projects.

It is possible to *Unflatten* layers, too, but doing so will not convert those layers into *Cut* files again. Instead, they'll become two separate *Print Then* Cut files.

If you want to change them back to *Cut* files, select them individually and change their *Operation* settings in the *Edit Bar.* It is good practice to always flatten your layers when finalizing your design for a *Print Then Cut* project.

Contour

This is an advanced feature for more complex images.

When you're working with many layers to create an image, Design Space shows cut lines to indicate the shapes that your Cricut needs to cut. The *Contour* feature gives you the option to show or hide these cut lines, effectively allowing you to tell your Cricut what you want to cut out and what not.

The *Contour* feature is a powerful tool that will serve you in many ways as your Cricut journey progresses. For now, though, you can acknowledge its existence but not worry about using it.

The *Attach/Detach*, *Flatten/Unflatten* an *Contour* functions are all accessible in the *Actions* category of your mobile app. With *Actions* active, swipe the secondary bar until you see the functions.

The Make It Screen

What It Looks Like on the Desktop Version

Once you have finalized your design, it's time to let your Cricut machine do its thing. When you're happy to go ahead, click on the green *Make It* button.

If you have a Cricut Joy, Explore 3, or Maker 3, you'll see a pop-up window that asks *"How will you load all of your materials for this project?"* as soon as Design Space takes you to the next screen. Below the question, there are three options:

1. *Without Mat* (Choose this if you're going to cut a Cricut Smart Material.)
2. *On Mat* (Choose this if you're going to cut any other material that needs to be attached to a cutting mat.)
3. *Multiple Ways* (When you want to cut Smart Materials and normal materials for the same project; this is for more complex projects.)

If you have a Cricut Explore Air 2 or Maker, you'll see the *Make It* screen (also called the Prepare Screen) immediately after clicking on the *Make It* button.

The *Make It* screen has the same anatomy as other screens in Design Space: it has a header with the hamburger menu on the left side, the project's name in the middle, and the model name of the machine you're going to cut with.

The most obvious thing you'll notice on the Make It screen below the header is the big cutting mat template with a preview of your design on it. To the left of the preview is a panel with information. In the panel, you can specify how many copies you want to make of the project, change your material load settings for the Joy, Explore 3, or Maker 3 machines, specify the material size, and indicate whether the image needs to be mirrored.

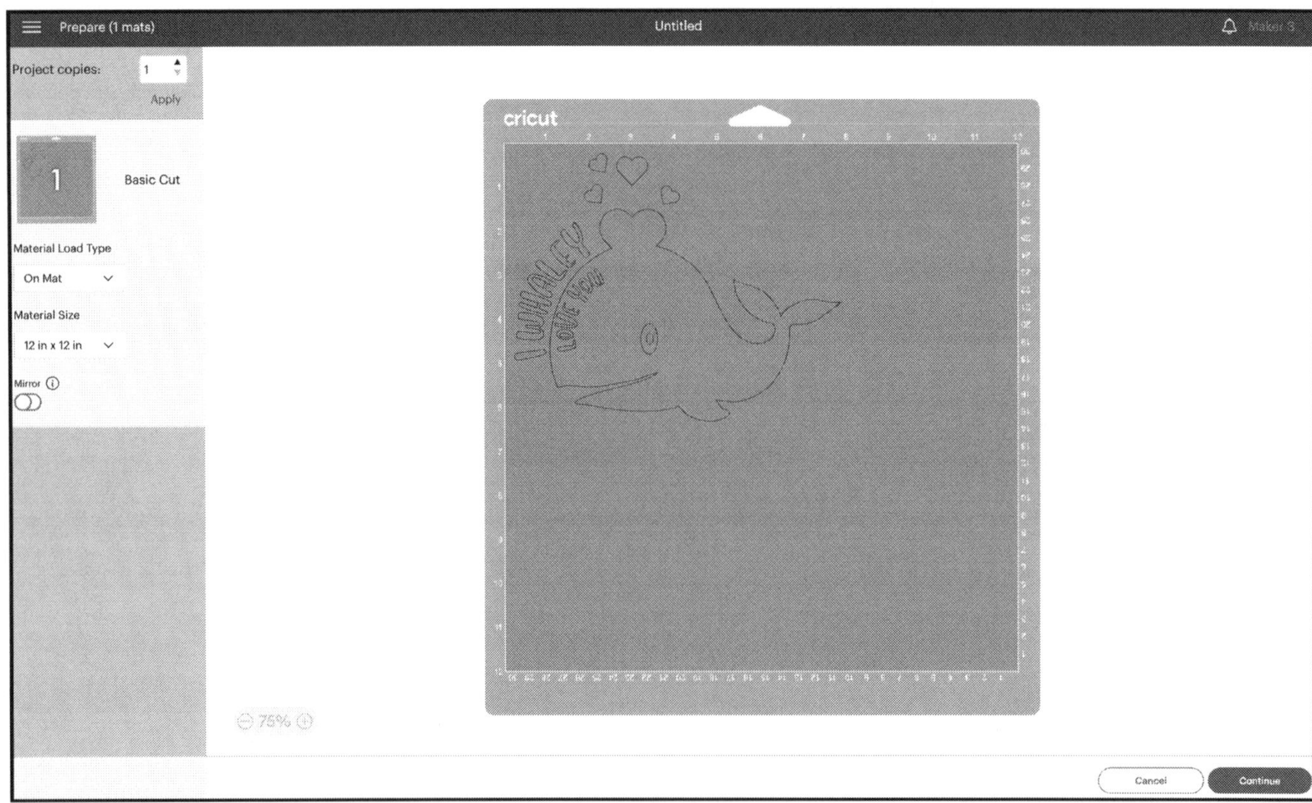

Material Size

Although you have different material size options to choose from, you can simply go with the cutting mat size you'll be using. For the Cricut Joy, the size will be either 4.5" by 6" or 4.5" by 12", and for the other machines it will be either 12" by 12" or 12" by 24". If you're going to cut *Smart Materials*, you'll see a set width and an option to specify the length.

Design Mirroring

You'll mirror images for Iron-on and other materials that require you to place them face-down on the cutting mat. The reason for mirroring designs has a lot to do with the transfer properties of the material (like Iron-On or heat transfer vinyl) or simply because it sticks better to the cutting mat when placed face-down (like leather). When you make a vinyl decal that you want to stick against the inside of a surface so it can be seen from the outside, like a window, you'll also mirror your design. Whenever you mirror a design, be sure to place your material face-down on the cutting mat. (There are no exceptions to this rule.)

At the bottom of the screen, to the right, you'll see a light gray Cancel and a green Continue button.

Don't Panic if Things Look a Little Weird on the Preview Mat

If the design on the preview mat looks nothing like the way you arranged it on the *Canvas*, it's easy to fix. Remember the *Attach* function? If you forget to apply it before moving on to the Make It screen, Design Space will automatically arrange each layer of your design to use the space on the cutting mat optimally. This is more or less what you'll see on the preview when you forget to apply the Attach feature:

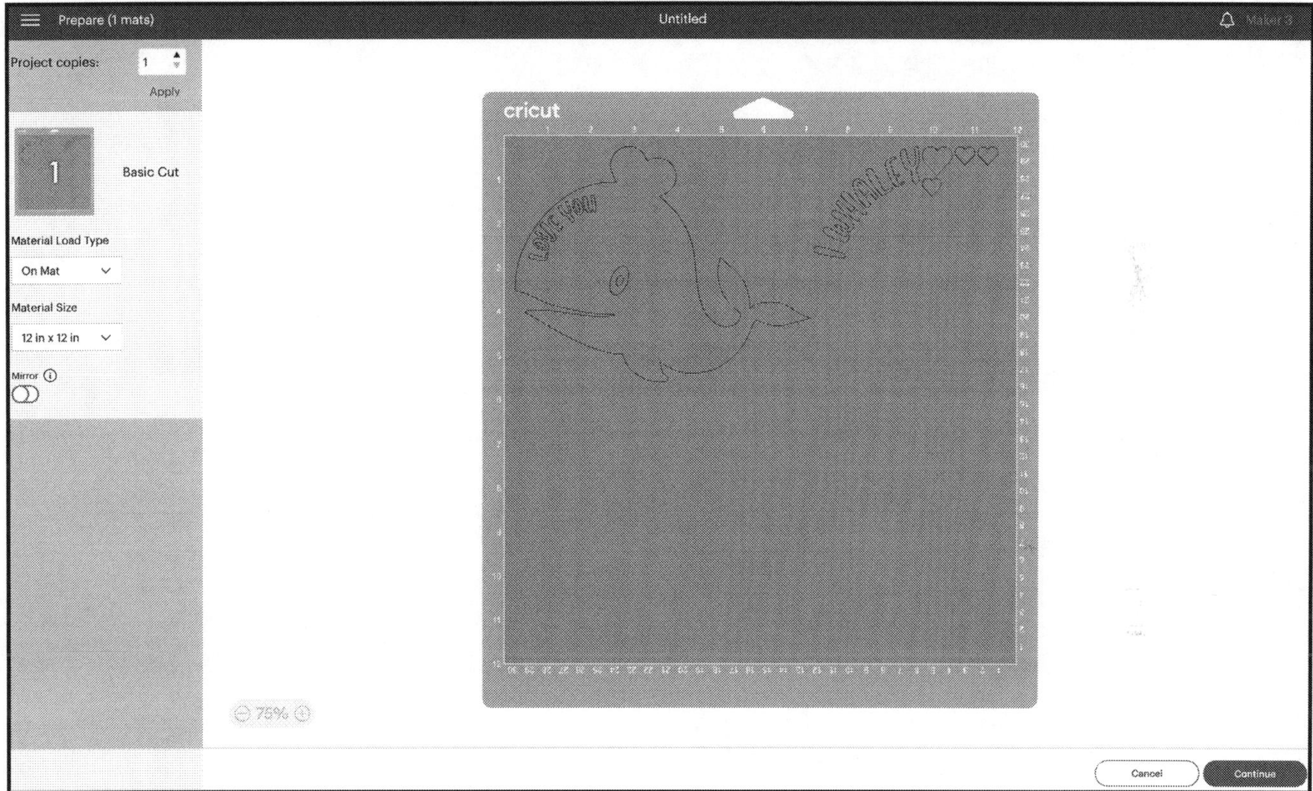

To get things back in order, click on the *Cancel* button; this will take you back to the *Canvas*. On the *Canvas*, select all your layers by clicking on the *Select All* feature in the *Edit Bar* and then click on *Attach* in the bottom of the *Layers Panel*. You'll notice that all your layers are now housed under an *Attached* label inside the *Layers Panel*. This time around, when you click on *Make It*, your design will be properly arranged on the preview mat.

The Make It Screen When You're Working with Different Colors

When working with different colors in your design, Design Space will separate each color onto its own mat on the *Make It* screen.

Note that you should not use the *Attach* feature when you want to cut materials with different colors, as you don't want the software to connect the different colored layers with each other. If you try to use the *Attach* feature after you make a design with different colors, you'll see that everything turns into one color (usually black or gray) the moment you click on *Attach*.

Naturally, when working with a design that has multiple colors, you'll have to rearrange your design manually after everything has been cut. When it comes to the cutting process, Design Space will guide you through getting each mat ready for your Cricut. You'll cut the different material colors one at a time.

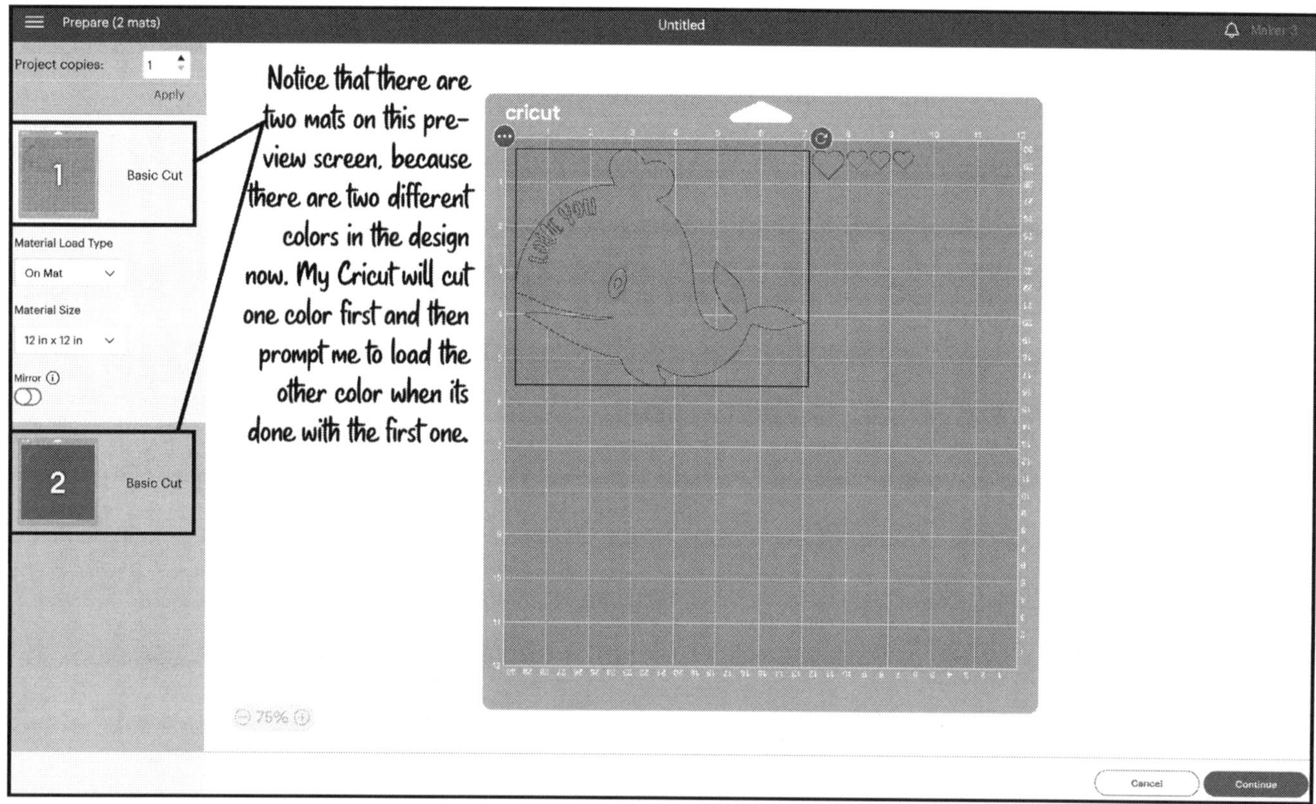

The Final Step before Cutting Your Project

When you're happy with everything on the Make It screen, click on the green *Continue* button.

Next, Design Space will ask you to specify a base material. The typical materials you'll work with as a Newbie include cardstock, vinyl, Iron-On/HTV, paper, and sticker paper. If you have the Explore Air 2, set your machine's *Smart Dial* to the appropriate material setting during this step.

Once you've selected the material you want to use for your project, Design Space will guide you to make sure you've got the right blade and tool (if needed) installed in your Cricut. When you're sure everything is in place, it's time to attach your material to the cutting mat and feed it to your machine. Remember to align the cutting mat using the guides on your machine that are near the opening. Once aligned, press the up/down button and watch as your Cricut measures the mat. At this point, Design Space will prompt you to press the *Go* button on your Cricut to let it cut the project.

As soon as you press the *Go* button, Design Space will show a screen that says *Preparing*. Then, as your Cricut does its magic, Design Space will keep you updated on its progress. Once your Cricut is done cutting, you'll see the progress indicator on Design Space has reached 100%, followed by an instruction to unload your cutting mat from the machine. Use your machine's up/down button to let your machine release the mat. All that's left to do now is to click on the *Finish* button in Design Space.

Pro Tip: Remember that the Cricut Joy doesn't have any buttons. You'll use Design Space to control the entire cutting process.

And you're done! Personally, I love the manual work that comes after the cutting process just as much as designing my projects and watching my machine do its thing. It all strikes the perfect balance.

What the Make It screen looks like on your mobile app

To go to the *Make It* screen on your mobile app, tap on the *Make It* button in top-right corner of the screen. (See the left-hand screenshot on the next page). Remember to apply the *Attach* feature if you want your design to cut out exactly the way you see it on the *Canvas*. If you forget, you'll have to go back to the *Canvas* to do it anyway.

Design Space will open a window that says *Select Material Load Type*. If you're working with a Cricut *Smart Material*, select the *Without Mat* option. If you're working with any other material, select the *On Mat option*. After making your selection, Design Space will take you to the preview mat. (See the right-hand screenshot on the next page.) When you're ready to start the cutting process, tap on the green *Continue* or *Next* button.

On the next screen, you'll have the opportunity to specify the material you want to use for the project, double-check the size, and indicate whether the image should be mirrored. The app will tell you which cutting blade to load and prompt you to press the *Go* button to move on to the cutting process.

While your Cricut cuts, you'll see how far the process is on your app. Finally, the app will notify you when your machine has finished cutting the design and prompt you to unload the cutting mat or *Smart Material*. It's important to always press the *Unload* button (the up/down arrow on your machine) after a cut, as this tells your Cricut to release the material from its grip. Trying to force the material out of the machine may damage it and ruin your design.

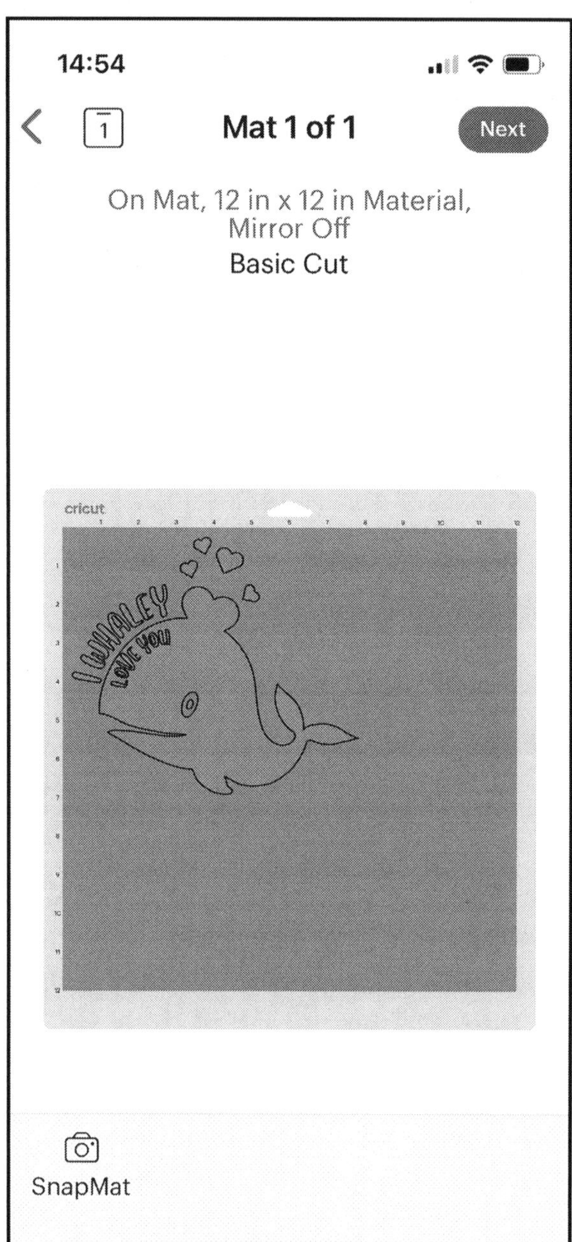

The Print Then Cut Feature

As the name suggests, *Print Then Cut* means that you will use your printer to print out your design before your Cricut cuts it.

Why Would You Want to Use Print Then Cut?

Some colorful designs can get really complex. If you want to make something that has 5, 10, or more colors, can you imagine the task ahead of you if you have to prepare a cutting mat for every one of them? On top of that, you would have to spend hours combining all those separate bits to reconstruct your design. Or, if you want to make cards with a lot of text on them, you'll wear out your precious Cricut pen in no time if you want it to write every single word.

Print Then Cut allows you to take on complex design projects and saves you a ton of time if you want many copies of the same design.

Which Materials Work with Print Then Cut?

In general, you can use printable vinyl, cardstock, paper, and sticker paper for *Print Then Cut* projects. You might be able to work with more materials, like printable magnets and printable fabric, but what you can and cannot print out depends on your printer and the Cricut machine you own.

Cricut recommends that you use an ink jet printer for these projects. Laser printers can damage materials like printable vinyl and sticker paper because of the heat it gives off.

How to Prepare for a Print Then Cut Project with Design Space

In most cases, you will upload the images you want to use for these kinds of projects (I'll tell you how to upload files in the next section). At other times, you might spot existing projects on Design Space to use. If you use an existing project, the settings will already be in place, so all you have to do is go to the *Make It* screen and follow the on-screen instructions.

If you upload images for your *Print Then Cut* project, the software will first prompt you to indicate the type of image and give you three options:

- Simple
- Moderately Complex
- Complex

For the best results, always choose the last option, Complex. On the next screen, you'll have a chance to remove the background behind the image. This is a Cricut Access feature, so you need a subscription to make use of it. That said, I encourage you to always upload images with the backgrounds already removed whenever possible.

When you click on *Apply & Continue*, you'll go to a new screen where Design Space will ask you whether the image you are uploading is a *Cut* image or a *Print Then Cut image.* Select the *Print Then Cut* option, give the image a name, and click on the *Upload* button at the bottom right corner of the screen.

Design Space will take you back to the Uploads screen, where you'll see your uploaded image below the *Recent Uploads* heading. Click on the box showing your new upload and then click on *Add to Canvas*. Once the *Canvas* screen opens, you'll be able to see your design's settings have already been set to *Print Then Cut*.

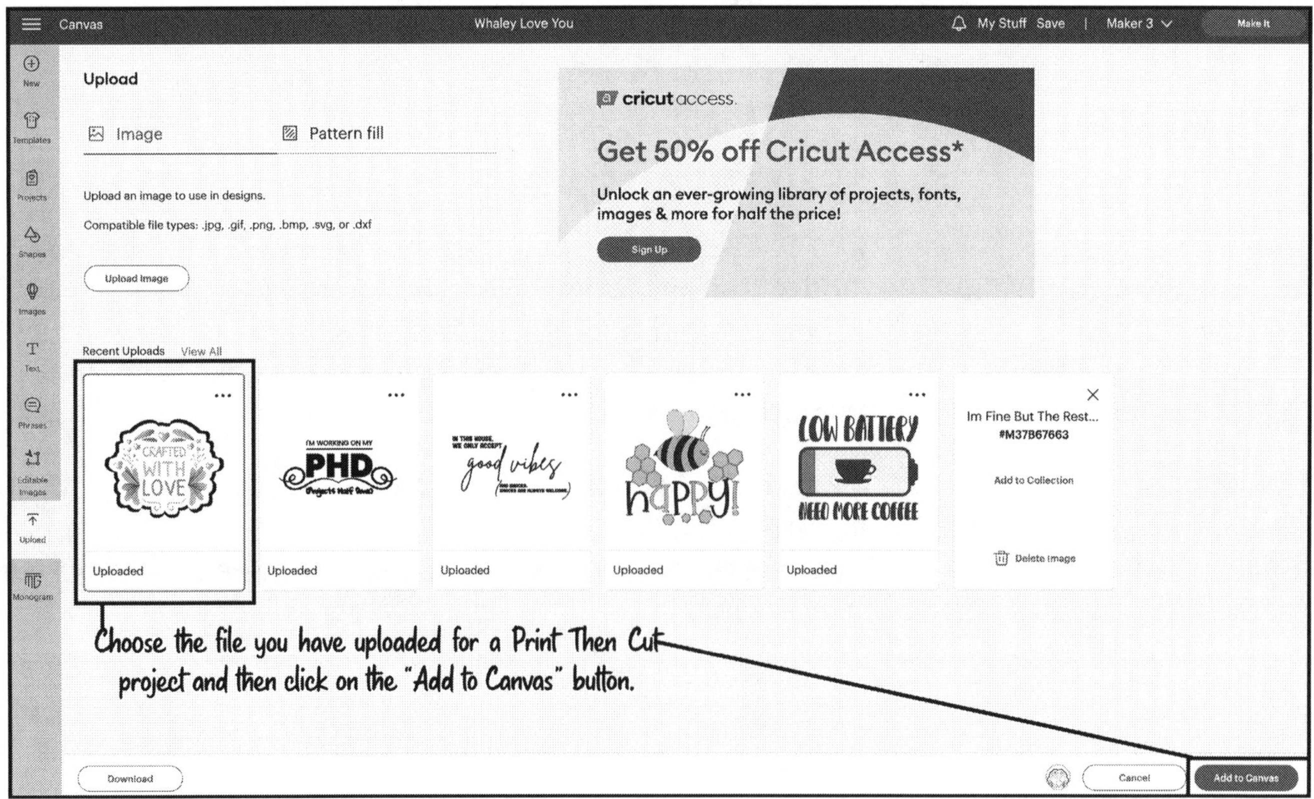

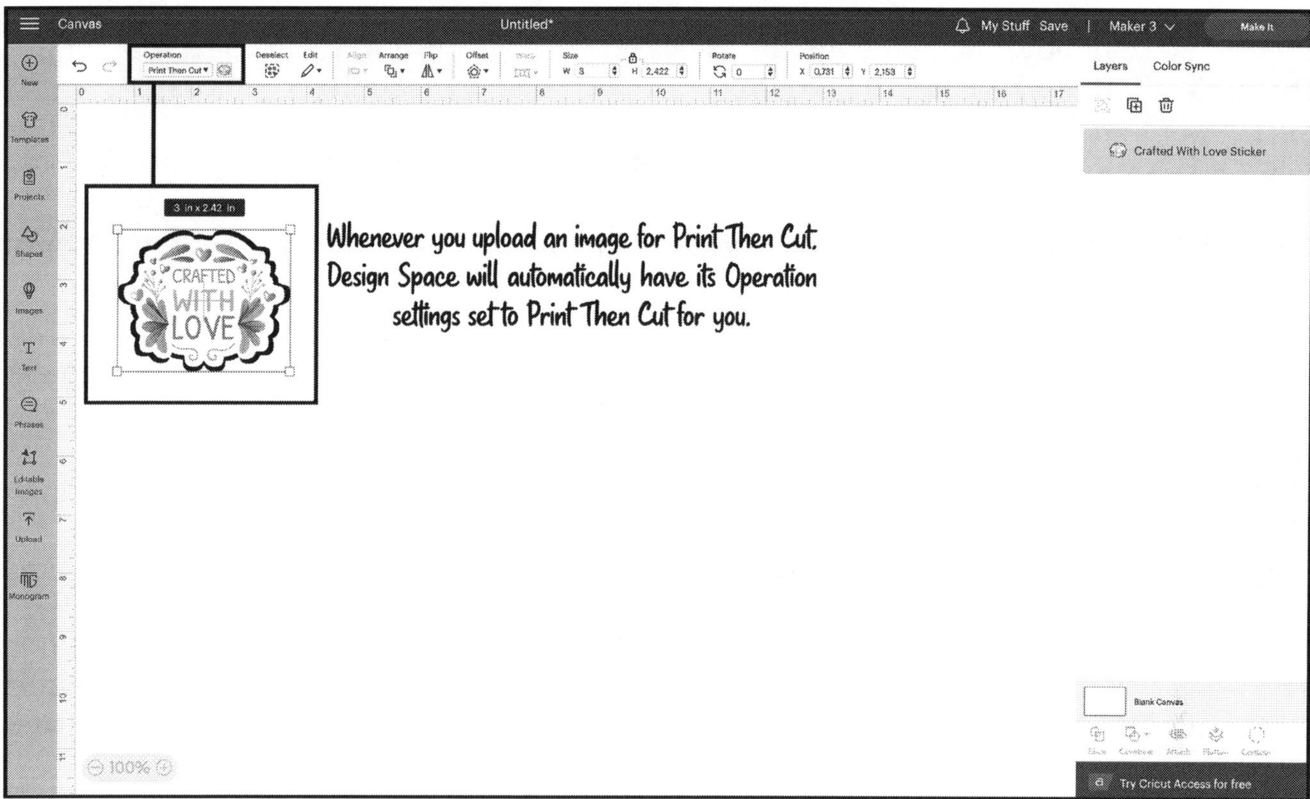

All you have to do now is resize the design until you're happy and then go to the *Make It* screen. If you want to fill up a sheet of paper with copies of your *Print Then Cut* design, you can do so on the *Make It* screen. Let's say we want to make a sheet of stickers. All you have to do is increase the number of *Project Copies* in the left-hand panel of the *Make It* screen. To confirm the duplicate copies, click on *Apply*. You'll see a bunch of copies pop up on the preview mat.

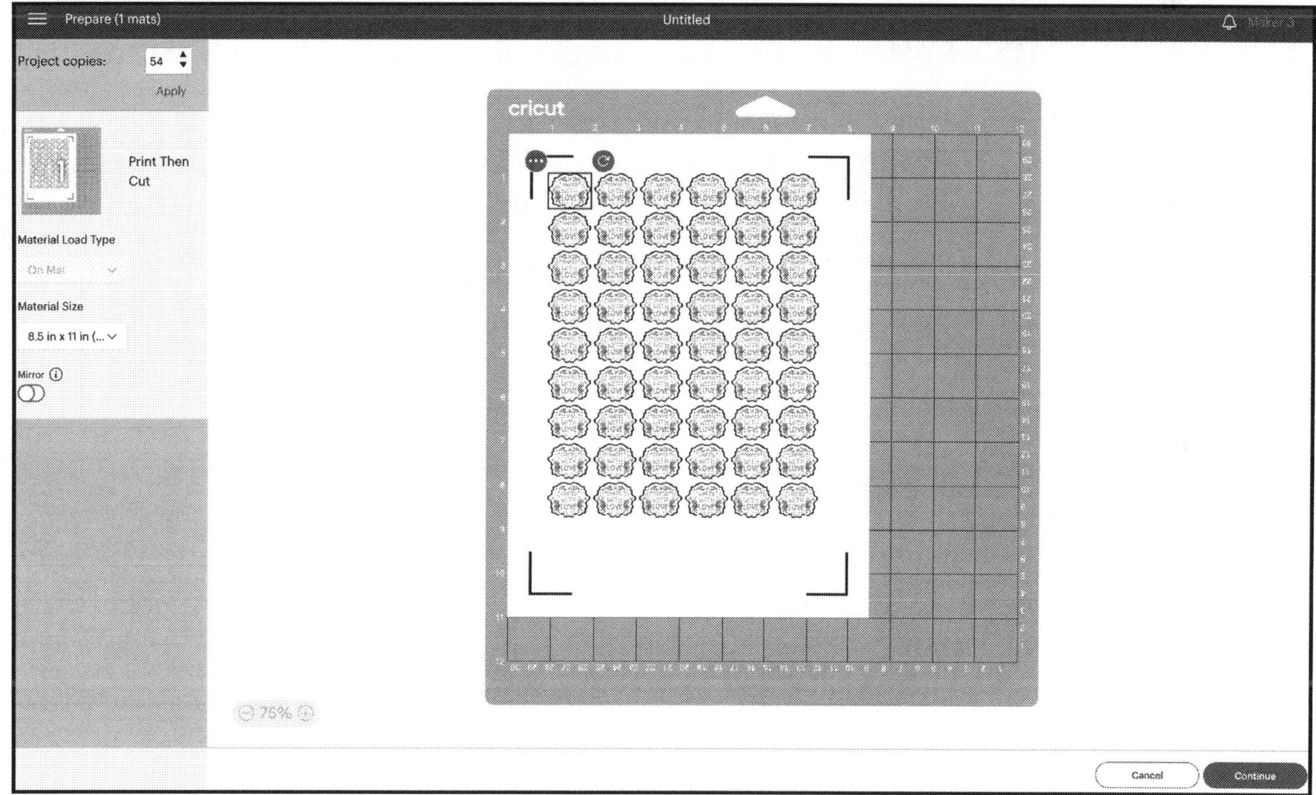

When you're happy, click on *Continue*. Design Space will prompt you to first print out the project, after which it will guide you through the normal cutting process.

Good to Know about the Print Then Cut Feature

The thick black line all around your design acts as a guide for your Cricut machine's sensors, so it can know where to cut.

If you have a Cricut Explore Air 2, you can only print designs on white paper. The sensors of the machine are not designed to deal with colored or patterned paper.

If you have a Cricut Explore 3, Maker, or Maker 3, its sensors can handle colored paper. Cricut recommends that their machines perform best with lighter colors as it gives better contrast for the sensors to see the print guide.

The above machines can even handle some patterned papers, but they were not designed with that functionality in mind. So, if it works for you, consider yourself lucky. But if it doesn't, it's not a manufacturing fault on Cricut's part. They do not guarantee that their machines will cut designs printed on patterned paper.

By default, *Image Bleed* is enabled for *Print Then Cut* projects. Bleed is like an extended border around the image which, according to Cricut, allows for more precise cutting. They recommend that you keep the bleed enabled but do give you the option to disable it. My advice is that you test which way works best for you. Do one project with the bleed enabled and another one with it turned off and then compare the results to decide whether or not you'll use it in future *Print Then Cut* projects.

How to Upload External Image Files to Design Space

Print Then Cut is not the only reason you may want to upload external files to Design Space. When I say "external," I'm referring to anything that you can't find inside the Design Space ecosystem. In your Cricut journey, you'll come across many websites and blogs that offer free SVGs which you can use for your Cricut projects. SVGs are, by far, the files you'll upload to Design Space most of the time.

What Is SVG Anyway?

SVG is short for Scalable Vector Graphics. In plain English, it's an image that can be enlarged indefinitely without losing its quality. This is very important for Cricut projects, as you don't want to be stuck with image files that can pixelate the moment you try to resize them. An SVG's simple and crisp qualities makes for the absolute best file to use for Cricut crafting.

A Note on the Ethical Use of SVG Files

The only time you should use SVG files (and any other image files, for that matter) without paying for them is when you have permission from its creator, even if you're only using the image for yourself.

Graphic designers spend a lot of time creating digital files for others to use, so, when they expect to get paid for it, it's only fair to do so. **Please don't ever save images from Google and upload them to Design Space for your projects**, because more likely than not, the images there are copyrighted. By using them, you're basically stealing. It sounds harsh, but it's true. It's kind of like your boss walking up to you and then casually saying, "Hey! I've decided not to pay you this week. But thanks for everything; keep up the good work!"

Seek out websites and blogs that give you permission to use their files. Also, be mindful of the terms under which you may use those files. Most of the time, you can use them for personal projects but not for commercial ones (projects you'll profit from). If you want to make money off your Cricut crafts, it's best to purchase commercial licenses for the files you want to use to sell products.

When SVG Is Not the Best Option for a Project

As I pointed out earlier, when working with complex designs, SVG files are not the way to go. The reason for this is that an SVG gets divided into layers the moment you upload it to Design Space; the more complex the image, the more layers you'll have. Some SVGs can have as many as 20 layers (and more!). While I can't get enough of Cricut projects, I can guarantee you I will not be a crafter if I have to load and unload my Cricut 20 or more times to finish one project. And neither will you!

You'll have to decide where you draw the line to define a complex image. All I can tell you is that when you're dealing with lots of little intricate bits that have to be brought back together to make up the image after everything has been cut, it's honestly not worth it. Remember how I talked about humans being apathetic earlier? If there's too much work involved, we look for excuses to avoid tasks—even fun ones.

Avoid *Cut* projects with five or more layers if they have different colors, and if an image you want to use looks really complex, consider doing a *Print Then Cut* project instead. When you upload an SVG file, Design Space assumes that it will be used for a *Cut* project, so it doesn't even give you the option to upload it as a *Print Then Cut* image.

So, if you want to do a *Print Then Cut* project, be sure to upload a PNG or JPEG file. When you do that, Design Space will give you a choice between whether the image should be uploaded as a *Cut* or *Print Then Cut* file.

The Upload Process

Apart from SVG files, Design Space will let you upload JPEG, GIF, PNG, BMP, or DXF files. Mostly, you'll upload PNG or JPEG files instead of SVGs.

How it Works on the Desktop Version

Click on *Upload* in the *Design Panel*. This will take you to a screen that shows all your uploaded images and files. In the upper-left part of the screen, you'll see an *Upload* button. Click on it and then add the image you want to use.

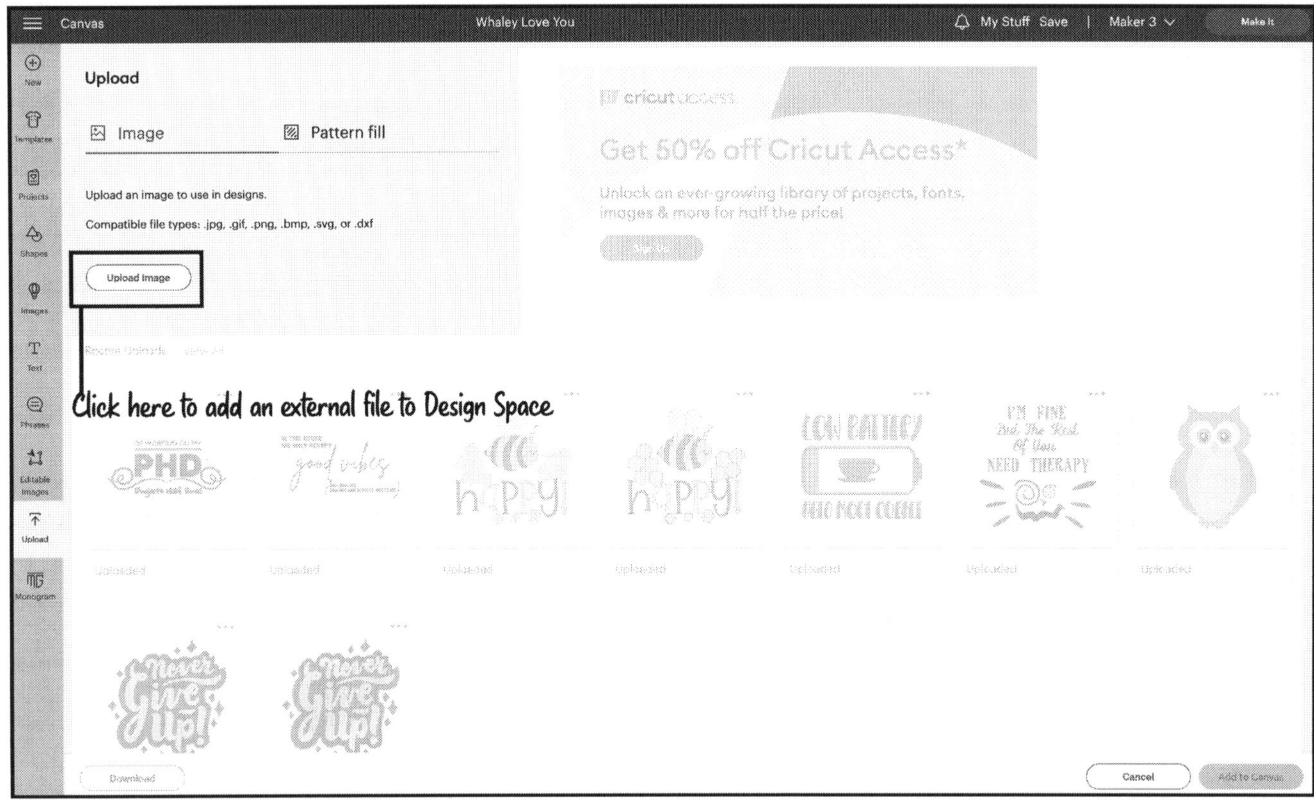

Now Design Space will ask you to specify the complexity of the image you want to upload. Like I mentioned earlier when we talked about uploading a file for *Print Then Cut*, always opt for the *Complex* option.

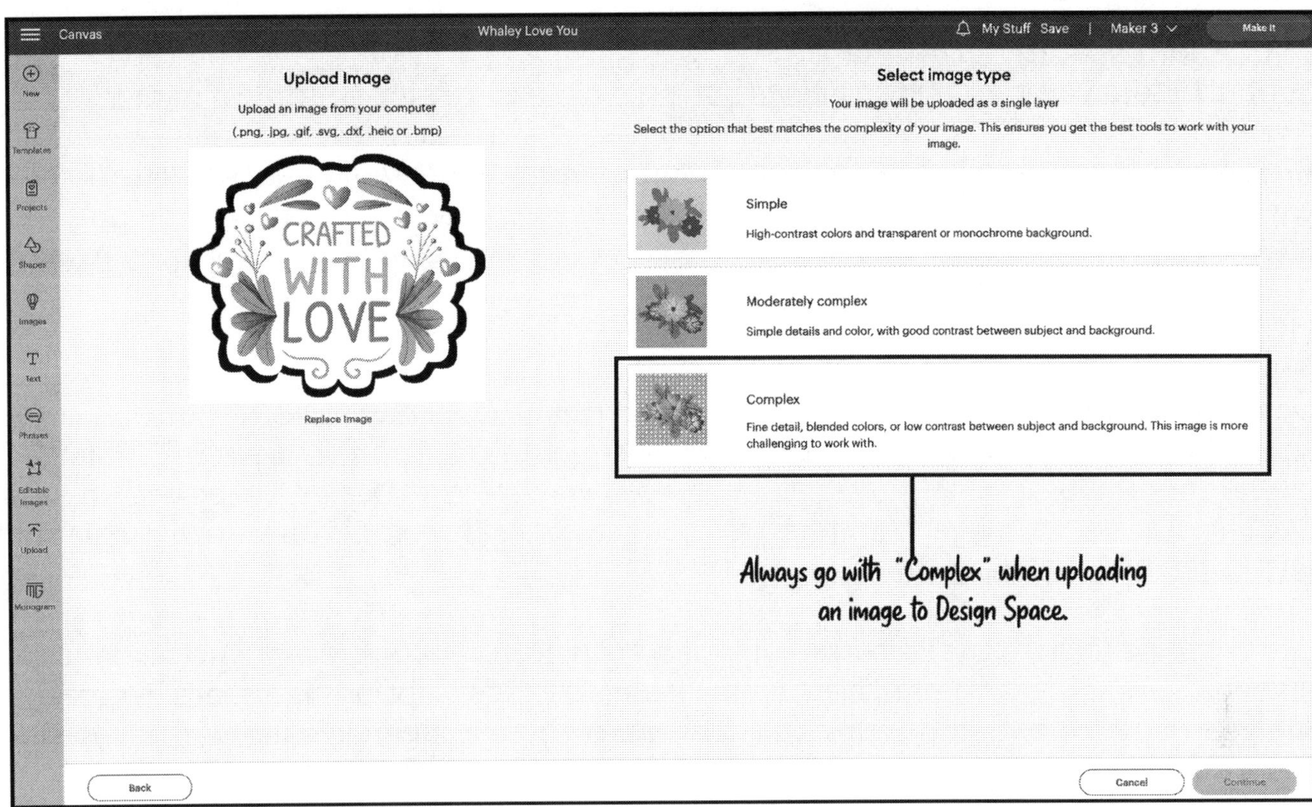

Click Continue. If you're uploading an image for Print Then Cut (a JPG or PNG file), Design Space will give you an opportunity to remove the image's background next.

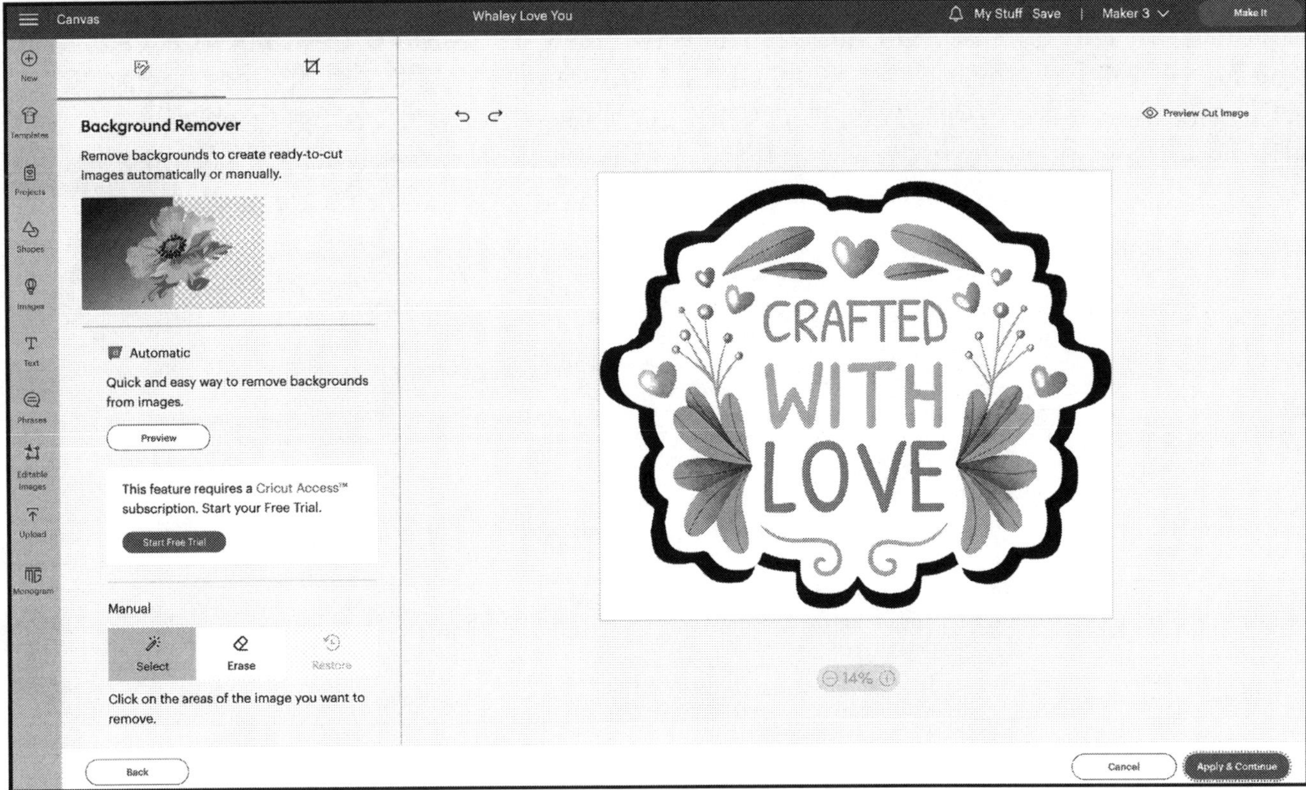

Click on *Apply & Continue*. If you are uploading a JPG or PNG file, Design Space will ask you whether you're uploading a *Cut* file or a *Print Then Cut file* (like you saw in the Print Then Cut section above). Very rarely will you choose *Cut* file when uploading a JPG or

PNG. And if you are uploading an SVG, Design Space will only give you the *Cut* file option. Before you click on the *Upload* button, you need to give your file a name.

After you click on the Upload button, Design Space will take you back to the *Upload* page and now display the file you have uploaded. From there, you can select it and add it to the Canvas.

How it Works on the Mobile Version

Go to the *Canvas* and choose the *Upload* option from the menu bar at the bottom of the screen. You'll see an option to take a photo or to select one from your photo library. Go to your photo library and select the image you want to use. Design Space will show a *Cleanup* screen, where you can remove the image's background if necessary. (See the left-hand illustration on the next page).

Click on *Next* to go to the *Prepare to Upload* Screen. Here, you'll specify whether you are uploading a *Cut* file or a *Print Then Cut* file. Beneath the two options is a space to give the image a name. Note that you can't save the upload before giving it a name. Once you've done that, click on Save (see the right-hand illustration on the next page).

The file will now be visible on your *Canvas* screen and also be saved to your Uploads folder in Design Space.

If you have the desktop version of Design Space, too, you'll be able to access your uploaded files from either of the versions. If you have an Android device, Design Space will inform you that *Print Then Cut* is not available after uploading a new file. You can still save the image for later use, though, but if you don't have the desktop app, you won't be able to do a *Print Then Cut* project with your Android mobile device.

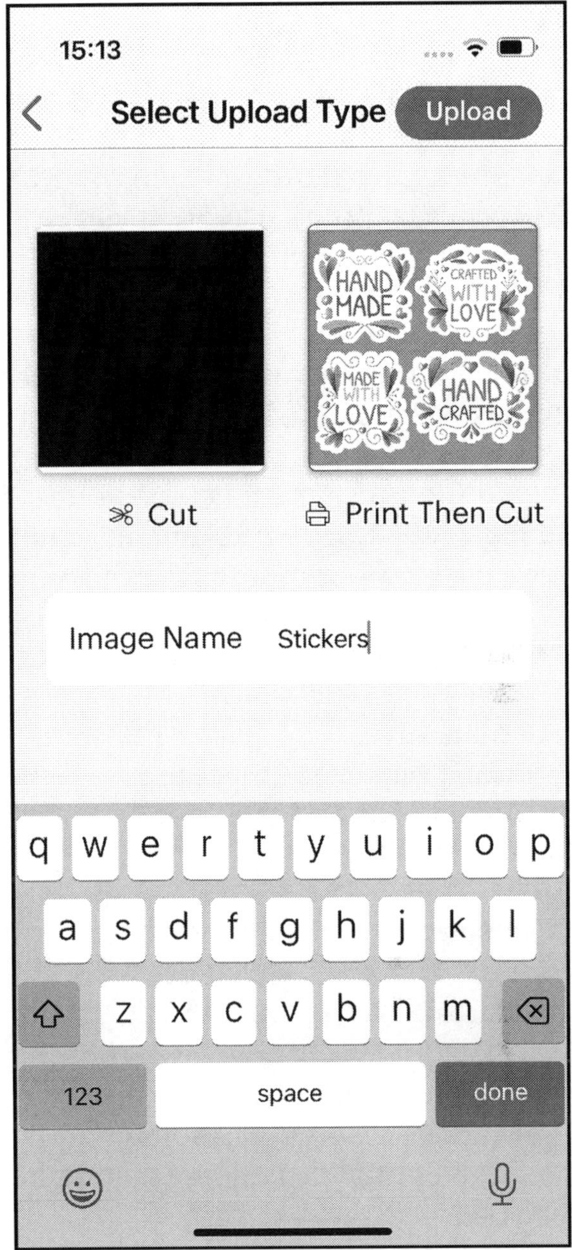

Cricut Access

As mentioned earlier, Cricut Access is a subscription-based service that allows you to use premium Design Space content. You have three options to choose from when you sign up.

The Free Plan

If you don't do many projects in a month, you could get away with the Free plan, as it gives you access to over 1,000 images, 15+ fonts, and a selection of over 250 ready-to-make projects. You can also buy any of the paid images, projects, and fonts for once-off fees if you want to use them.

The Standard Plan

At 9.99 USD per month, you'll have access to all the images, fonts, and ready-to-make projects available on Design Space. Unlike the Free plan, you don't need to purchase anything at an extra cost when you want to use it. Also, Cricut does not limit the number of resources you can use. So, if you're having a super creative day and want to do 5, 6, 7, or more projects, you can do so with the assurance that no disappointing notifications will pop up, telling you that you've reached your daily limit.

On top of access to all the Design Space resources, you'll qualify for a 10% discount on purchases you make from Cricut's website.

If you'd like to save money on your subscription, you can even pay a year in advance and pay 95.88 USD, which means you'll pay 24 USD less than what you would have paid over a period of 12 months for the monthly subscription.

The Premium Plan

This plan gives you everything the Standard plan offers, plus 20% off all Cricut materials, plus free shipping on all your orders over 50 USD. The Premium plan costs $119.88 per year and does not have a monthly subscription like the Standard plan.

Note that all the prices quoted above are accurate at the time of writing this book and may change over time.

Is Cricut Access Worth It?

Your circumstances will determine whether joining is really worth it. If you don't craft often and don't spend at least 9.99 USD per month on digital files to create your projects, then you'll probably feel like having a subscription service is a waste of money.

However, if you're spending time with your Cricut at least once or twice a week and find yourself spending more than 9.99 USD per month on digital files, I think you'll really appreciate everything Cricut Access offers for such a low price.

As a new Cricut owner, you can access everything Design Space has to offer absolutely free for 30 days, and there are no obligations to buy a subscription when your trial period ends. With such a generous offer, I encourage you to make use of it. It's a risk-free way to test whether you'll really need the Cricut Access service in your crafting journey.

Go to https://cricut.com/en_us/cricut-access-free-trial to sign up for the free trial.

BONUS: Cool Design Space Tips & Tricks

Always Save Your Progress

Sadly, Design Space has no auto-save function built in to save a project you are working on. So, if you've been working on the cutest, coolest, best design ever and something goes wrong, well ...

I know, it's a painful thought.

To avoid heartache and frustrations, make a habit of saving the design you're working on after every few edits.

How to Save Your Progress on the Desktop Version

On the *Canvas* screen, in the header section, you'll see a *Save* link next to the *My Stuff* link. When you click on it, Design Space will prompt you to name the file. After saving, you'll see a notification appear at the top of the screen informing you that the file has been saved successfully. (See the desktop screenshot at the top of the next page.) From the moment you save your design, it becomes available in your *My Stuff* library. As you tweak your design on the *Canvas* screen, click on the *Save* link every now and then to commit the changes you make.

How to Save Your Progress on the Mobile Version

On the *Canvas* screen, you'll see a little floppy disk icon at the top of the screen, right next to your profile picture. Click on it to save your project. The first time you click on it, you'll be asked to name the project. After naming it, you can simply tap that Save icon regularly as you design. (See the mobile screenshots on the next page.)

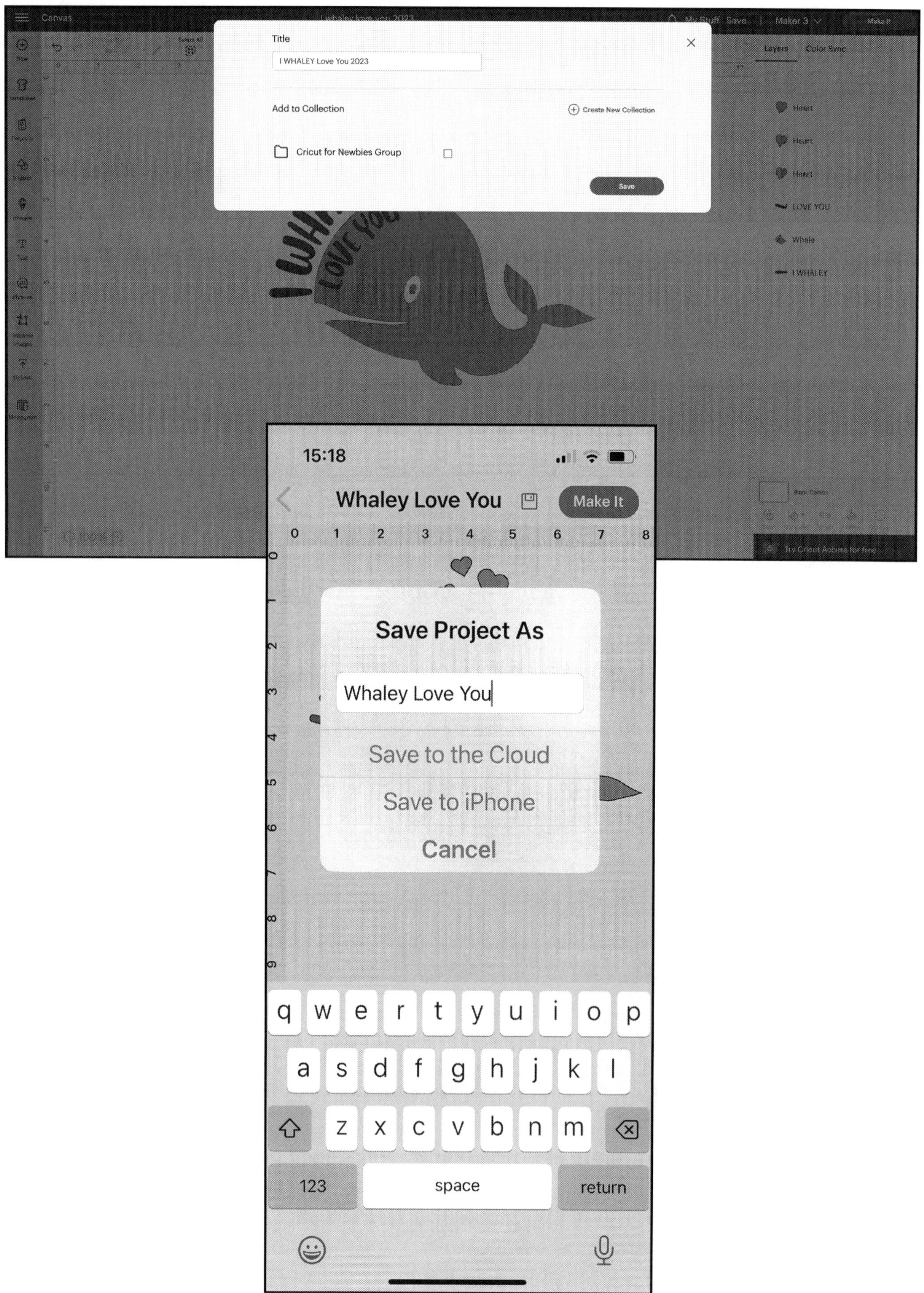
Title
I WHALEY Love You 2023
Add to Collection
Create New Collection
Cricut for Newbies Group
Save
Layers
Color Sync
Heart
Heart
Heart
LOVE YOU
Whale
I WHALEY
15:18
Whaley Love You
Make It
Save Project As
Whaley Love You
Save to the Cloud
Save to iPhone
Cancel
space
return
123

Keyboard Shortcuts

If you're working on the desktop version of Design Space, you can get things done a teeny bit faster with some useful keyboard shortcuts. The shortcuts below are not all of them, but they're the ones you'll use (and come to love) the most.

DESIGN SPACE FUNCTION	WINDOWS COMPUTER SHORTCUT	APPLE COMPUTER SHORTCUT
Select All Layers	Control (CTRL) + A	Command (CMD) + A
Group Layers	Control (CTRL) + G	Command (CMD) + G
Ungroup Layers	Control (CTRL) + U	Command (CMD) + U
Copy Element	Control (CTRL) + C	Command (CMD) + C
Cut Element	Control (CTRL) + X	Command (CMD) + X
Paste Element	Control (CTRL) + V	Command (CMD) + V
Duplicate Element	Control (CTRL) + D	Command (CMD) + D
Undo	Control (CTRL) + Z	Command (CMD) + Z
Redo	Control (CTRL) + SHIFT + G	Command (CMD) + SHIFT + G
Save	Control (CTRL) + S	Command (CMD) + S

DESIGN SPACE FUNCTION	WINDOWS COMPUTER SHORTCUT	APPLE COMPUTER SHORTCUT
Delete Element	DELETE (DEL)	DELETE/BACKSPACE
Select more than one element at a time, but not all of them.	Hold SHIFT + click on layers you want to select in the Layers Panel or on the Canvas.	Hold SHIFT + click on layers you want to select in the Layers Panel or on the Canvas.

* * *

Design Space is the backbone of your Cricut crafting journey, so it's well worth your time getting to know the program. I hope this chapter has helped you understand the software and made you comfortable with the things you can do with it.

Chapters 9 Notes

Use this space to jot down the best take-aways you learned from Chapter 9. Use these notes as your personal quick-reference guide whenever you want to refresh your memory ons something specific.

PARDON THE INTERRUPTION, BUT ...

I was wondering if I could steal you away from the book for five minutes. Did you know that people who help others can live longer and experience levels of fulfillment others only dream of? You're nodding your head in agreement because you are someone who loves helping your fellow humans—I just know it. With that in mind, I was wondering...

Would you help someone you have never met, even if you get nothing in return apart from the knowledge that their lives are better off because of you?

If yes, I'd really appreciate it if you could lend a hand to a complete stranger. My goal with this book is to inspire creativity and encourage people to do the things that make them happy, no matter what. But to achieve that goal, Cricut for Newbies needs to reach the people who need it most.

Somewhere out there, someone is feeling lost and discouraged to use their Cricut because of complete overwhelm. They don't know what to do or where to start, kind of like how you felt way at the beginning of this book. They're looking for answers, and they're desperate to start crafting, but they don't know who or what can help them overcome the obstacles.

You can nudge them in the right direction by simply writing a quick, honest review of Cricut for Newbies. The person who reads your review will probably never meet you, but your words could be the reason they find the hope and courage to unbox their Cricut and take action. That, my friend, is a priceless gift to give.

If you agree, please take a moment now to visit your favorite book review site and share your opinion.

Thank you wholeheartedly.

***

Now we need a drum roll ... You're about to start your first project! See you in Chapter 10.

CHAPTER 10

YOUR FIRST CRICUT PROJECTS

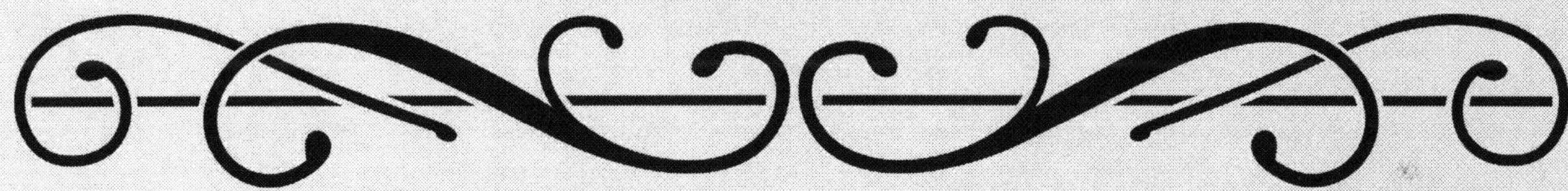

To practice any art, no matter how well or badly, is a way to make your soul grow. So do it.
—Kurt Vonnegut

In this chapter, you'll find three detailed Cricut project tutorials. Whatever Cricut Machine you own, you can take part in all three of them. Each project focuses on different ways in which you can source, create, and apply designs. You'll also learn how to source and download fonts and SVG design files on any device and get to practice your new Design Space skills.

Excited? Let's get started!

Project 1: Make a Personalized Mug

The Goodies You Need

- Any Cricut Machine.
- Cricut *StandardGrip* Cutting Mat (the green one).
- Cricut Premium Vinyl–Permanent (any color).
- Cricut *StandardGrip* Transfer Tape.
- A blank mug (avoid mugs with textured surfaces).
- Weeding Tool.
- Scraping tool.
- A bit of rubbing alcohol.

The following information builds on the five basic steps involved in the cutting process you learned in Chapter 2. Instead of walking you through the process again, the steps for this and other projects will show you where and how to get designs, how to handle specific materials, and how to transfer materials to specific surfaces.

Step 1: Find and Prepare a Ready-to-Make Image in Design Space

This is by far the easiest and quickest way to create a Cricut project. And, since you're just starting out, I encourage you to use this method as much as possible for now. Going through this process will help you get comfortable with and see even more of what you can do with Design Space. Design Space offers many images, fonts, and projects you can use for free, so always look out for these freebies when creating your designs.

A quick note before we dive in: If you don't remember exactly where to go in Design Space as we work through the projects, it's OK! Simply head back to Chapter 9 for a quick refresher on the interface. Remember that this is all new, so it will take some time to find your bearings. Trust the learning process and be patient with yourself.

To start, click on *Images* in the *Design Panel*. When the *Images* library opens, the first thing you'll want to do is to filter the results so you can only see designs that will cost nothing to make. In the left-hand panel, tick the *Free* box. Notice that you can get very specific in the filters panel. For example, you can specify materials and even the language you want to see. Let's tick the *Cut Only* box too, which you'll see under the *Operation Type* category. Finally, let's refine our search with a keyword in the search bar, too. I'll type *craft*, but you can type anything you have in mind to put on your mug. Have a look at the available option and choose your favorite design. Click on your choice and then click the *Add to Canvas* button.

Pro Tip 1: For now, go with a design that has one color only. When you gain more experience as a Cricut Crafter, you can start experimenting with multiple color projects.

Pro Tip 2: If you're not seeing something you like in the *Images* library, you can always go and see what the *Phrases* library has to offer.

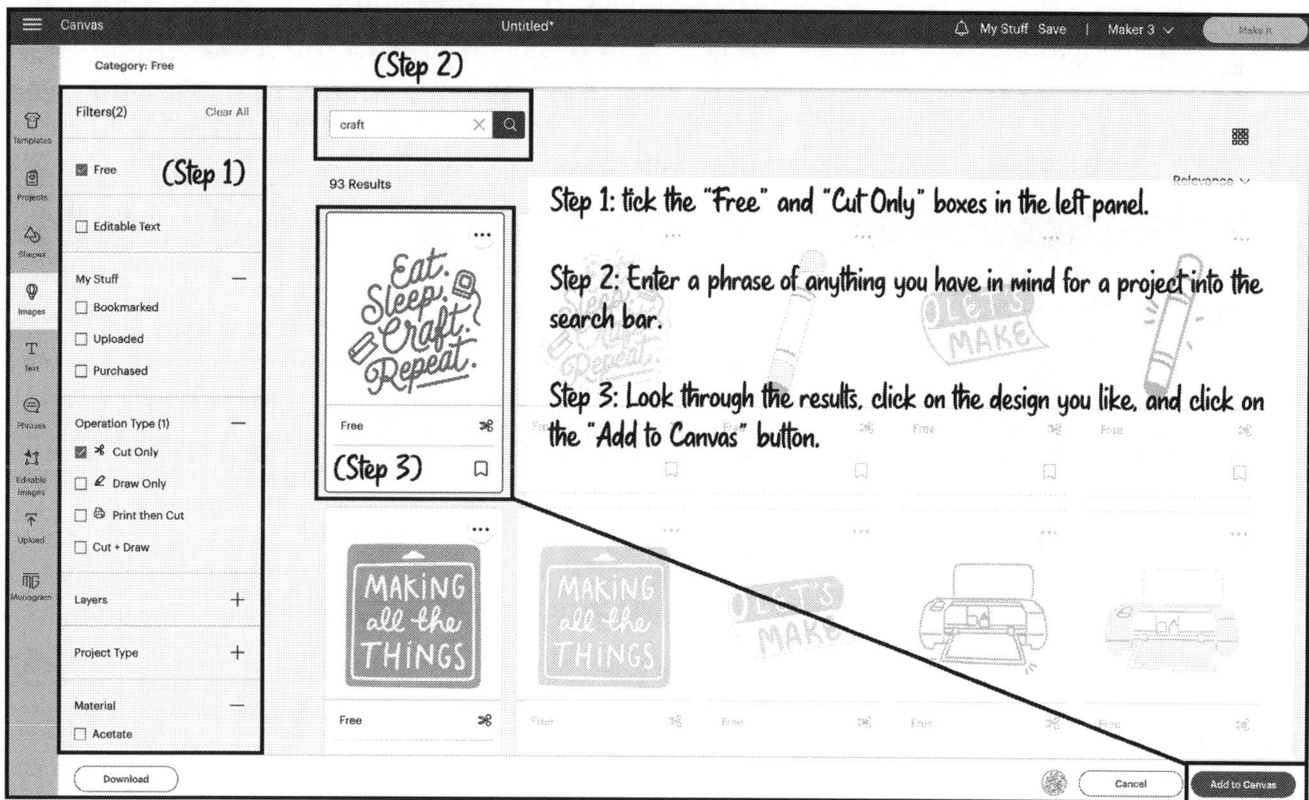

If you're on the mobile app, open your *Canvas* and tap on *Images* in the bar at the bottom of the screen. A screen will pop up with images to choose from. Tap the filters icon and switch on the *Free* toggle. Go back to the results page. To refine your search, tap on the search icon and enter a keyword or phrase that best describes what kind of image you're looking for. Scroll through the results and tap on the image you want to use, then tap on the *Add* button at the bottom of the screen.

If you can't find an image you like, or if you'd rather play it safe for this project, go ahead and use the same image that I'm using for this example. To find it quickly, copy it's unique number and paste it into the search bar in your Images library: #M422499D2

Every design asset on Cricut Design Space has a unique number by which it can be identified. To see an asset's unique number and other information.

Back on the Canvas, the image or phrase you chose will be on the grid area. Now it's just a matter of making sure the image's size is good to fit the surface of your mug. Select the image and change its size to 3.5" wide. (Remember that you can specify the exact size you want in the *Edit Bar.*)

Next, change the image's color to the color of your vinyl, whether it's black, blue, red, or whatever. On your mobile device, select the image and tap on Edit in the bar at the bottom of the screen. In the secondary bar, change the width to 3,4" and change the image's color to match your vinyl's color.

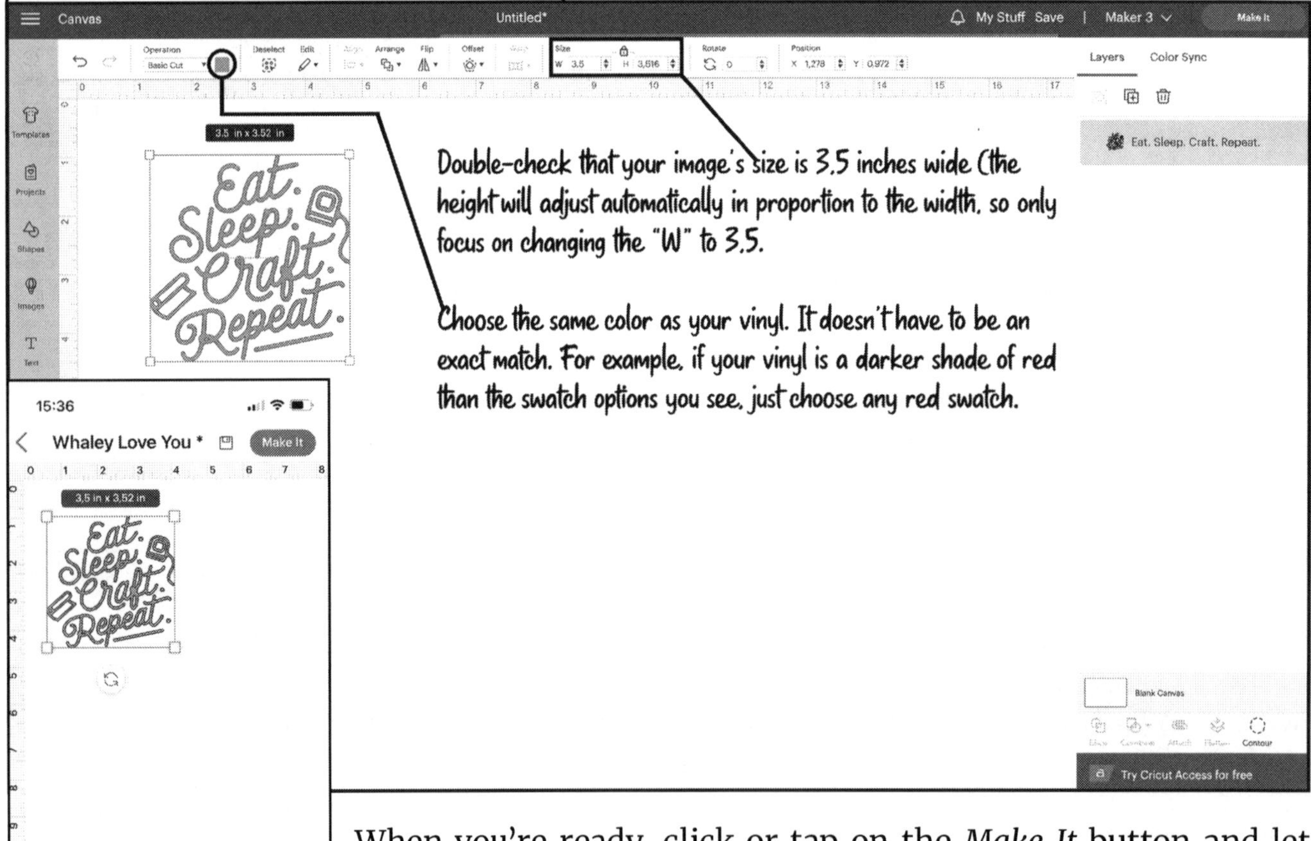

When you're ready, click or tap on the *Make It* button and let Design Space Guide you through the cutting process.

When Design Space prompts you to set the base material, choose *Premium Vinyl – Permanent* from the predefined list. If you don't see it in the predefined list, Click on the *Browse All Materials* link above the list and then find the right option.

Pro Tip: The exact name of the material you're using is on the back side of your material sheet. Flip it around to double-check what you're working with and make sure you choose the right option in Design Space. Each option comes with predefined settings perfect for that material. If you choose the wrong one, your Cricut may not cut out your design properly.

Step 2: Prepare Your Vinyl for the Cutting Process

Cut a piece of vinyl large enough for the design, around 4" by 4". Always make sure your material is slightly bigger than the design, but not too much, otherwise you'll have a lot of wastage.

Remove the protective film from your cutting mat and set it aside. You'll use it to cover your cutting mat again when your Cricut has finished cutting out the design.

Apply the vinyl to the cutting mat with the shiny side facing you. The other side, which has a grid and the vinyl's name printed on the back, is the backing. When applying the vinyl to the mat, start by positioning the vinyl in the upper left-corner of the grid border on the mat. To secure the vinyl on the mat, press down on it and smooth it out with a flat palm or with your Cricut scraper tool (you can also use a brayer if you have one).

Step 3: Let Your Cricut Cut the Vinyl

When you're ready to go ahead, align your cutting mat with the guides on your Cricut machine's opening and give it a slight push until the rollers grip the mat. Click or tap the *Load* button on Design Space if you're working with a Cricut Joy. If you have one of the other models, press the flashing up/down arrow button. After the machine scans the material, press the *Go* button on your app (for the Cricut Joy) or machine (for the other models).

When your Cricut has finished cutting, press the *Unload* button on your Design Space app (Cricut Joy) or the up/down button on your machine (other Cricut models) to release the cutting mat from your machine.

Step 4: Remove the Vinyl from the Cutting Mat

When separating materials from the cutting mat, it's natural to want to peel the material from the mat. But this causes your precious creations to curl, bend, and (sigh...) get damaged sometimes. The answer to this dilemma is to simply flip the mat over and peel *it* away from the material. The material will remain straight and separate from the mat so much easier.

When doing this, chant the words "easy does it." Flip the cutting mat over, bend it toward you, and, as it detaches from the vinyl, press the vinyl against the table with one hand while you continue to pull the mat away with the other hand. Be sure that you're pulling away the vinyl with its backing, and not the vinyl alone.

Reattach the protective film over your cutting mat as soon as you're done using it and put it away.

Step 5: Weed your Design

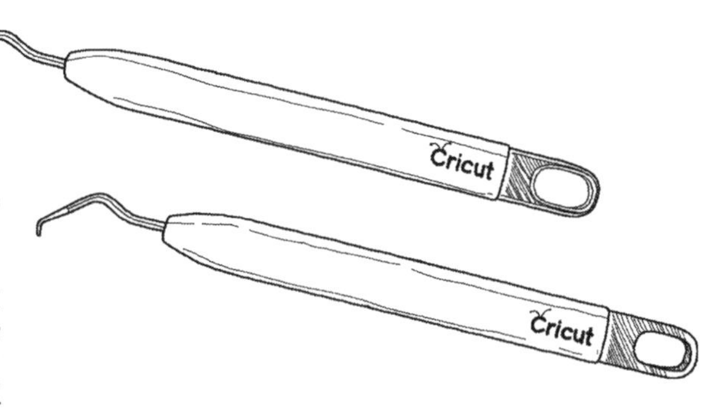

If you ever get confused about which parts of the material you're supposed to remove, just think of weeds growing in a garden. Like you get rid of unwanted growth, your goal is to remove the parts you don't want as part of your project. Cricut vinyl is forgiving, so if you accidentally weed a wrong piece, re-stick it to the backing and continue weeding the unwanted bits.

The weeder is the tool with the hook-like metal end that looks like a dentist's pick. If you don't know what that is because you've never visited the dentist before, you need to let me know what your secret is!

Basically, the weeder's metal tip is pointy and sharp. These days, Cricut has two types of weeders, called the classic weeder and the hook weeder. The hook weeder comes in the Cricut Weeding Tool Set and looks the same as the classic weeder, except that its end has an extra angle to it. They say the hook weeder works well for really, really intricate projects. That said, I have worked with a lot of vinyl and have not come across a project that my trusty classic weeder could not handle. The classic weeder is by far the most popular and perfect for you as a newbie.

To start, remove the largest part of the excess vinyl from the backing first, starting in a corner—the upper-left corner if you're right-handed and the upper-right corner if you're left-handed. If you're having trouble getting hold of the vinyl, use your weeder. Press the sharp point against the vinyl in the corner and lift it up. As you remove the excess vinyl from the backing, work slowly. Don't pull the excess upward. Instead, keep it close to the surface and pull it toward you, using your fingers to remove it as evenly as possible. Be careful not to allow the sticky part of the vinyl you're pulling away to come in contact with the vinyl that stays behind (the design you want to use). If the adhesive side of permanent vinyl gets a hold of the non-adhesive side, it will not let go. Nine times out of ten, if this happens, it leads to everything landing in the bin.

If your design has many intricate parts or letters, some excess bits will probably stay behind after you have pulled away the larger part. Use your weeder to pick up and remove those bits.

Bonus Tips for Weeding

Use Baby Powder to Identify Cut Lines

When working with a complicated design, it can become hard to see the parts that must stay and the parts that must go. To make it easier, sprinkle baby powder over the vinyl and brush it over with a make-up brush. The powder will fall into the gaps and reveal the cut lines. After weeding, clean the remaining vinyl (your design) with a damp cloth to get rid of all the powder before you transfer it to the mug's surface. Make sure everything is dry before you transfer your design.

Have a Copy of the Final Design Nearby for Reference

You can print out your design or have a copy of it open on your computer, laptop, or smartphone. Glance over it while you weed to make sure you're weeding the right parts. You'll find that the more complex your design, the more useful it is to have this copy nearby for referencing.

Cut the Excess Vinyl when Working with Larger Projects

The risk of accidentally sticking the excess vinyl to the design itself increases when your project requires a large sheet of vinyl. To avoid this, cut the excess vinyl with scissors as you remove it. You can form a sticky ball with the cut vinyl and use it to gather the smaller excess bits as you work. When you remove pieces with the weeder, press it into the sticky ball to make the process easier.

Step 6: Cover Your Design with Transfer Tape

Transfer tape is a transparent, sticky film that makes it easy to transfer a vinyl design from its backing to the surface you want to apply it to. Use Cricut's *StandardGrip* transfer tape, as the *StrongGrip* transfer tape is, well... strong. While *StrongGrip* transfer tape is perfect for heavier materials like glitter vinyl, it's way too sticky for most vinyl projects.

Cut a piece of transfer tape just large enough to cover your design. Remove the tape from its backing the same way you removed the excess vinyl in the previous step. When applying transfer tape, your goal is to avoid air bubbles in between the tape and the vinyl. You'll find the way that works best for you with practice. In my experience, I have had the best results when applying the transfer tape from the center of the design. Align the transfer tape with the design from above and stick it unto the center, then rub the tape over the design toward the edges. Next, rub over the transfer tape with your Cricut scraper (or your open palm) to ensure there are no air bubbles trapped in between the transfer tape and your design. Flip the sheet and rub over the back, too. When doing this, apply a good amount of pressure. (The process of rubbing over a design is also called burnishing.)

Step 7: Prepare Your Mug

Determine where you want to place the design on the mug before removing the vinyl from its backing. To find the best spot, move the design around on the mug and imagine what it would look like once applied. Keep in mind that if you want other people to see the design while you hold the mug, it has to go on the opposite side from your viewpoint when drinking from it. Once you've decided on the perfect spot, it's time to prepare the mug for the design's application.

It's important to ensure the surface you want to transfer the design to is clean and free from dust and other particles. Rubbing alcohol is perfect for this task. Dip cotton or a piece of tissue in some rubbing alcohol (but don't soak it) and wipe the mug's surface where the design will go, as well as the surrounding area. Let the mug dry for a minute or two before you apply the vinyl.

Step 8: Apply Your Design to the Mug

Lift the transfer tape by starting in the upper-left (if you are right-handed) or upper-right (if you are left-handed) corner. It should be easy to lift, but if you struggle, use your weeder to get it loose from the vinyl's backing. Pull the transfer tape up at a steady pace. As you get to the design, be extra careful to check whether it lifts with the transfer tape. If parts of it stay behind on the backing, it means that the vinyl did not adhere to the transfer tape. In that case, let the tape down again and burnish that area with some extra pressure. Afterward, lift the tape again.

Be prepared for frustrating moments the first few times you work with vinyl and other materials. You might mess things up, and that's really OK. I didn't learn by getting everything right all the time, and neither will you. As weird as it seems, we learn best when we make mistakes. To save yourself from feeling disheartened, all you have to do is manage your expectations. Do this with a *I'll do my best* attitude, but at the same time, tell yourself everything will be fine if blunders slip in.

Once you have lifted the entire design with the transfer tape, position it over the area of the mug you want to place it. To apply the design, stick it onto the mug from the center and rub it on toward the edges, just like you did when you applied the transfer tape to the vinyl in step 6 above. Since you're now dealing with a curved surface, the scraper or brayer will not work as effectively as it would on a flat surface. To make sure the vinyl stays behind when you peel off the transfer tape, spend some time rubbing over the design with a bit of pressure. This is to get rid of air bubbles trapped in between and to make the vinyl stick to the mug. Peel the transfer tape away from the mug, starting in a corner. As the transfer tape loosens, pull it away from the mug at a low angle by keeping it close to the mug's surface. Sometimes, a piece of the vinyl will pull away with the transfer tape. If this happens to you, stop peeling, stick the vinyl to the mug, rub it with pressure, and slowly peel again.

When your design has been applied to the mug, rub over the vinyl with your fingers to make sure everything is sticking to the surface. Let the mug rest for at least 24 hours before you use it, as this will give the adhesive on the vinyl to settle.

Did you complete this project? Head over to the Cricut for Newbies Facebook group to share it with your fellow crafters. The community is friendly and, above all, supportive and encouraging, so you have nothing to be afraid of!

When you share your picture, use the #MugProject hashtag.

Mug Project Notes

Use this space to jot down a checklist of things you need to do this project. Maybe write down a date you'd like to complete it, too. And if you're having trouble with something, make notes and then head over to the Cricut for Newbies Facebook group to ask for help.

Project 2: Make a Witty T-Shirt

For this project, I'll show you how to download and use SVG files for Cricut projects on your computer or mobile device.

Downloading files for your Cricut projects is another easy way to get things done. It takes a little longer than using design assets directly from within the Cricut ecosystem, since there are a few extra steps involved, but it's still easy and convenient. There are many places where you can find free SVG files. I'll share a treasure trove of websites where you can get lots of freebies in Chapter 11.

Now let's take a plain t-shirt and make it awesome!

The Goodies You Need

- Your Cricut machine.
- Cricut Smart Iron-On (any color) if you have a Cricut Joy, Explore 3, or Maker 3.
- Everyday Iron-On (any color) if you have a Cricut Explore Air 2 or Maker.
- Weeding Tool.
- One cotton t-shirt.
- An iron or the Cricut EasyPress or EasyPress 2.
- A heat-safe surface.
- Parchment or Teflon paper to act as a protective barrier between the heat press and your design when transferring it to the t-shirt.

Important Factors to Consider before You Start

Iron-On is Cricut's Heat Transfer Vinyl

The standard term for vinyl that needs heat to adhere to a surface is *Heat Transfer Vinyl* or *HTV* for short. Cricut has their own HTV that they trademarked, called *Iron-On*. Many crafters use the terms *HTV* and *Iron-On* interchangeably. Whenever you see me use the term *Iron-On*, I'm referring to Cricut's product specifically. If I want to refer to Heat Transfer Vinyl in the general sense, I'll use *HTV*.

No EasyPress? No Problem!

An EasyPress is Cricut's heat-press machine, an ideal tool to have if you plan on using *Iron-On* or other heat transfer materials for many or most of your projects. However, if you want to put a design on a t-shirt, tote bag, or other surfaces every now and then, you can get away with using your trusty household iron instead.

Choose Your Pressing Surface Wisely

The surface you use to apply *Iron-On* to a t-shirt needs to be flat, sturdy, not too high, and heat safe. An ironing board is not going to help you in this project, as it might buckle under the pressure you need to apply when pressing the *Iron-On*. If the surface is too high, you'll have a harder time pressing, as you won't be able to use your body weight to do most of the work. A waist-high surface is ideal, but you can go lower. Heat-safe surfaces include metal, granite, and concrete. For other surfaces, like wood, you'll need a protective barrier like a heat mat.

Use Cricut's Heat Guide for All Heat-Transfer Projects

Cricut takes the guesswork out of projects that need heat to make materials stick to surfaces. You never have to scratch your head over how to prepare a surface, the amount of heat you need, or for how long you need to apply heat. Bookmark the Cricut *Heat Guide* and always consult it when taking on these kinds of projects.

https://cricut.com/en_us/heatguide

Alternatively, you can access the *Heat Guide* directly from your Design Space home page if you have the desktop app. (There's a link to the *Heat Guide* in the panel on the left of the home page screen)

Use T-Shirts Made from High-Quality Materials

If you want your *Iron-On* to stick properly and last a long time, you have to give it a good base surface. The best t-shirt materials for Cricut *Iron-On* projects are:

- 100% Cotton
- 100% Polyester

This is true whether you plan on using Cricut's regular range of *Iron-On* vinyls or their *Smart Iron-On* vinyls. I like to use Bella & Canvas shirts because they're really soft, durable, and easy to get a hold of from stores like Michaels, Amazon, or directly from the Bella & Canvas website.

If you're planning on putting a design on active-wear or any stretchy material, always go for the Cricut *SportFlex Iron-On*, as they designed it to stretch with those fabrics. *SportFlex Iron-On* is not available as a *Smart Material* at the time of writing this book, so you have to use a cutting mat with it.

Pre-wash Your T-Shirt

Fabric shrinks after its first wash, so it's best to get that done before you apply a design to your t-shirt. Also, pre-washing helps to get rid of chemicals that might interfere with how well the vinyl will adhere to the t-shirt. Don't use any fabric softeners for this wash, as that may interfere with the vinyl's adhesiveness, too.

Don't Waste Time Browsing through Endless Design Options

It's always good to have a general idea of what kind of design you want to use for your upcoming project. If you don't, you can end up spending hours upon hours browsing. Get into the habit of brainstorming four to five project ideas and picking a theme for each one before you go hunting for designs. This will help you stay focused and prevent you from getting lost in the sea of options.

Step 1: Download A Design

How to Download and Extract SVGs on your Computer or Laptop

For this project, we'll use an SVG from Creative Fabrica's collection of freebies. This is actually one of few websites that allows you to use their free assets for commercial purposes, meaning you're allowed to make money off some of the designs you download for free.

Go to https://www.creativefabrica.com/. On the right side of the menu bar, you'll see a *Freebies* link with a dropdown arrow. When you hover over *Freebies*, a list of options will pop up. Click on *Free SVGs*. I've chosen the image you see on the next page, but feel free to choose anything you'd like to put on yours. If you're going with the same design as me, you can find it here: https://www.creativefabrica.com/product/i-was-going-to-take-over-the-world-but-then-i-got-distracted/

Click on the green *Download* button next to the design preview.

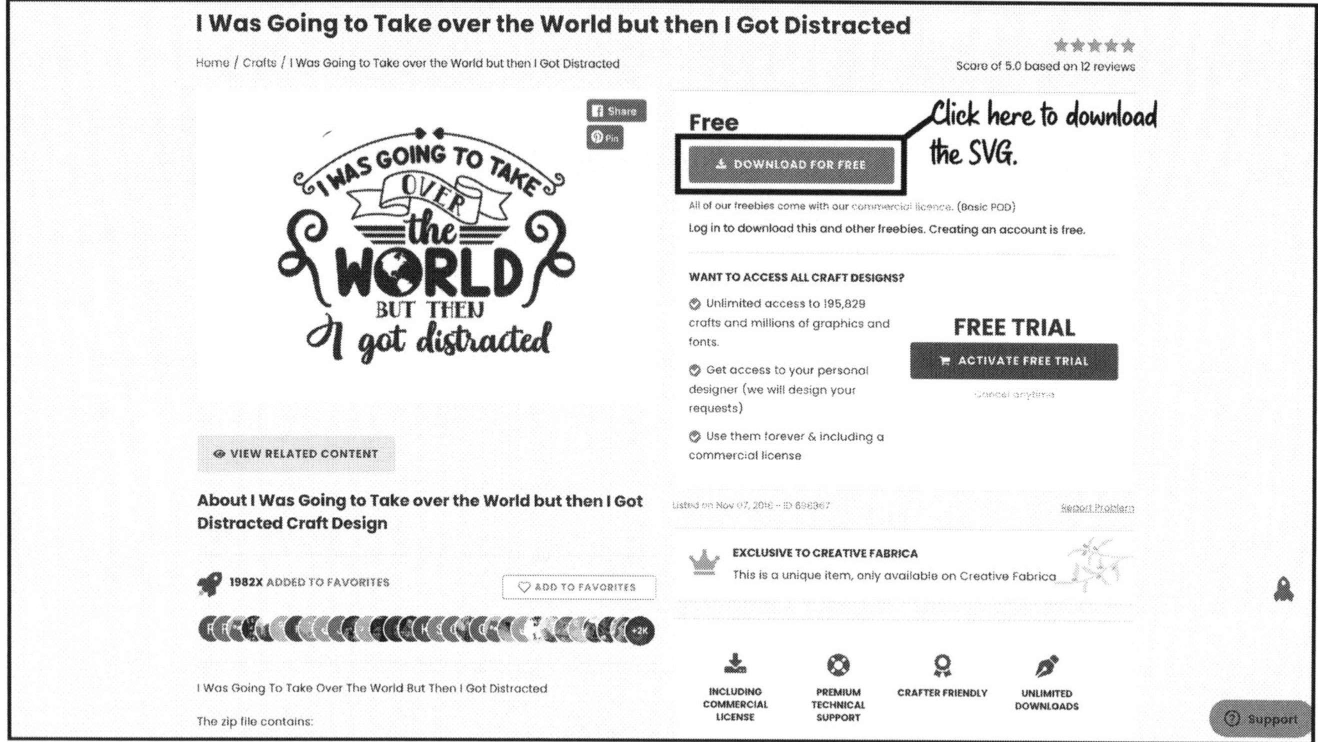

How to Extract an SVG on a Windows Computer

Unless you have specified otherwise, all downloaded files on a Windows computer usually go to the *Downloads* folder or to your Desktop. Go to your *Downloads* folder or the folder you usually send new downloads to. In there, you should see the ZIP file for the SVG. Right-click on the ZIP file and click on *Extract All*. Windows will prompt you to specify where the file should be extracted to. If you click on the *Extract* button without specifying a location, it will extract in the same location as the ZIP file. You'll see a folder appear next to the ZIP file when the extraction is complete. From there, you can move the new folder to a location on your computer you'll remember. You can delete the ZIP file after the file extraction.

Some windows computers will display a browser thumbnail for SVG files like the Internet Explorer or Google Chrome icon. This usually happens when there is no program installed on the computer for previewing SVGs. However, you'll still be able to upload the file to Design Space and see it just fine on the app's *Canvas* screen.

How to Extract an SVG on an Apple Computer

Go to your *Downloads* folder, locate the SVG's ZIP file and double-click on it. This action will extract the file, after which you'll see a new folder appear with the SVG's name. Move the new folder to a location you'll remember and delete the ZIP file.

Whether you use a Windows or Apple computer, downloaded SVG folders contain three to five different files most of the time. There is usually a *.png*, *.eps*, *.svg*, and sometimes a *.jpeg* file, too. When you upload the design to Cricut, you'll choose the *.svg* file.

It's also a good idea to have a folder for everything design-related on your computer where you can store downloads after they have been extracted from ZIP files. The most accessible place for such a folder is your computer's Desktop. That way, you'll always know where to go when you want to upload files to Design Space.

How to Download and Extract SVGs on your iOS or Android Device

Open your smartphone or tablet's Internet browser and go to the following URL to download the design file: https://www.creativefabrica.com/product/i-was-going-to-take-over-the-world-but-then-i-got-distracted/

Tap on the green *Download* button.

How to Extract an SVG on an iOS Device

If you have iOS version 11 or higher, you can download SVG files and upload them to Design Space. Versions older than 11 don't support SVG files.

After tapping on the download button at the above URL, your device will prompt you to confirm the download. Once you tap on *Download*, the process will start and you'll see a blue circle with a downward-pointing arrow appear at the bottom of the screen.

Go to your device's *Files* app—its icon is a blue folder on a white background. Inside the app, locate the *Downloads* folder.

Locate the downloaded ZIP file, press and hold on to it until a menu pops up, and then choose the *Uncompress* option. A new folder that has the same name will appear next to the ZIP file. To open the folder, tap on it. Inside, you'll find a *readme* file and two to five image files. The *readme* file typically contains license information that tells you how you may and may not use the free design. The other files all represent the image or design, just in different formats. The only one you need for this project is the one that ends with *SVG*.

Follow these Instructions if Your iOS Device is a Little Older

The above instructions work for the latest iOS versions; that is, iOS 14 and up. If you have an older version than 14, things may look different for you.

On the browser screen, you should see the ZIP file with its name and a couple of options below it when you tap on the *Download* button. Choose the *Open in Files* option. This will prompt you to choose a location to save the file. Typically, your options are *iCloud Drive*, *On My iPhone*, and third-party services like Google Drive or Dropbox if your device is connected to them. Whatever you choose, you need to be sure you'll be able to locate the file afterward. Tap on your choice and then tap on *Add* in the upper-right corner of the screen.

On the next screen, tap on *Preview Content* below the ZIP file's name. If the ZIP file came with a license agreement, this is probably what you'll see when you tap on *Preview Content*. Tap on the three stacked lines at the bottom-right corner of the screen; now you'll be able to see everything inside the ZIP file. Locate the SVG file and tap on it. This will open a new screen with a preview of the design, where you can tap on the upload (or share) icon at the bottom-left corner of the screen. (It's the icon of a little box with an upward-facing arrow coming out of it.) A window will pop up with applications, like Messages and Mail, to choose from. Below the applications are more options; scroll sideways until you see the *Save to Files* option and tap on it. Don't tap on *Save Image*, because it will not save the actual SVG file. A new window will open and prompt you to choose a location to save the file, similar to what you saw when you were prompted to choose a location for the ZIP file right after you downloaded it. Tap on the location in which you want to save your SVG file, then tap *Add* on the next window (be sure to pick a location you will remember). The SVG is now available to use in specialized apps like Design Space.

How to Extract an SVG on an Android Device

Depending on your device's settings, it will either download the file immediately after you tap the *Download* button, or it will ask you to confirm the download. When the download is complete, you should see a notification.

Go to your *Files* application and tap on the *Downloads* category. The ZIP file you just downloaded should be the first item you see. If not, scroll down until you locate the file name and tap on it. A window will pop up to ask whether you want to extract the ZIP file. Tap on the *Extract* button.

When the extraction is done, a new window will pop up containing a list of all the extracted files. Tick the box at the bottom of the pop-up window that says *Delete ZIP file*, and tap on *Finished*. You should now be able to see the .svg file, along with other formats of the design, in your *Downloads* folder.

Step 2: Upload the SVG to Design Space & Prepare it for Your Cricut Machine

Unless you want to add extra shapes or text to a ready-made design, this step requires almost no effort on your part. We talked about how to upload external files to Design Space in chapter 9, so instead of repeating those steps, I'll just remind you of the following:

- Upload your image as a *Cut* file and not a *Print Then Cut* file.
- Choose *Complex* as the image type.
- Be sure to choose the right file type for your project (in this case, choose the one that ends with .svg.

Once the design has been uploaded, it's time to make sure its size is right for the t-shirt. Since t-shirts come in many forms and sizes, I like to measure the available space on the blank t-shirt to make sure I get the size of my design just right. While I suggest you do the same, here is a general rule you can follow:

T-SHIRT SIZE (CLASSIC ADULT)	DESIGN SIZE
Small	9,5" (max 10,5")
Medium	10" (max 11")
Large	10,5" (max 11,5")
X-Large	11" (max 12")
2 X-Large	12,5" (max 13,5")
3 X-Large	13" (max 14")
4 X-Large	13,5" (max 14,4")

If you're working with teen or youth t-shirts, subtract 1'' to 1,5'' from the above guidelines for the best results

The desktop version of Design Space allows you to work with templates, allowing you to visualize what the design will look like once applied to the t-shirt. Many crafters find this feature very helpful. If you need to visualize this design, click on *Templates* in the Design Panel to see all the template options.

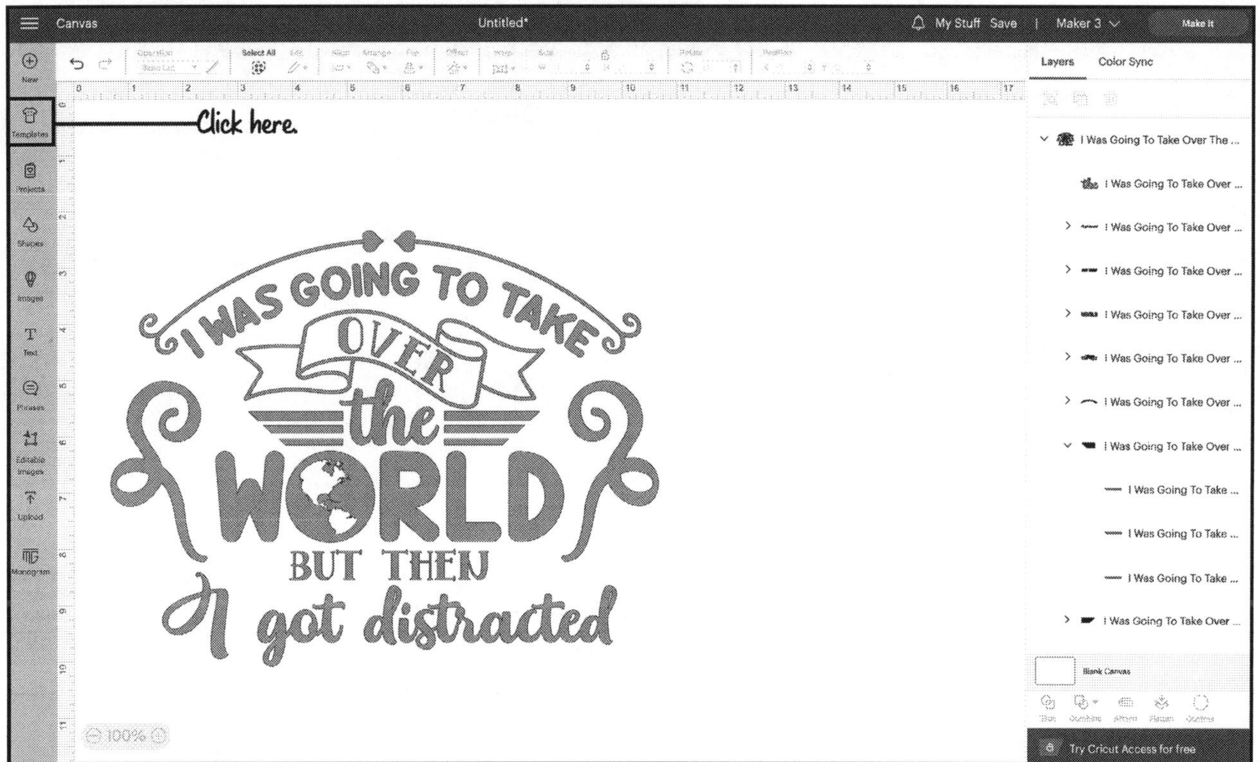

Type *shirt* into the search bar in the upper-right corner of the window and choose the *Classic t-shirts* option. If another template represents your blank t-shirt better, choose that one instead. When you click on your choice, Design Space will take you back to the Canvas screen, where you will see outlines of the template you chose. At the top of the window, you'll see a notification from Design Space informing you that the template is for reference only. The outline serves as a guide, but your Cricut machine will ignore it when it's time for the cutting process. One outline shows the front of the t-shirt while the other shows the back. Drag your design to an appropriate spot on the template to get an idea of what it will look like after being applied.

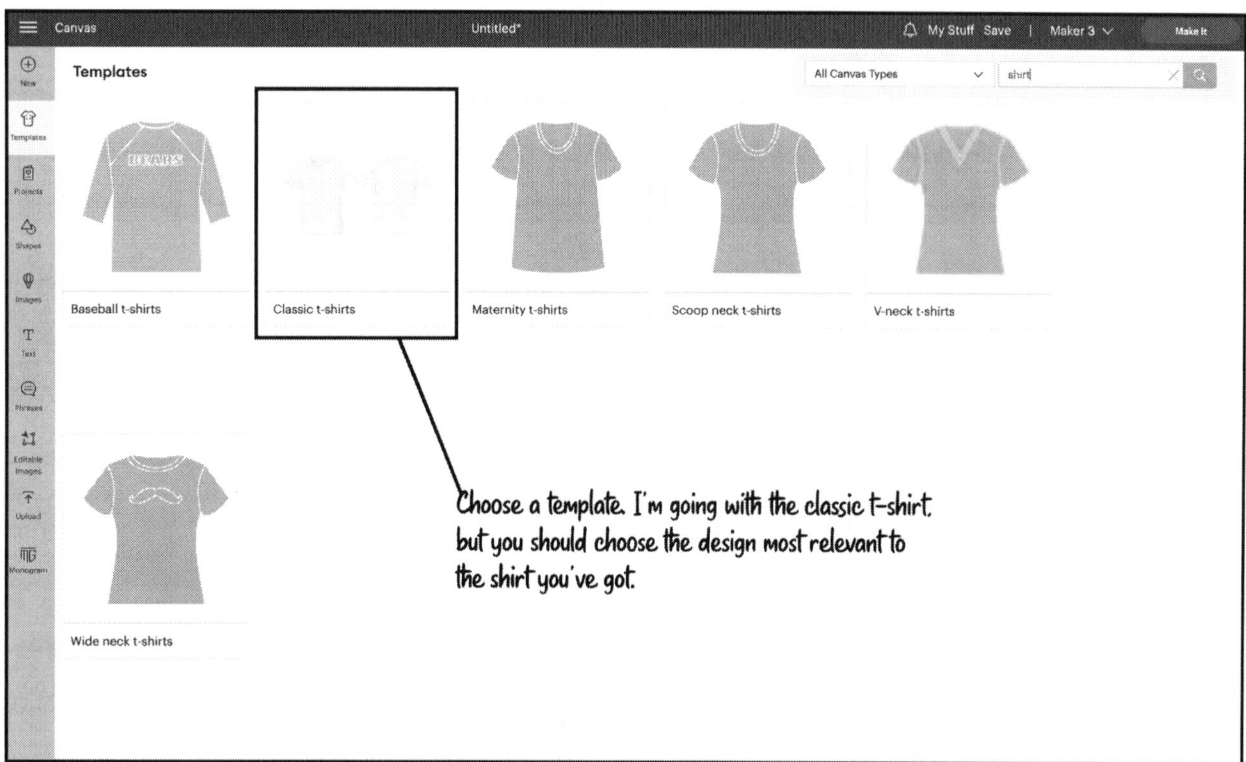

My design will be 10 inches wide, but you can make yours smaller if you want to. If you want to go bigger, keep the recommended maximum sizes from the above table in mind.

When you look at your *Layers Panel*, you'll see a lot of separate layers stacked on top of each other. Most of the time, this is how Design Space will import an SVG file. The final design is made up of many individual elements, each represented by a layer. To keep the design intact (as you see it on the Canvas), you'll have to use the *Attach* function before you click on the *Make It* button, otherwise Design Space will separate and arrange the layers in any way it thinks will make the best use of the available space on the cutting mat. After linking the layers with the *Attach* function, go ahead and click (or tap) on the Make It button.

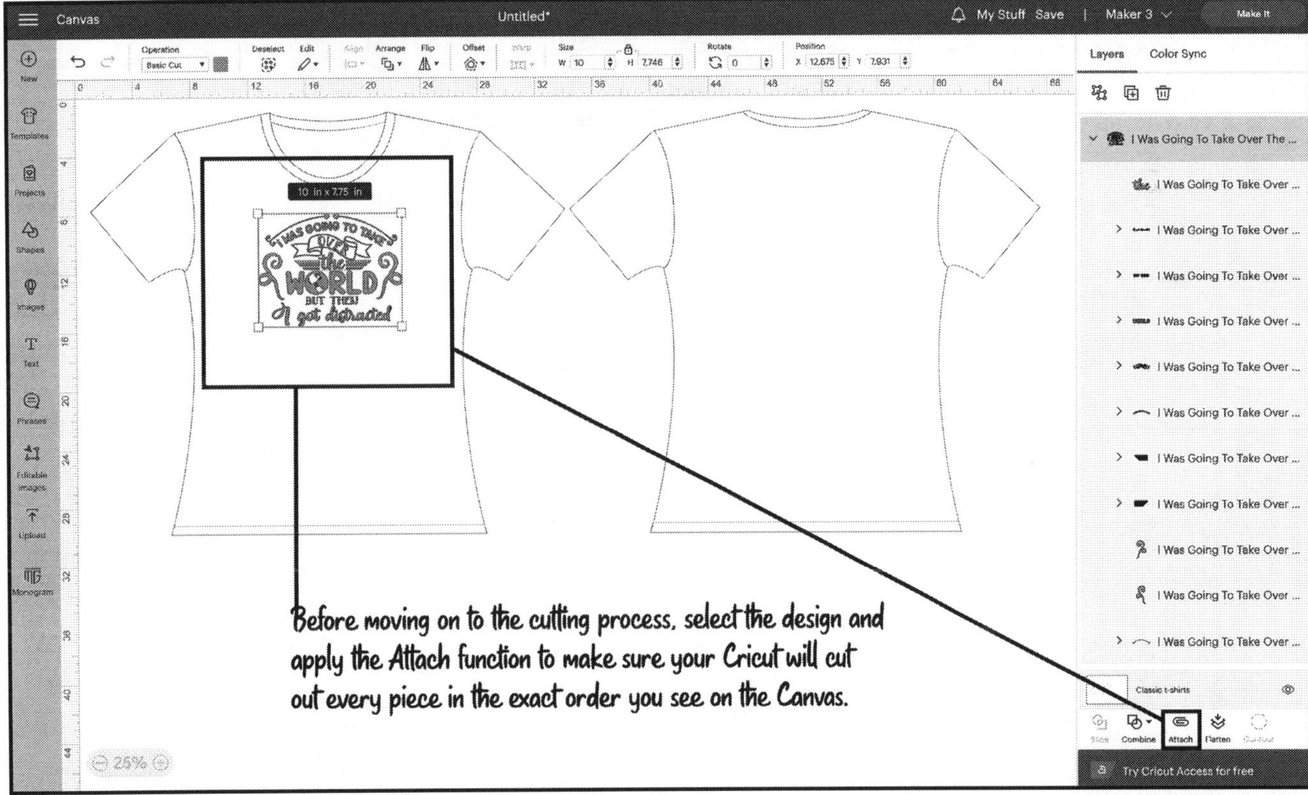

Earlier in the book, we briefly talked about when to mirror images. *Iron-On* and other heat transfer materials always need to be mirrored, because the material's adhesive layer, which gets activated by heat, is on the front (the colorful or shiny side you look at when opening the roll). When you mirror an image, you flip it face-down so it looks as if it was created the wrong way around. Then, when it gets applied to a surface, it will look the way it did when you first worked on the design. On the preview screen (the one you see after clicking on the *Make It* button), you'll see *Mirror* with a toggle switch underneath it. Click on the toggle switch to activate it. You'll know it is switched on when the circle moves from left to right. If you're still not sure, look at the preview mat, which should now show your design flipped the wrong way around.

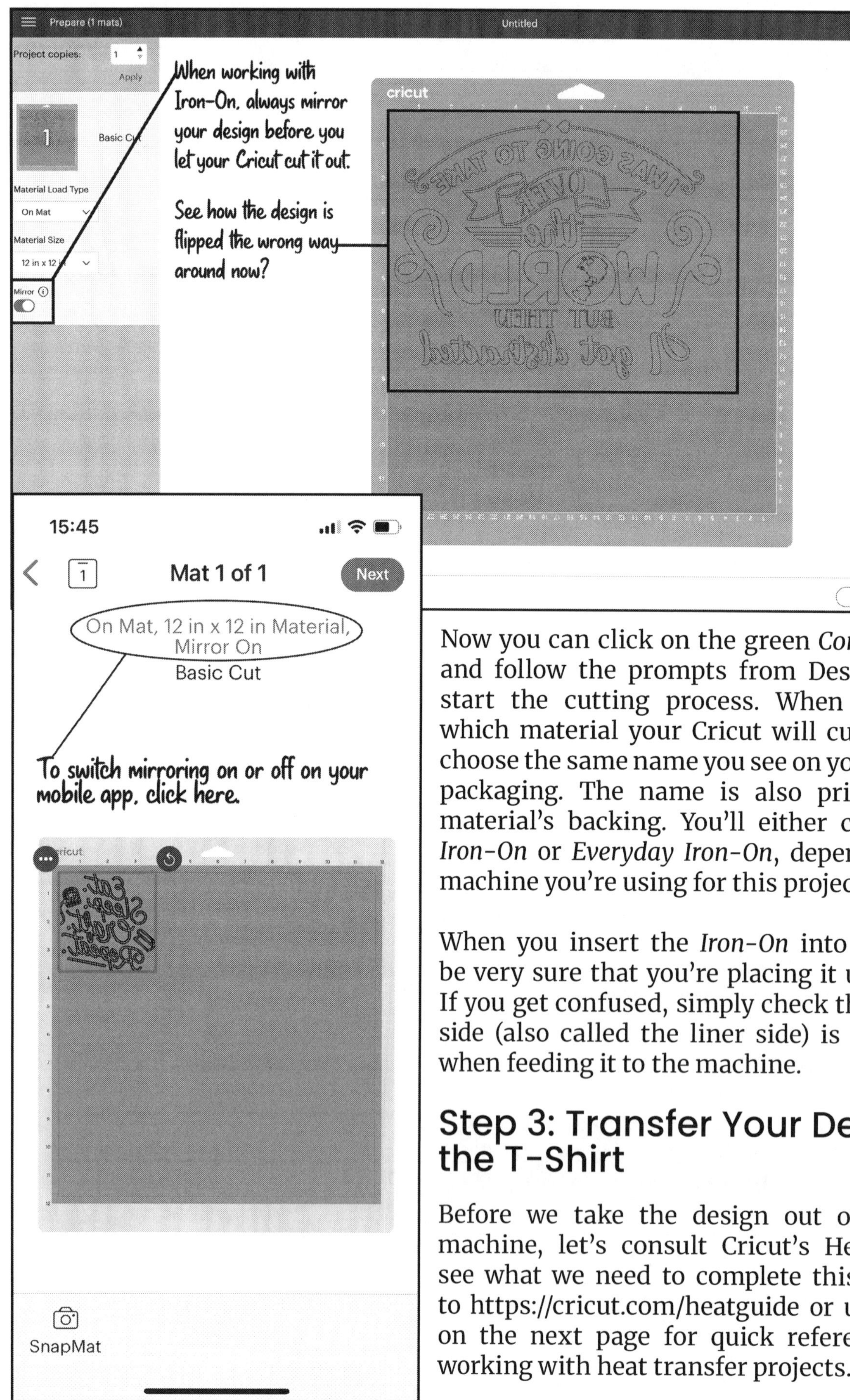

Now you can click on the green *Continue* button and follow the prompts from Design Space to start the cutting process. When you specify which material your Cricut will cut, be sure to choose the same name you see on your material's packaging. The name is also printed on the material's backing. You'll either choose *Smart Iron-On* or *Everyday Iron-On*, depending on the machine you're using for this project.

When you insert the *Iron-On* into your Cricut, be very sure that you're placing it upside down. If you get confused, simply check that the shiny side (also called the liner side) is facing down when feeding it to the machine.

Step 3: Transfer Your Design to the T-Shirt

Before we take the design out of the Cricut machine, let's consult Cricut's Heat Guide to see what we need to complete this project. Go to https://cricut.com/heatguide or use the table on the next page for quick referencing when working with heat transfer projects.

HEAT TRANSFER MATERIAL	BASE MATERIAL	IDEAL HEAT	PRESS TIME & PRESSURE	COOL/WARM PEEL
Everyday Iron-On/Light/ Metallic *Remember to flip fabrics over and to press their backsides for 15 to 20 seconds.	100% Cotton; Cotton/ Poly Blend; Polyester	315°F / 155°C	30 seconds; light	Cool
	Faux Leather; Nylon	280°F / 140°C	30 seconds; light	Cool
	Wood	300°F/ 150°C	40 seconds; firm	Cool
Express Iron-On *Remember to flip fabrics over and to press their backsides for 15 to 20 seconds.	Cardstock; Chipboard; Corkboard; 100% Cotton; Cotton Canvas; Cotton/Poly blend; Faux leather; Felt; Mesh; Muslin; Neoprene; Polyester; Silk; Wool; Cricut Blanks	300°F/ 150°C	15 seconds; firm	Cool
Foil Iron-On *Remember to flip fabrics over and to press their backsides for 15 to 20 seconds.	Cardstock	270°F / 130°C	30 seconds; firm	Cool
	100% Cotton; Cotton/Poly blend	295°F / 145°C	30 seconds; firm	Cool
	Cotton Canvas; Muslin	290°F / 145°C	30 seconds; firm	Cool
	Faux Leather	255°F / 125°C	30 seconds	Cool

HEAT TRANSFER MATERIAL	BASE MATERIAL	IDEAL HEAT	PRESS TIME & PRESSURE	COOL/WARM PEEL
Foil Iron-On	Felt; Mesh	280°F / 140°C	30 seconds; firm	Cool
	Neoprene	280°F / 140°C	20 seconds; firm	Cool
	Nylon; Silk; Wool	255°F / 125°C	30 seconds	Cool
	Polyester;	295°F / 145°C	30 seconds; firm	Cool
Glitter Iron-On *Remember to flip fabrics over and to press their backsides for 15 to 20 seconds.	100% Cotton; Cotton/Poly Blend; Polyester;	330°F / 165°C	30 seconds; light	Cool
	Faux Leather	270°F / 130°C	20 seconds; light	Cool
	Wood	300°F / 150°C	40 seconds; firm	Cool
Holographic Iron-On *Remember to flip fabrics over and to press their backsides for 15 to 20 seconds.	100% Cotton; Cotton/Poly blend; Polyester	330°F / 165°C	30 seconds; light	Cool
	Faux Leather	285°F / 140°C	30 seconds; light	Cool
	Wood	300°F / 150°C	40 seconds; firm	Cool

HEAT TRANSFER MATERIAL	BASE MATERIAL	IDEAL HEAT	PRESS TIME & PRESSURE	COOL/WARM PEEL
SportFlex Iron-On *Remember to flip fabrics over and to press their backsides for 15 to 20 seconds.	Nylon; Polyester	305°F / 150°F	30 seconds; light	Cool
Smart Iron-On *Remember to flip fabrics over and to press their backsides for 15 to 20 seconds.	100% Cotton; Cotton/Polly blend; Polyester	315°F / 155°C	30 seconds; light	Cool
	Faux Leather; Nylon	280°F / 140°C	30 seconds; light	Cool
	Wood	300°F / 150°C	45 seconds; firm	Cool
Smart Iron-On – Glitter *Remember to flip fabrics over and to press their backsides for 15 to 20 seconds.	100% Cotton	330°F / 165°C	30 seconds; light	Cool
	Cotton/Poly Blend	330°F / 165°C	30 seconds; light	Cool
	Faux Leather	270°F / 130°C	20 seconds; light	Cool
	Polyester	330°F / 165°C	30 seconds; light	Cool
	Wood	300°F / 150°C	40 seconds; firm	Cool

HEAT TRANSFER MATERIAL	BASE MATERIAL	IDEAL HEAT	PRESS TIME & PRESSURE	COOL/WARM PEEL
Smart Iron-On – Holographic *Remember to flip fabrics over and to press their backsides for 15 to 20 seconds.	100% Cotton; Cotton/Poly blend; Polyester	330°F / 165°C	30 seconds; light	Cool
	Faux Leather	280°F / 140°C	30 seconds; light	Cool
	Wood	300°F / 150°C	40 seconds; firm	Cool
Smart Iron-On – Patterned *Remember to flip fabrics over and to press their backsides for 15 to 20 seconds.	100% Cotton; Cotton/Poly blend	340°F / 170°C	30 seconds; firm	Cool
	Faux Leather	265°F / 130°C	20 seconds; firm	Cool
Infusible Ink Transfer Sheet **Infusible Ink Pen / Marker on Copy Paper** *Remember to flip fabrics over and to press their backsides for 15 to 20 seconds.	Aluminum Sheet	385°F / 195°C	40 seconds; no pressure	Cool
	Baby Bodysuit; Tote bag; T-shirt	385°F / 195°C	40 seconds; firm	Cool
	Ceramic Coaster	400°F / 205°C	240 seconds; no pressure	Cool
	Cosmetic bag; Pillow cover; Wine bag	385°F / 195°C	60 seconds; firm	Cool
	Square Coaster	400°F / 205°C	60 seconds; no pressure	Cool

Note: The table I shared above is based on Cricut's heat guide and is meant to be used as a guideline for their range of *EasyPress* products. When using a household iron, the guide is still useful. However, you will need to experiment to get the best results. The table also doesn't contain all the materials and settings applicable to heat transfer projects, so be sure to check out Cricut's *Heat Guide* when working with these kinds of projects.

An important note about *Infusible Ink* from Cricut: "*Use in a well-ventilated area—vapors from heating process may be irritating to sensitive individuals. In case of skin irritation, immediately wash skin with soap and water; for contact with eyes, immediately flush with water. If irritation persists, seek medical attention.*"

If you are consulting the *Heat Guide* and own a Cricut *EasyPress*, select the model from the available options on the *Heat Guide* web page. If you're doing this with a household iron, choose the regular *EasyPress* (second option from the left). Below the heat press options, you need to choose a heat transfer material and a base material (In this case, the heat transfer material will be Everyday *Iron-on/Lite/Metallic* or *Smart Iron On* and the base material will be whatever kind of t-shirt you have). Next, tick the circle next to *Cricut EasyPress Mat*—even if you don't have one, as you can't continue without doing so.

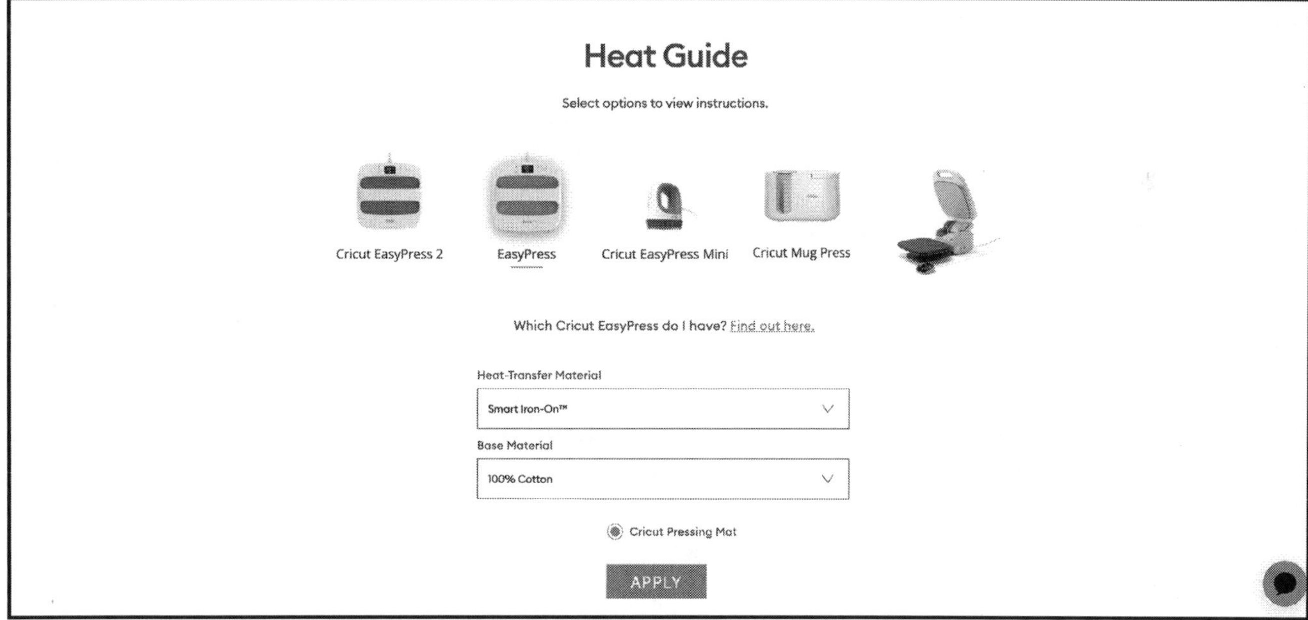

When you click on *Apply*, Cricut will give you information such as the ideal temperature needed to transfer the *Iron-On*, how long to press down, and how to prepare and apply the design to your chosen surface. Although the Cricut *Heat Guide* is aimed at giving you information related to their heat press machines, it is still useful for general guidelines whenever you take on heat transfer projects, no matter the method you use to apply materials to surfaces.

If you are using any kind of heat press, follow the instructions from the *Heat Guide* to complete your project. If you are using a household iron, use the Heat guide for pointers and the guidelines below to ensure you get the best results.

Switch On Your Iron

According to the *Heat Guide*, we'll need around 315ºF (or 155 ºC) to transfer our design. Generally, an iron produces the most heat on the Linen or Cotton setting, so set yours on either of those. (Some irons have one setting for both linen and cotton and will read something like Cotton/Linen.)

Make sure there is no water in your iron and that the steam setting is turned off. Set the iron aside and give it time to heat up.

Remove the Design from Your Cricut and Weed the Excess Vinyl

Now it's time to unload the *Iron-On* from your Cricut and weed out the excess bits from the design. Take your time with the weeding process and work carefully. As you weed, you'll notice that the mirrored (backward) design remains on a clear sheet, also known as the liner or carrier sheet. If you flip the sheet over, you'll see your design facing you right-side up from underneath the liner.

Prepare your T-Shirt

Make sure the surface where you will do the press-work is clean and free of clutter, then place the t-shirt on it, making sure the side where you want to put the design is facing you.

Cricut's Heat Guide says that you need to preheat your t-shirt for a few seconds before applying the design. The reason for this is to even out the part where the design will go and to remove possible moisture from the t-shirt.

Now you need to position the design to make sure it will look great once applied. The easiest way is to find the t-shirt's center with one of these two methods:

1. Use the t-shirt's label as the center and align the design with it.
2. Fold the t-shirt in half so the sleeves align with each other and then iron over the fold line. Open the t-shirt again and use the line you made as the center and align the design with it.

In terms of height, an effective rule of thumb is to place the design two to three inches below the t-shirt's collar.

Press the Design

When you're happy with the design's position, place a Teflon sheet or piece of parchment paper over it. This barrier is important to protect both your design and the iron's sole plate from damage, especially when working with multiple layers of *Iron-On* or HTV.

At this stage, the natural thing you'll want to do is to iron over the design. However, this is the least effective way to get the vinyl to adhere to the t-shirt. It needs pressure to really stick. Starting at one end of the design, place the iron on it and press down with moderate pressure for around 15 seconds. Make sure your iron covers the entire end of the design that you've chosen as the starting point. After 15 seconds, lift the iron (don't slide it over!) and place it on the next part of the design for another 15 seconds. Continue doing this until you've reached the other end of the design.

With tall designs, it's a good idea to press all around the design's edges, too. Many crafters like to flip their t-shirts around after the initial press and iron over the back with pressure for good measure. You can't go wrong by doing that, as the extra heat will definitely help the vinyl adhere to the fabric better.

Once the pressing is over, remove the parchment paper or Teflon sheet and wait 20 to 30 seconds, or until the liner on top of the Iron-On is cool to the touch. Take hold of a corner and gently pull the liner away from the design. You'll want to do this slowly, as you'll still need to have it in place if some of the vinyl did not stick to the fabric properly. You'll know the vinyl did not bond with the fabric if some of it sticks to the liner instead of staying behind on the t-shirt as you pull. If that's the case, simply reapply the liner, being mindful that the vinyl does not wrinkle, cover it with the parchment paper again, and press with the iron for another 10 to 15 seconds on the spot where the vinyl pulled away. Wait for the liner to cool and then pull it away again. If necessary, repeat this process on other spots. This might be your first go at applying *Iron-On* or HTV to a surface, so be patient with yourself if things don't go as you had planned it in your head. (Spoiler alert: things rarely go as planned in crafting, but that's where the beauty comes in.)

Caring for Your T-Shirt

Congratulations! You just made your very own witty t-shirt. To let the vinyl settle and bond with the fabric completely, let the t-shirt rest for 24 hours before you wash and use it. The following tips will extend your t-shirt's life and ensure that you get the best out of it. Be sure to share these tips with others if you plan on gifting or selling similar projects:

- Wash and dry your t-shirt inside-out.
- Use cold or warm water to wash the t-shirt in, but not hot water.
- Do not dry clean your t-shirt.
- Never iron directly on the design.

Did you complete this project? Head over to the Cricut for Newbies Facebook group to share it with your fellow crafters.

When you share your picture, use the #ShirtProject hashtag.

T-Shirt Project Notes

Use this space to jot down a checklist of things you need to do this project. Maybe write down a date you'd like to complete it, too. And if you're having trouble with something, make notes and then head over to the Cricut for Newbies Facebook group to ask for help.

Project 3: Design Your Own Greeting Card from Scratch

With a more hands-on approach, this project will give you a decent exercise in using more Design Space features than you do when working with ready-made design files from Cricut and other sources like Creative Fabrica. It will also help you see how you can bring your creative ideas to life as your Cricut journey progresses.

The Goodies You Need

- Any Cricut Machine.
- Cricut *StandardGrip* Cutting Mat (the green one).
- Cricut Cardstock (any two colors).
- Scraping Tool.
- Weeding Tool.
- Cricut Scoring Stylus (optional).
- Cricut Fine Point Pen or Cricut Marker (any color of your choice, as long as it will be clear on your choice of cardstock).
- Glue that will become clear when it dries.

Step 1: Create Your Card's Foundation in Design Space

Let's create the basic shape for our greeting card. Click on *Shapes* in the Design Panel and choose the standard square shape.

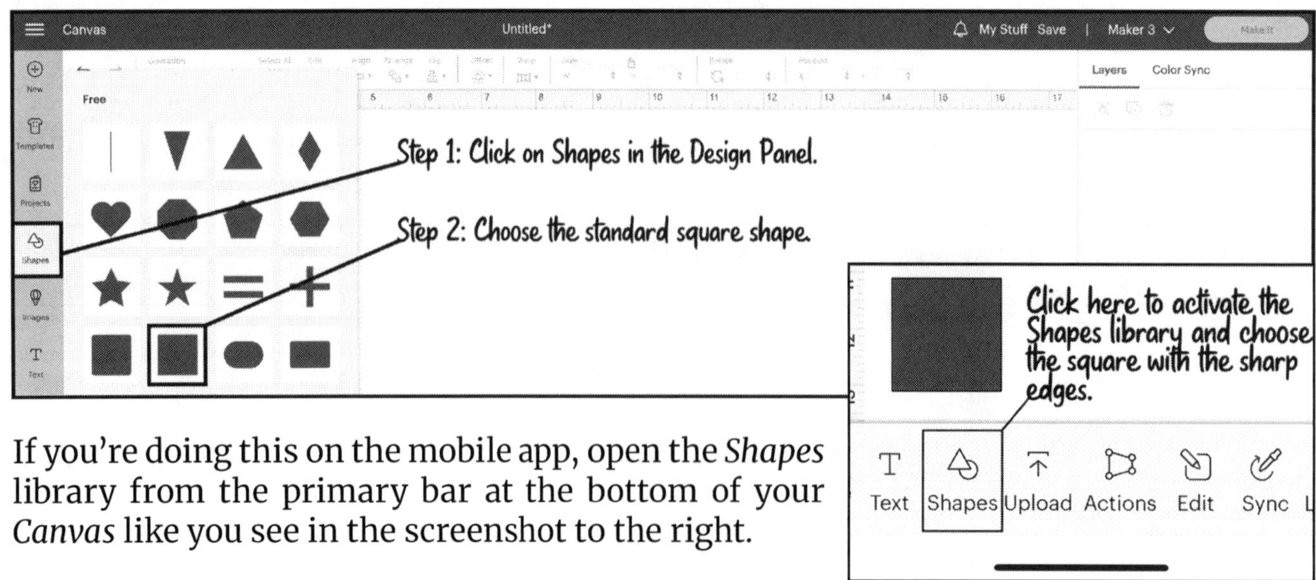

If you're doing this on the mobile app, open the *Shapes* library from the primary bar at the bottom of your *Canvas* like you see in the screenshot to the right.

When the shape shows up on the grid area, change its color to whatever color of cardstock you will use for your greeting card's cover (the outside of the card). Note that the color you choose on Design Space need not match the color of your cardstock exactly. Simply choose a color similar to the cardstock so you can visualize the result as you develop the design.

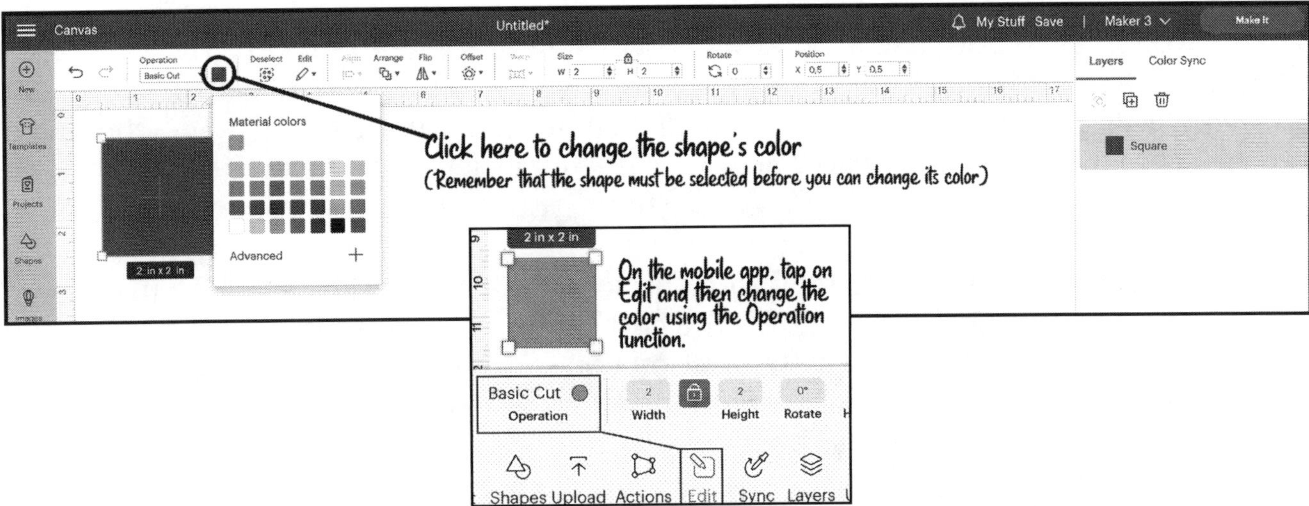

The next step is to unlock the square's aspect ratio by clicking on the padlock icon in between the width and height settings of the shape in the *Edit Bar*. You'll know the aspect ratio is unlocked when the padlock's loop or shackle looks like its open. Now, change the square's width to 10 inches and its height to 7 inches in the *Edit Bar.*

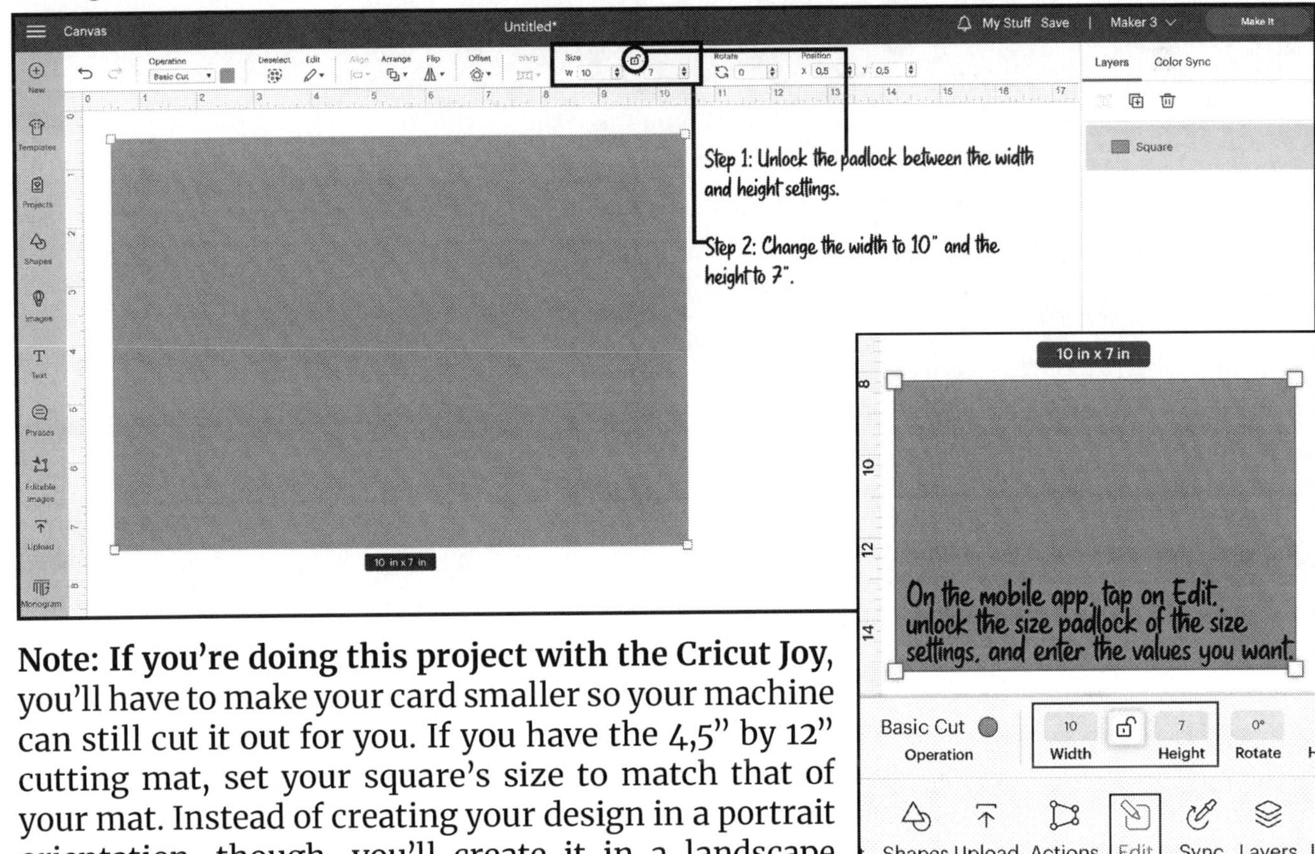

Note: If you're doing this project with the Cricut Joy, you'll have to make your card smaller so your machine can still cut it out for you. If you have the 4,5" by 12" cutting mat, set your square's size to match that of your mat. Instead of creating your design in a portrait orientation, though, you'll create it in a landscape orientation. Remember to arrange your design elements accordingly as you work through the tutorial. If you have the Cricut Joy and plan on making lots of personalized cards, it will be worth your while to invest in the Cricut Joy Card Mat and Cricut Joy Insert Cards. Although we won't do a Cricut Joy Insert Card tutorial in this book, you can learn all about it from Cricut at this link: https://help.cricut.com/hc/en-us/articles/360040664534-Cricut-Joy-Insert-Cards-and-Card-Mat-101

The next step is to add a score line. This will be the guideline where the cardstock should be folded to make the greeting card. If you have the Cricut *Scoring Stylus* or *Scoring Wheel*, your machine will make a crease or indent on the cardstock where you set the score line in Design Space. However, it's not essential to have these tools to do this project. If you don't have Cricut scoring tools, you'll simply fold your card the good-old-fashioned way by bending the cardstock to align the four corners and then folding it into a card. Besides, the main goal with the score line in Design Space is to make sure you get the design's position right for the cutting process. You can find the score line in the *Shapes* library. It's the very first option you see when opening the *Shapes* library (the thin line). Add it to your *Canvas* now. With the score line selected, change its height to 7" so it matches the height of the rectangle.

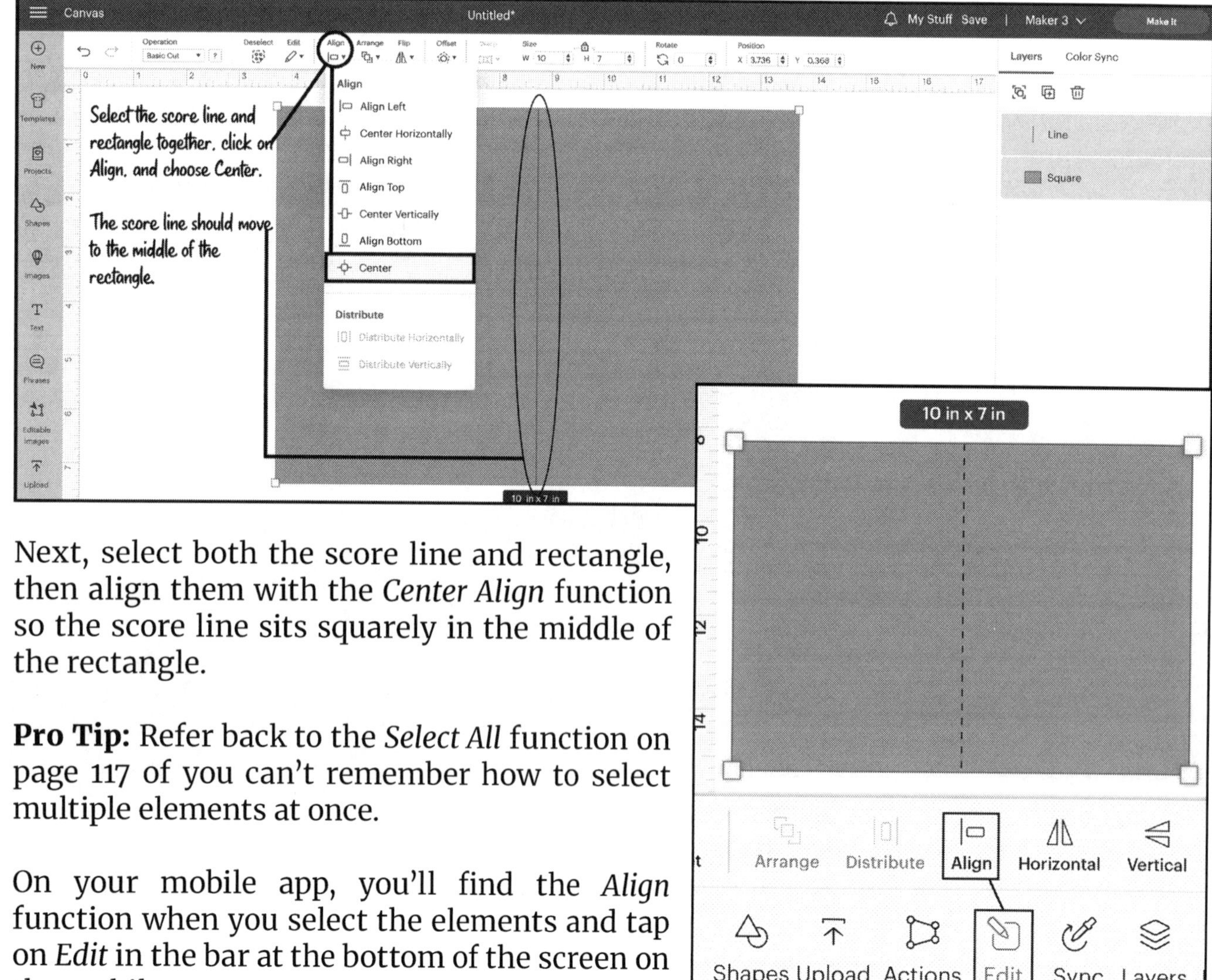

Next, select both the score line and rectangle, then align them with the *Center Align* function so the score line sits squarely in the middle of the rectangle.

Pro Tip: Refer back to the *Select All* function on page 117 of you can't remember how to select multiple elements at once.

On your mobile app, you'll find the *Align* function when you select the elements and tap on *Edit* in the bar at the bottom of the screen on the mobile app.

Let's make the rectangle and score line act like a unit so they can stick together if we need to move them around. Select both elements and click on the *Group* icon at the top of the *Layers Panel*. On your mobile app, you'll find the *Group* function in the secondary bar that pops up when you select the rectangle and score line.

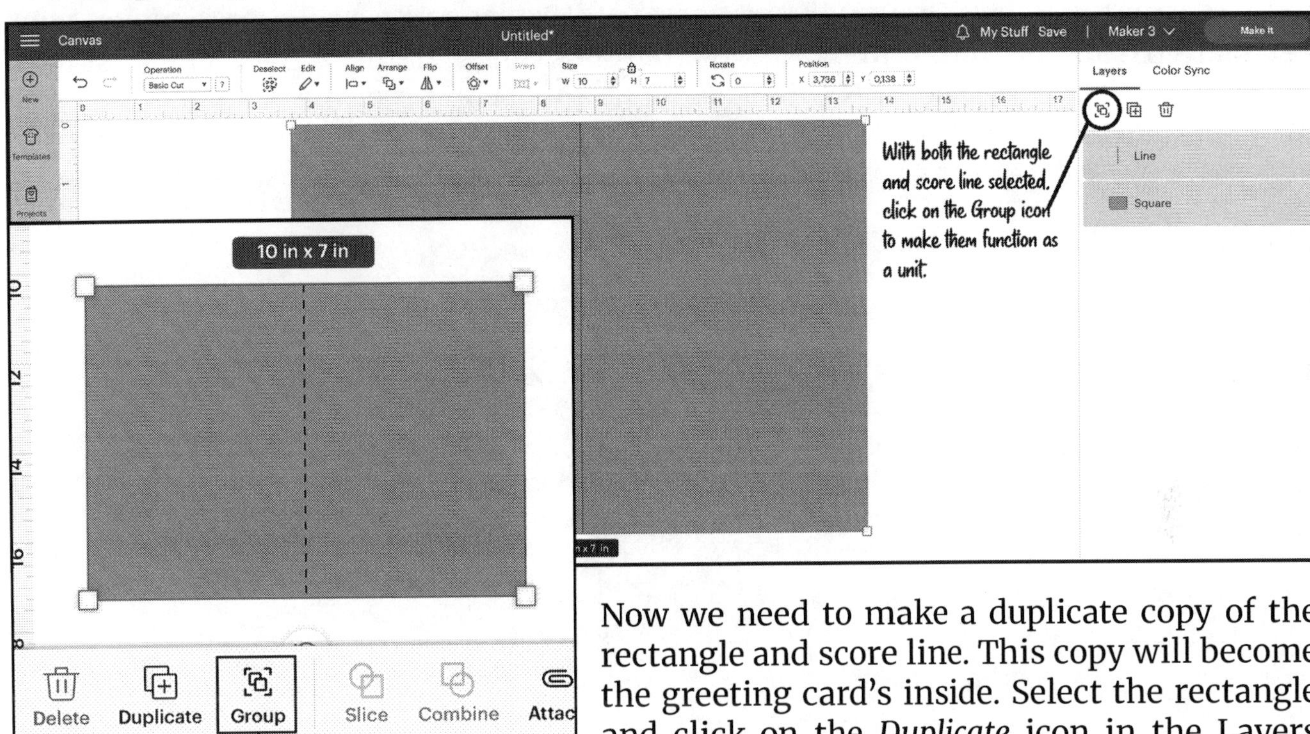

Now we need to make a duplicate copy of the rectangle and score line. This copy will become the greeting card's inside. Select the rectangle and click on the *Duplicate* icon in the Layers Panel. Since the rectangle and score line are grouped, the duplicate copy will automatically include both of them.

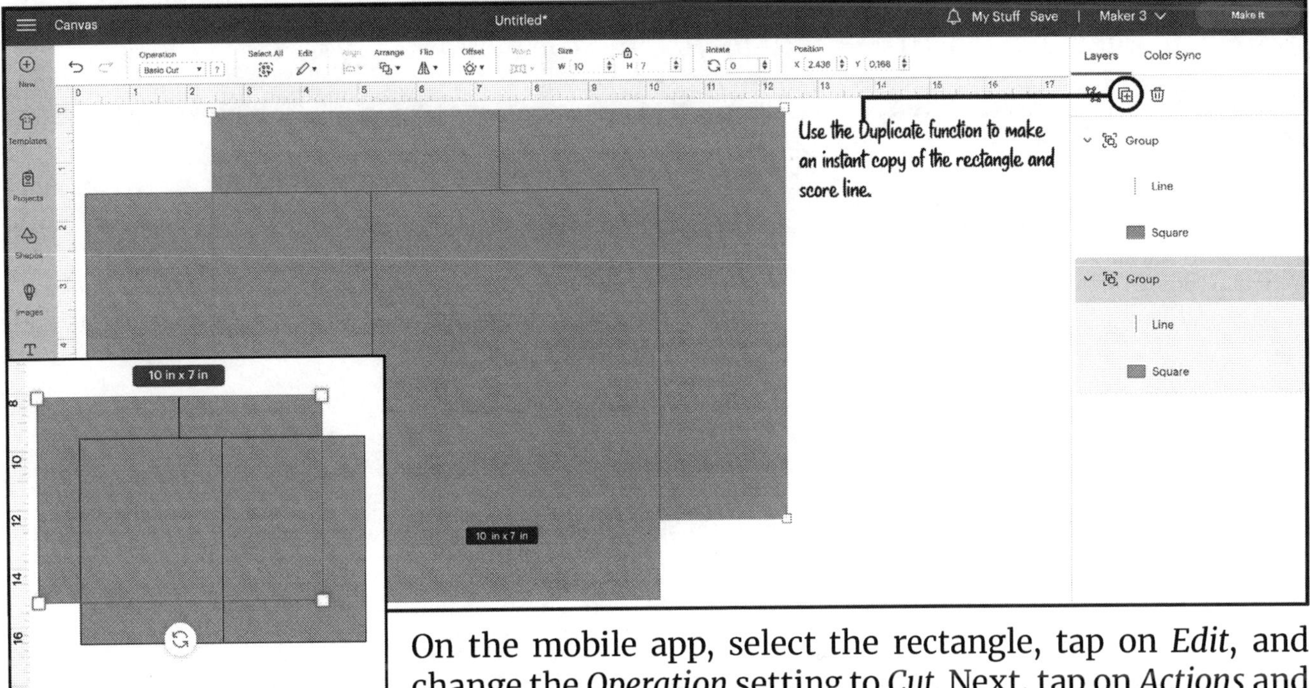

On the mobile app, select the rectangle, tap on *Edit*, and change the *Operation* setting to *Cut*. Next, tap on *Actions* and then *Duplicate* to make an instant copy of the rectangle.

Let's rename the items that we've got so far in the *Layers*

Panel so we don't get confused. Click on the rectangle that's in front on the grid area and then look at the *Layers Panel* to see which list item is highlighted (it should be the one on top). The highlighted item tells you that it's the same one you have currently got selected in the grid area. Double click on the name of the highlighted item in the *Layers Panel* (currently, it says *Group*). Type *'Inside of Card'* and press the Enter key on your keyboard to rename the list item. Now double click on the name of the second list item in the *Layers Panel* (it also says *Group* at the moment) and rename it *'Card Cover'*. You won't be able to rename the layers on the mobile app as this feature is not available yet.

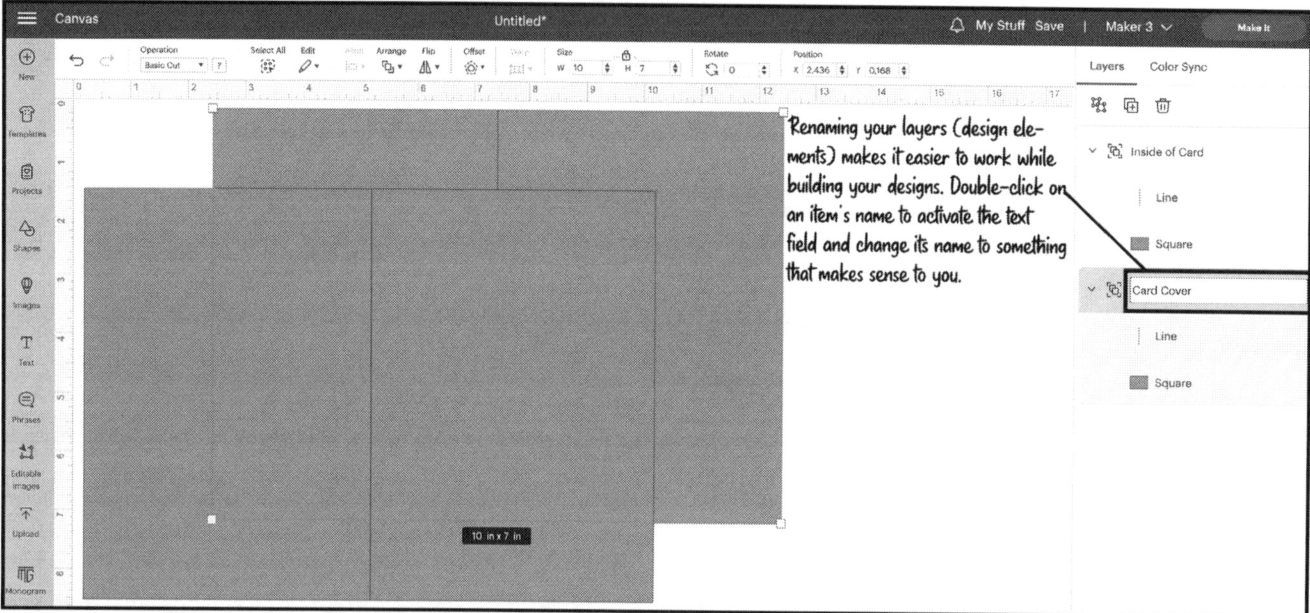

Let's select the layer named *Inside of Card* to change its color and adjust its size. Select it by clicking on its name in the *Layers Panel* and make its color the same as the other piece of cardstock you have for this project. When you're done, unlock the size padlock in the *Edit Bar* and change the width to 9.7" and the height to 6.7".

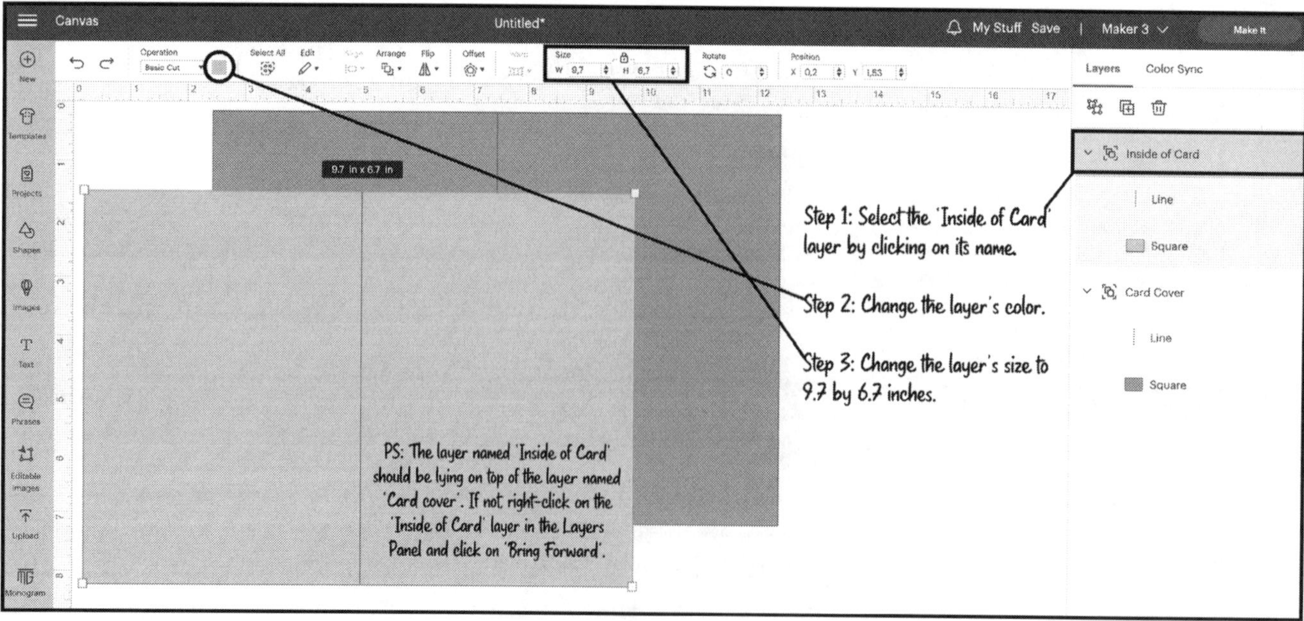

Since you can't rename layers nor see the *Layers Panel* without activating it on your mobile app, you'll have to work with the elements directly on the grid area. The duplicate copy we made of the rectangle and score line is the one you see on top. Select it, change its color to match that of your other piece of cardstock, and change its size to 9.7" by 6.7" (remember to unlock the size padlock to change the width and height independently).

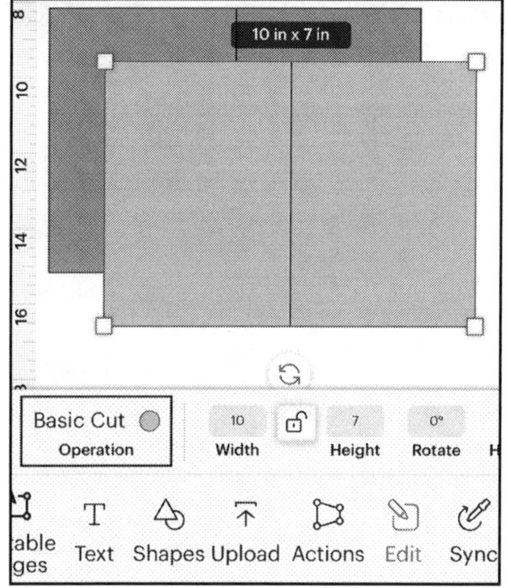

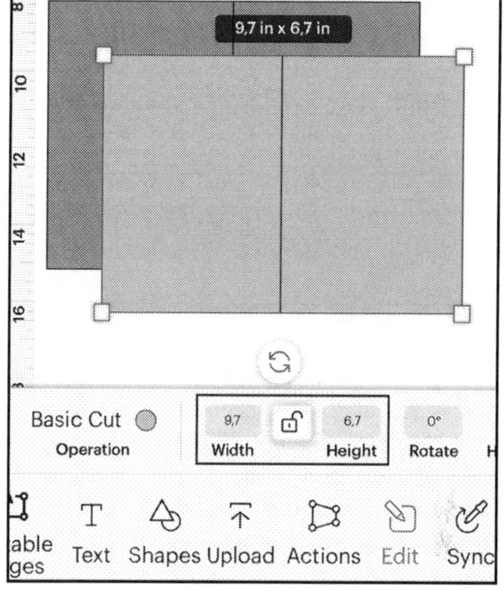

Now we can align the two rectangles so the smaller one sits squarely in the middle of the larger one. Select both rectangles and apply the *Center Align* function.

This is what you should see after applying the Center Align function to both rectangles.

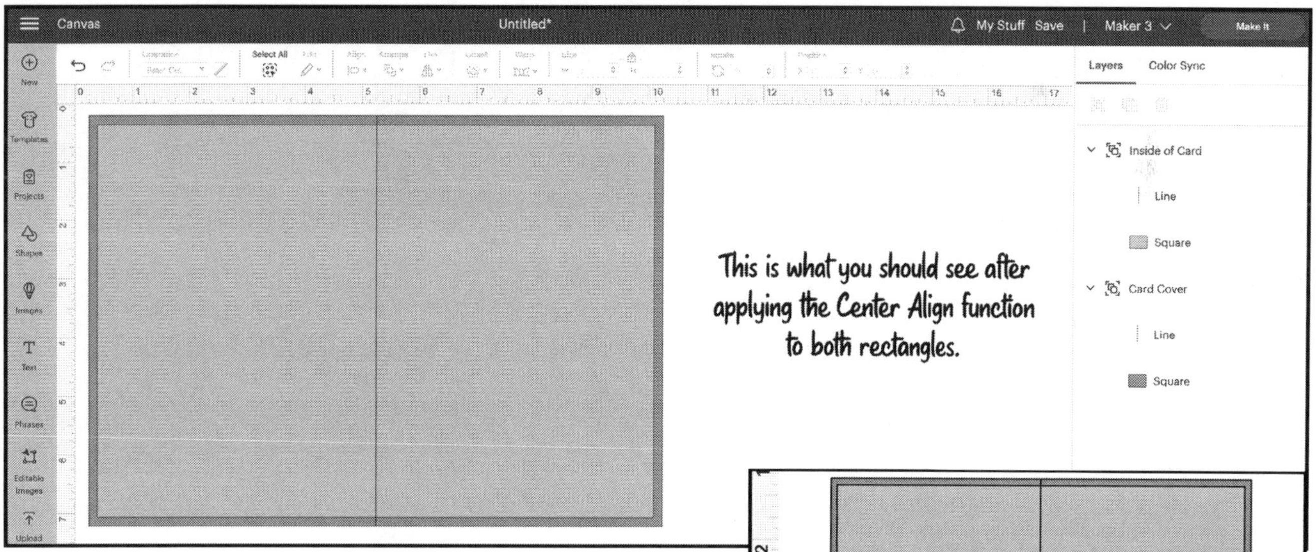

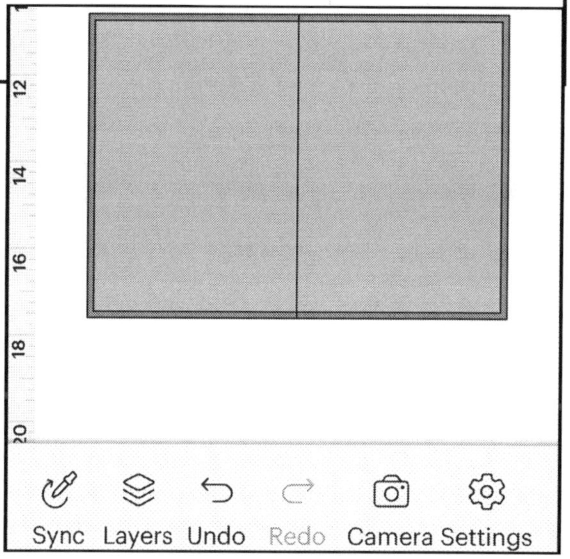

Let's save the project before moving on. Click on *Save* in the menu above the *Edit Bar.* In the window that pops up, name the project *Greeting Card Project* and then click on the *Save* button. To save the project in the mobile app, tap on the save icon in the menu bar above the grid area. Design Space will then prompt you to name and save it.

From now on, remember to click on *Save* every few minutes while working, as Design Space will not save your progress automatically. If you're worried that you might forget to save your work, put a sticky note (or Post-It-Note) reminder where you can see it often.

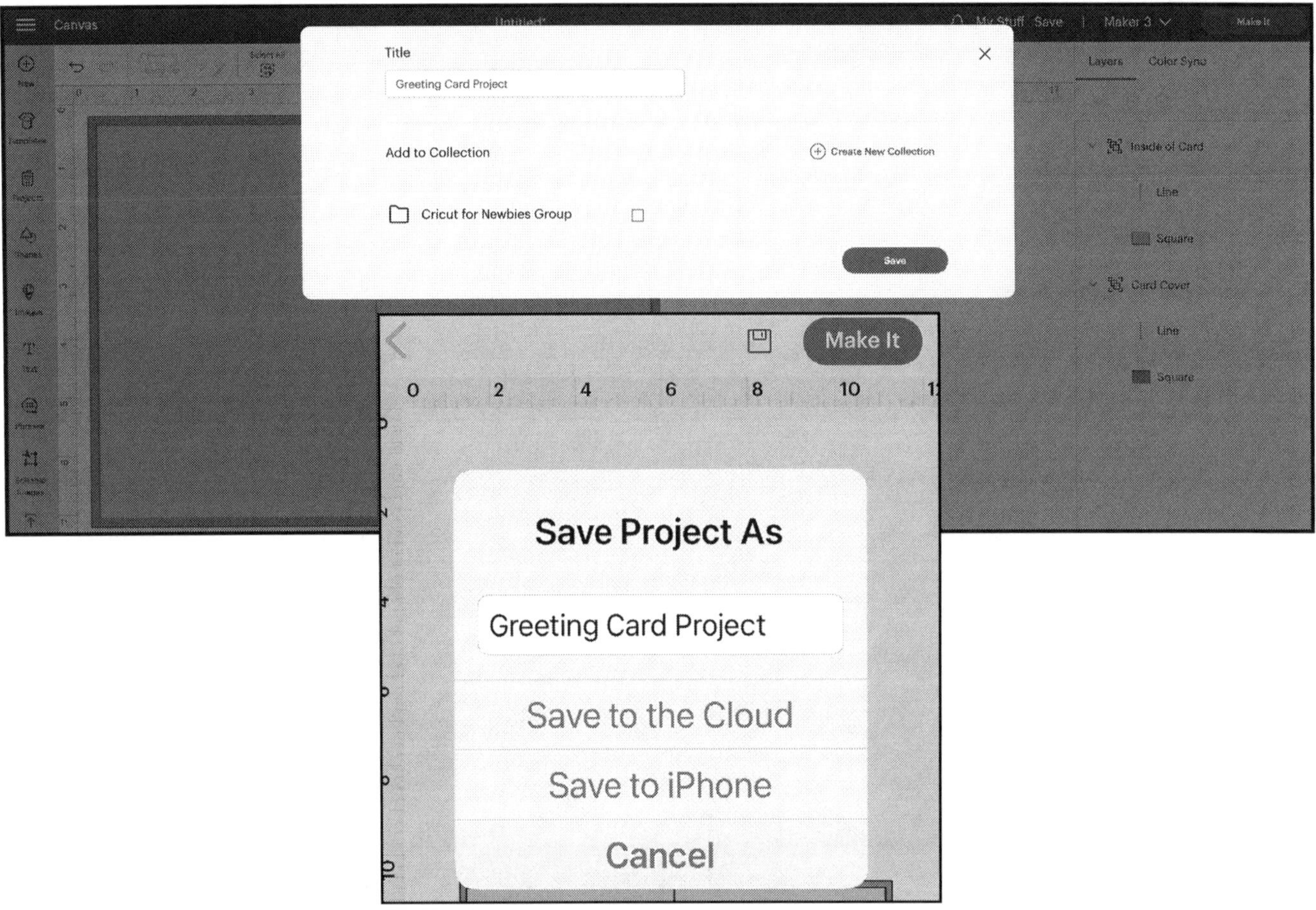

Step 2: Add Your Design Elements

Now we'll spice up our card with a cute whale and some hearts and combine them to make up a unique image. Let's start with the whale.

Click on *Images* in the *Design Panel*. Type '*whale*' into the search bar and hit the Enter key on your keyboard. Tick the *Free* box at the top of the left-hand panel. On your mobile app open the Images library, tap on the filters icon at the top-right corner of the screen, and toggle the Free switch on. Go back to the library, tap on the search bar next to the filters icon, and type in 'whale'.

Choose the cute guy with the big head.

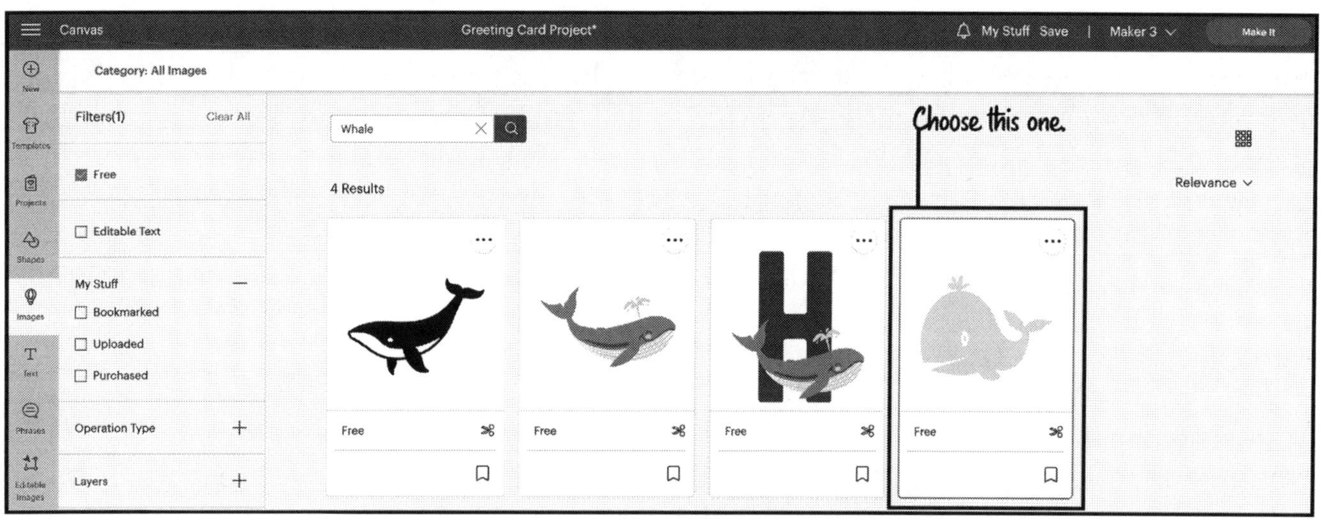
Canvas
Greeting Card Project*
My Stuff Save
Maker 3
Make It
Category: All Images
Filters(1)
Clear All
Free
Editable Text
My Stuff
Bookmarked
Uploaded
Purchased
Operation Type
Layers
Whale
4 Results
Choose this one.
Relevance
Free
Free
Free
Free

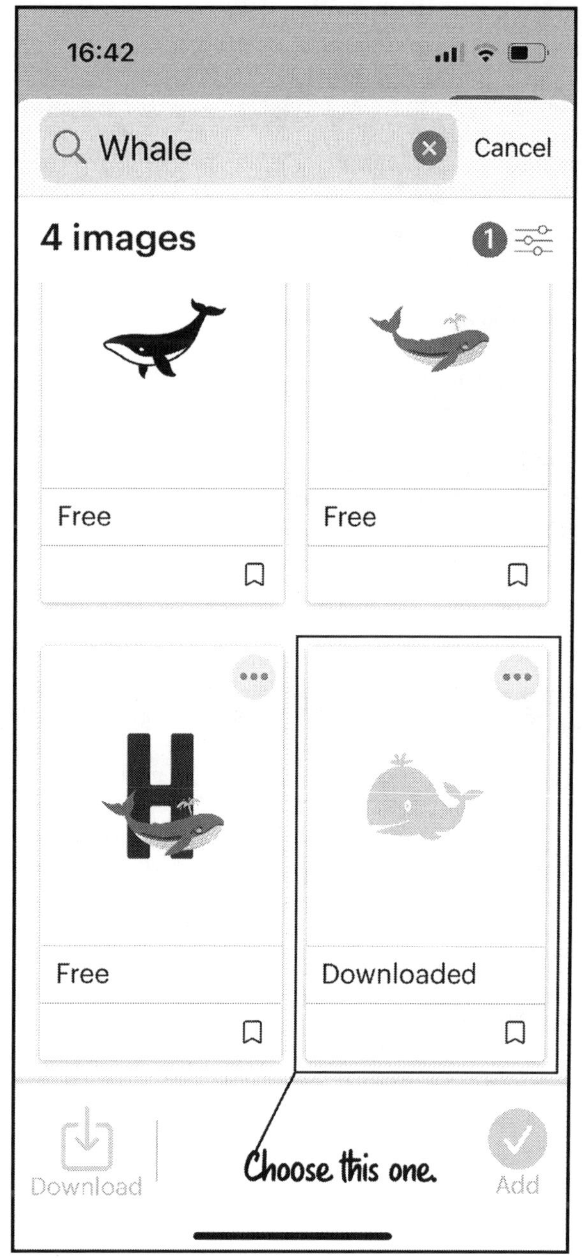
16:42
Whale
Cancel
4 images
Free
Free
Free
Downloaded
Download
Choose this one.
Add

Since we'll be making a cutout of the whale, it doesn't really matter what color it is. My suggestion is that you change it to a neutral color like black so that it doesn't distract you as you continue to build the design. Let's change its width to 4". The size padlock should be closed for this, as you want the whale to resize proportionally. And let's move the whale so it sits on the right side of the rectangles (anywhere is fine for now).

Let's add a heart to the *Canvas*. To do this, click on *Shapes* in the *Design Panel* and choose the heart. On your mobile app, tap on *Shapes* in the bar at the bottom of the screen to find the heart.

Make the heart the same color as the whale. We're going to combine the heart and the whale so that it looks like the whale is squirting hearts out of its breathing whole. Move the heart over to the whale and position it over the part where it looks like it's squirting out water. This is more or less what you should see:

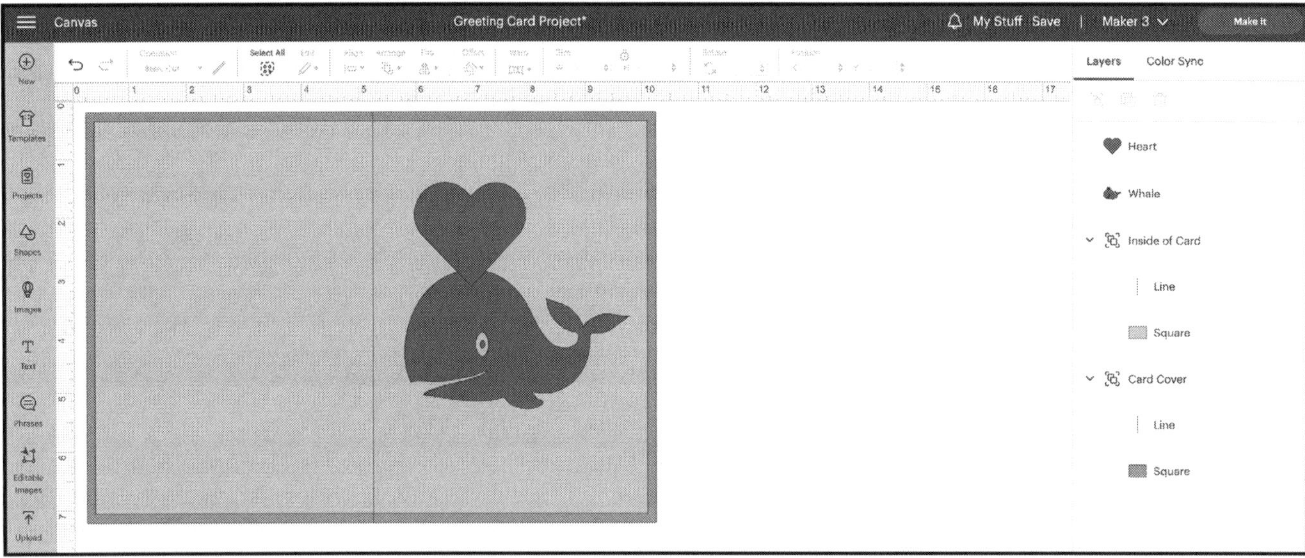

Use heart's selection box to shrink it down. Something like this:

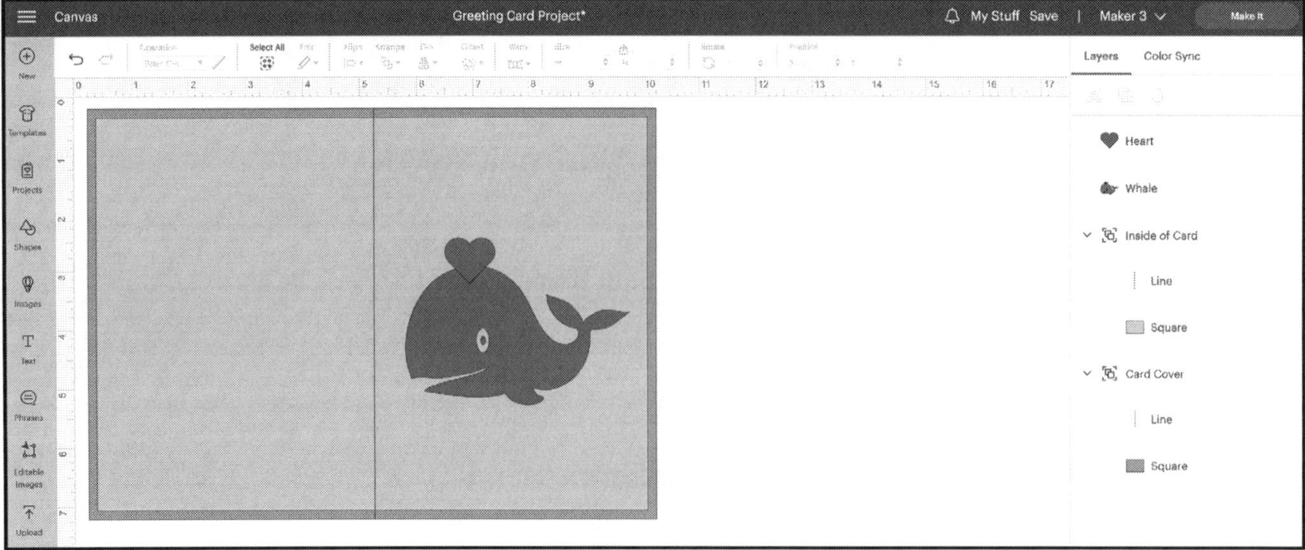

Duplicate the heart, make it smaller than the one coming out of the whale, and position it above the first heart.

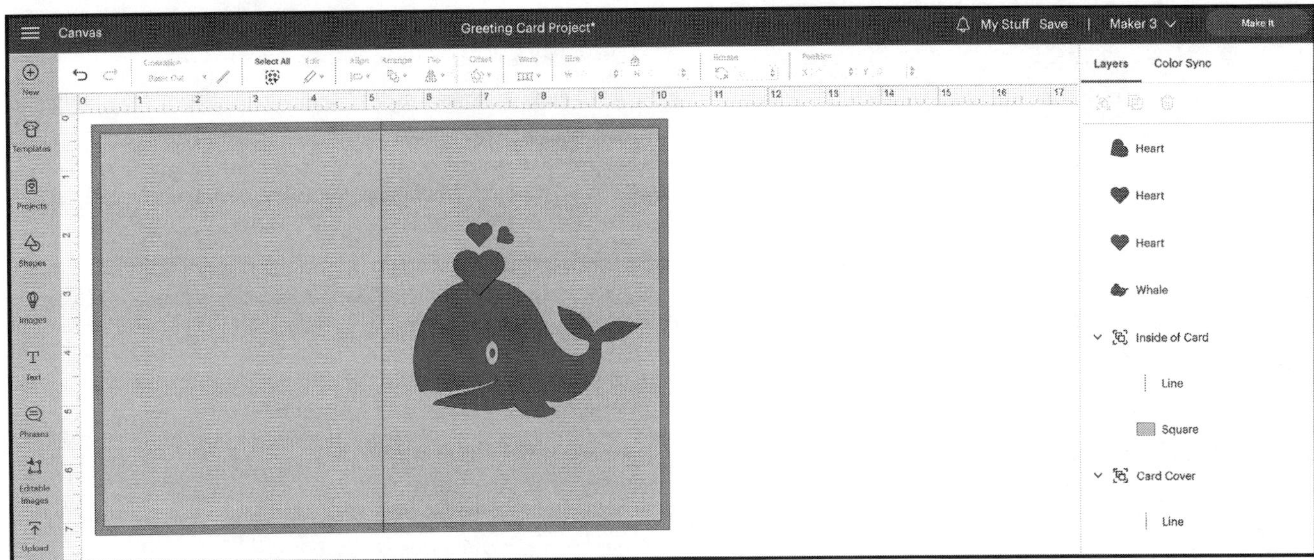

Make a duplicate of the small heart, shrink the duplicate copy a bit, tilt it to the right, and position it somewhere in between the other two hearts.

Duplicate the smallest heart, tilt it to the left, and position it somewhere to the left of the two bigger hearts. Make a duplicate of the heart you just made, make it a teeny bit smaller, and move it upward just a bit. Tilt its angle, too, to make the design a little more dynamic.

Now that we have the whale and hearts in position, we can use the Unite them into a single image. Select the whale and all the hearts. To do this, click on the highest heart, then press and hold your keyboard's Shift key, then click on the rest of the hearts one by one (moving from top to bottom), and finally click on the whale. When you have them all, let go of the Shift key. The next step is to click on *Combine* at the bottom of the *Layers Panel* and to choose the *Unite* action.

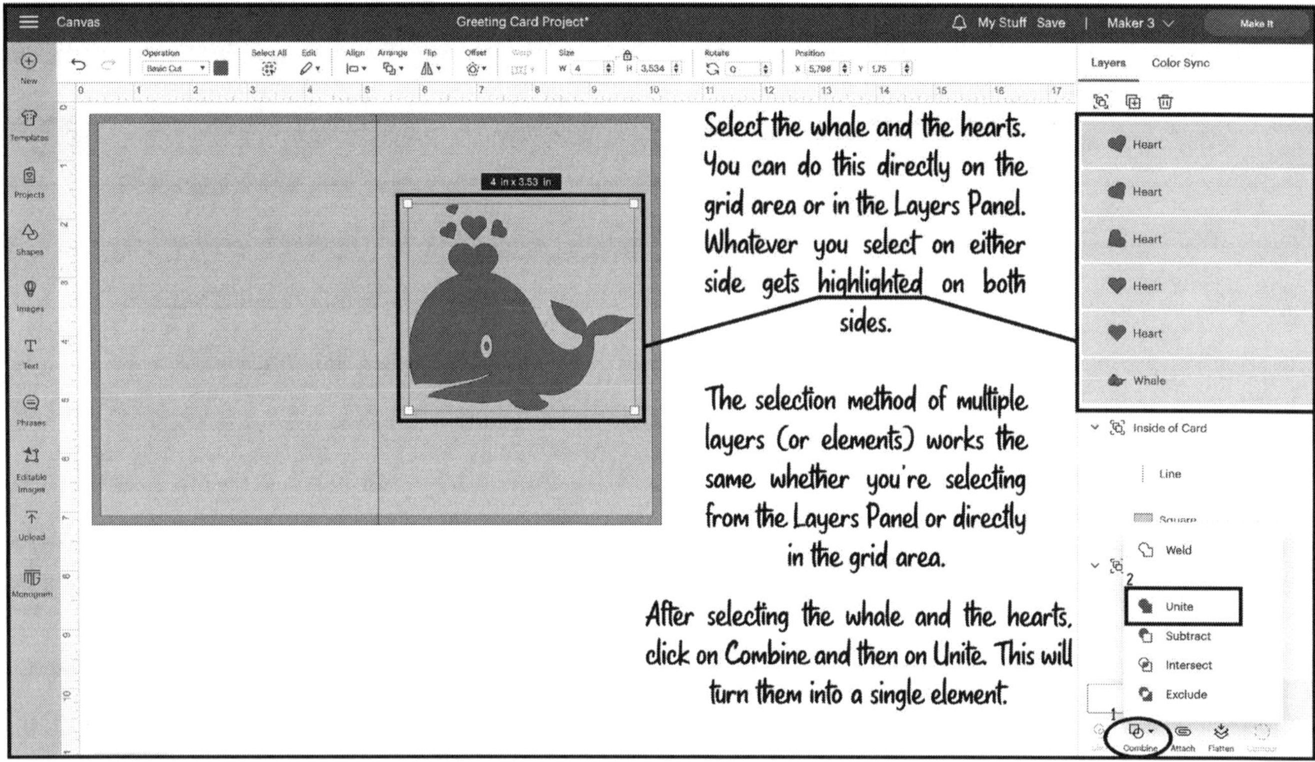

Notice that the action created a new item in the *Layers Panel* (at the very top) named *Unite*. Let's rename this item to *United Whale and Hearts*. Do you see that the hearts and whale are still listed underneath the *Unite* item? So, although it looks and acts like one element now, the *Layers Panel* is showing you that the item is really made up of all those individual elements. The same thing happens when you *Group* or *Attach* layers.

You can combine the whale and hearts with the mobile app, too. If you have an iOS device, you'll find the *Combine* options in the *Actions* category. Select the whale and hearts, make sure you're in the *Actions* category, and then look for *Unite* in the secondary bar (see the left-hand screenshot below). If you have an Android device, the *Combine* options aren't available yet. However, you can apply the original *Weld* action, which does the same thing as *Unite* (see the right-hand illustration below).

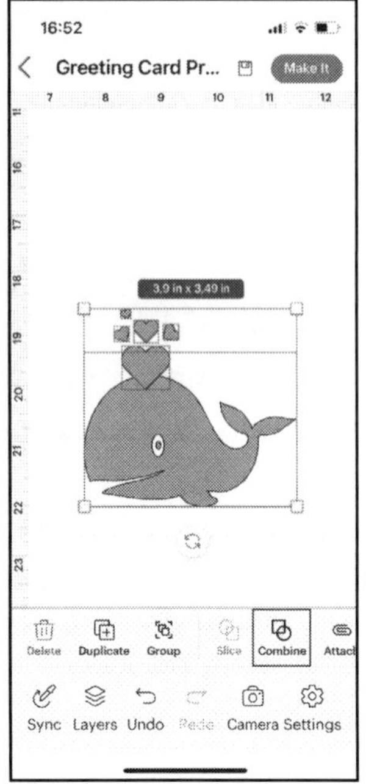

Let's tilt the whale now, using the *Edit Bar* instead of swinging it with the selection box. The reason is that we want a specific angle. Select the whale (remember, it's combined with the hearts now) and then enter a value of 25 in the box underneath *Rotate* in the *Edit Bar*. To achieve the same result with the whale in your mobile app, select the whale, tap on Edit in the bar at the bottom of the screen, and then find *Rotate* in the secondary bar. Enter the value of 25 in the box above *Rotate*.

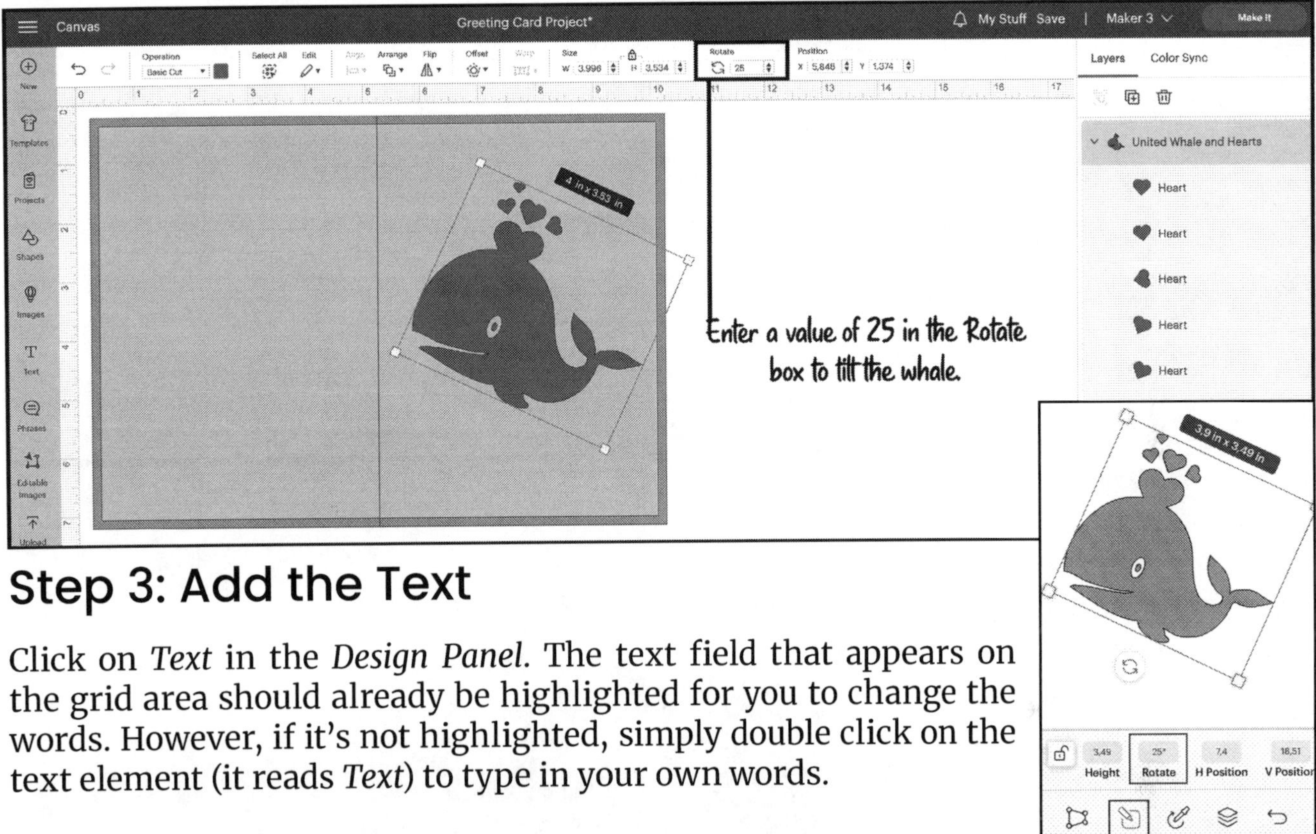

Step 3: Add the Text

Click on *Text* in the *Design Panel*. The text field that appears on the grid area should already be highlighted for you to change the words. However, if it's not highlighted, simply double click on the text element (it reads *Text*) to type in your own words.

Type 'I WHALEY'.

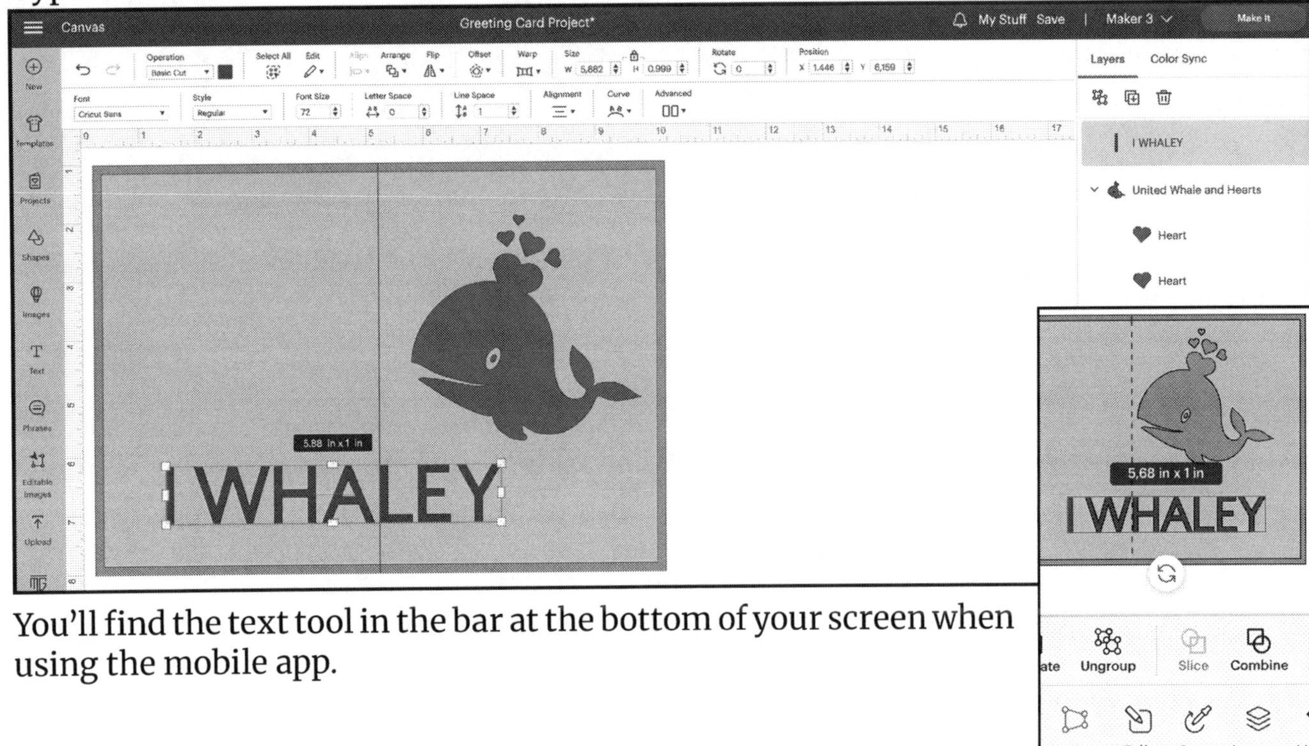

You'll find the text tool in the bar at the bottom of your screen when using the mobile app.

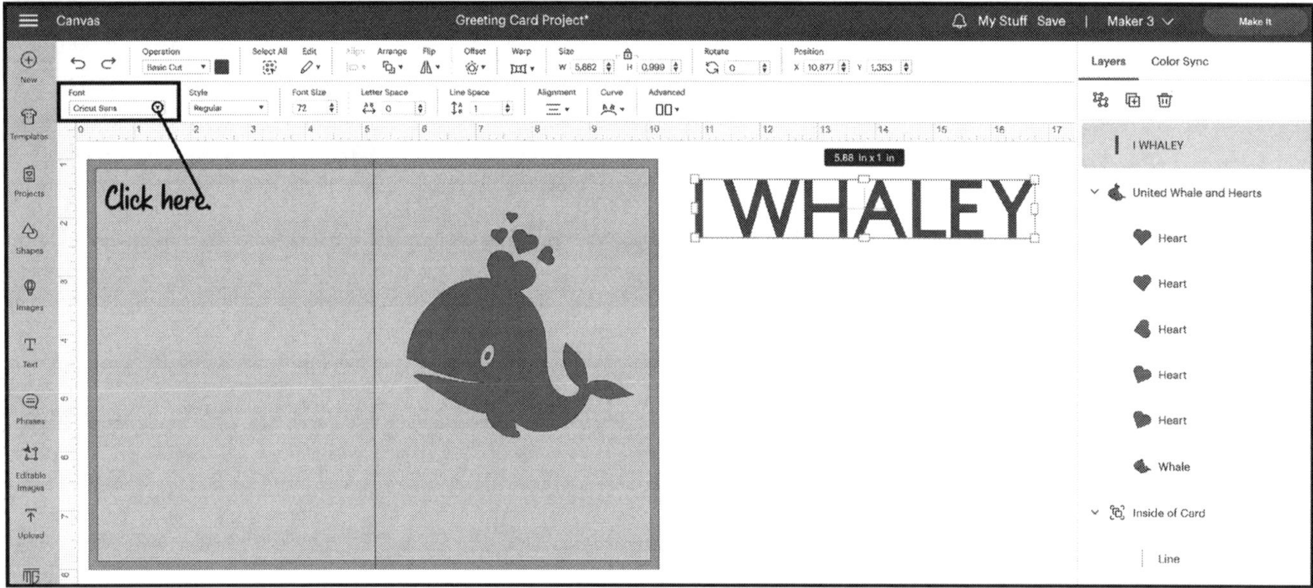

With the text selected, click on the drop-down menu below *Font* in the *Text Bar.*

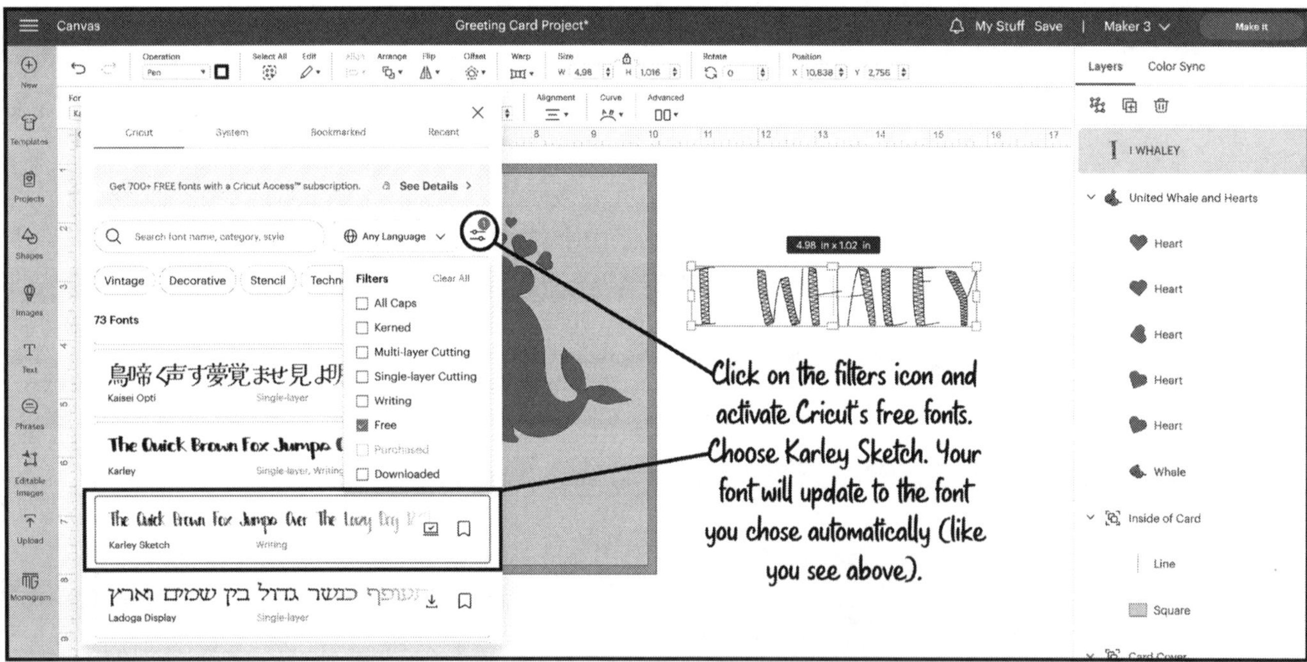

When the font menu comes up, click on the filters icon and tick the *Free* box. Scroll down the list of results and choose the font called *Karley Sketch.*

On the mobile app, you'll find the font settings when you select the text element and tap on Edit in the bar at the bottom of the screen. From there, you'll see the font options in the secondary bar. Tap on *Font Name.* You can follow the same steps as above, or you can simply type *Karley Sketch* into the search bar and tap on the font when it appears.

Now we're going to position the text near the whale's beautiful big head and let the text curve in harmony with it. The first step is to drag the text over to the whale. Next, use the text's selection box to tilt the text to the left.

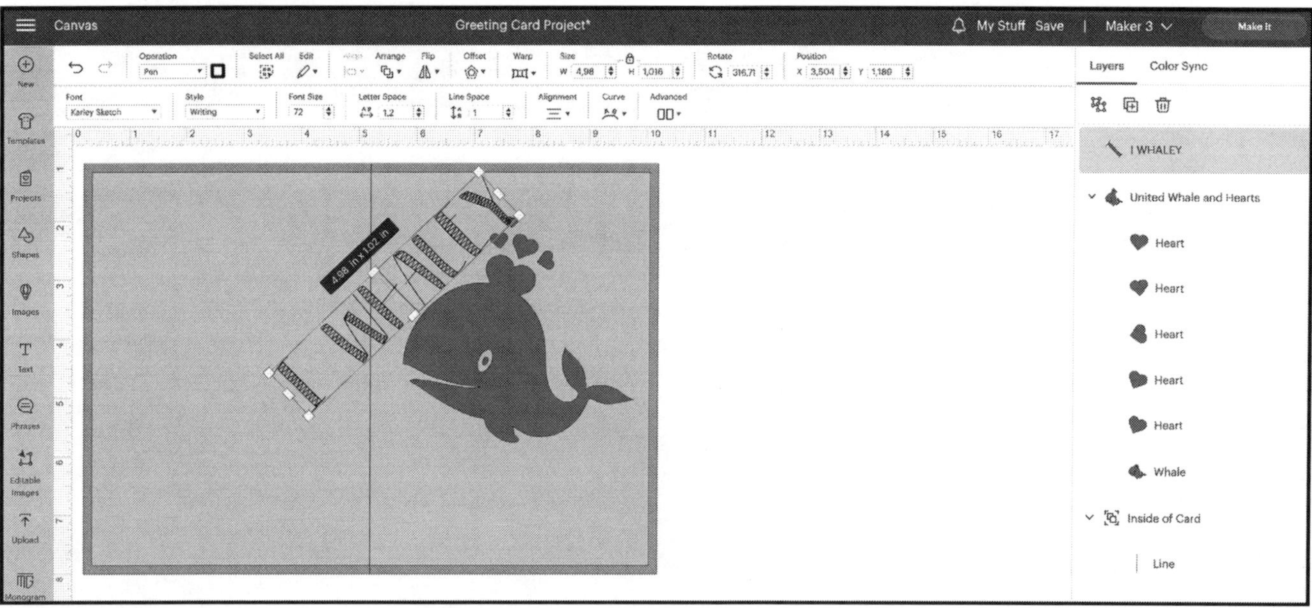

Let's make the text a bit smaller. Here, you can decide how large you want the text to be in relation to the whale's head. Let your creativity guide you.

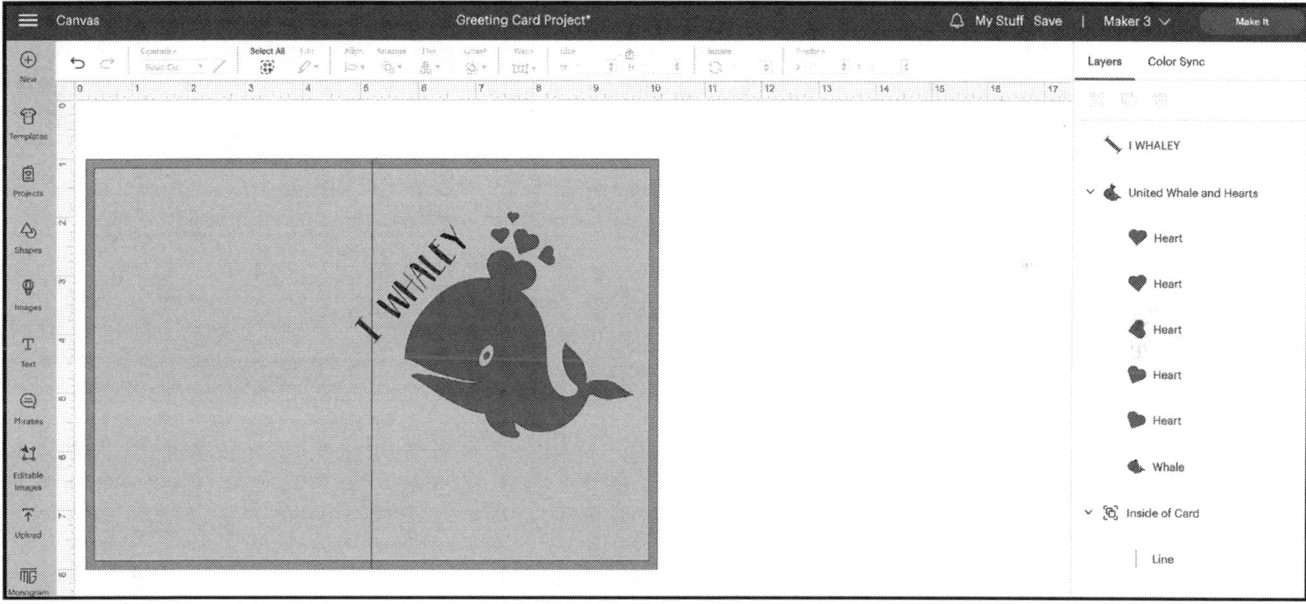

The second last option in the Text Bar is *Curve*. That's the function we'll use next. With the text selected, click on *Curve*. A slider bar will appear. To make the text curve around the whale's head, slide it to the right. Do this slowly until you like what you see.

Pro Tip: You can continue to tilt the text element to the left or right to get the angle the way you want it.

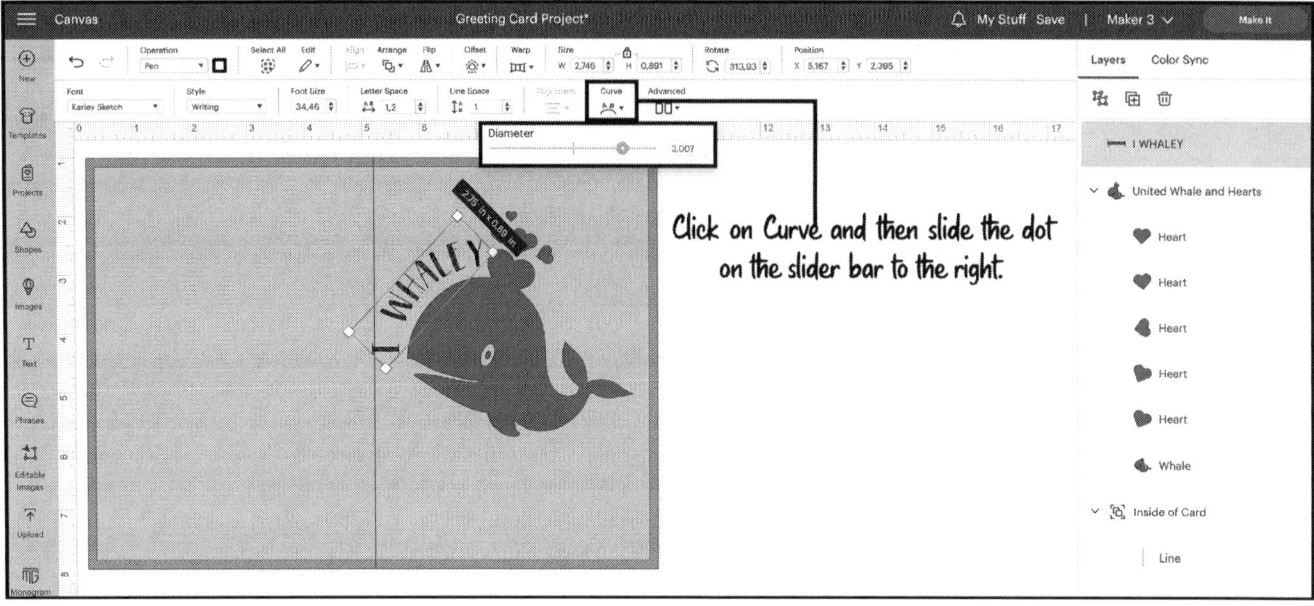

Add a new text element to the *Canvas*. Notice how, this time, Design Space remembered your previous font settings, so there's no need to change the font again. Write 'LOVE' in the new text element and make a duplicate copy of it. Change the duplicate copy to 'YOU'. The reason we're doing it this way instead of just writing 'LOVE YOU' in one go is that the font has really large spaces between words. So, we want these two closer together.

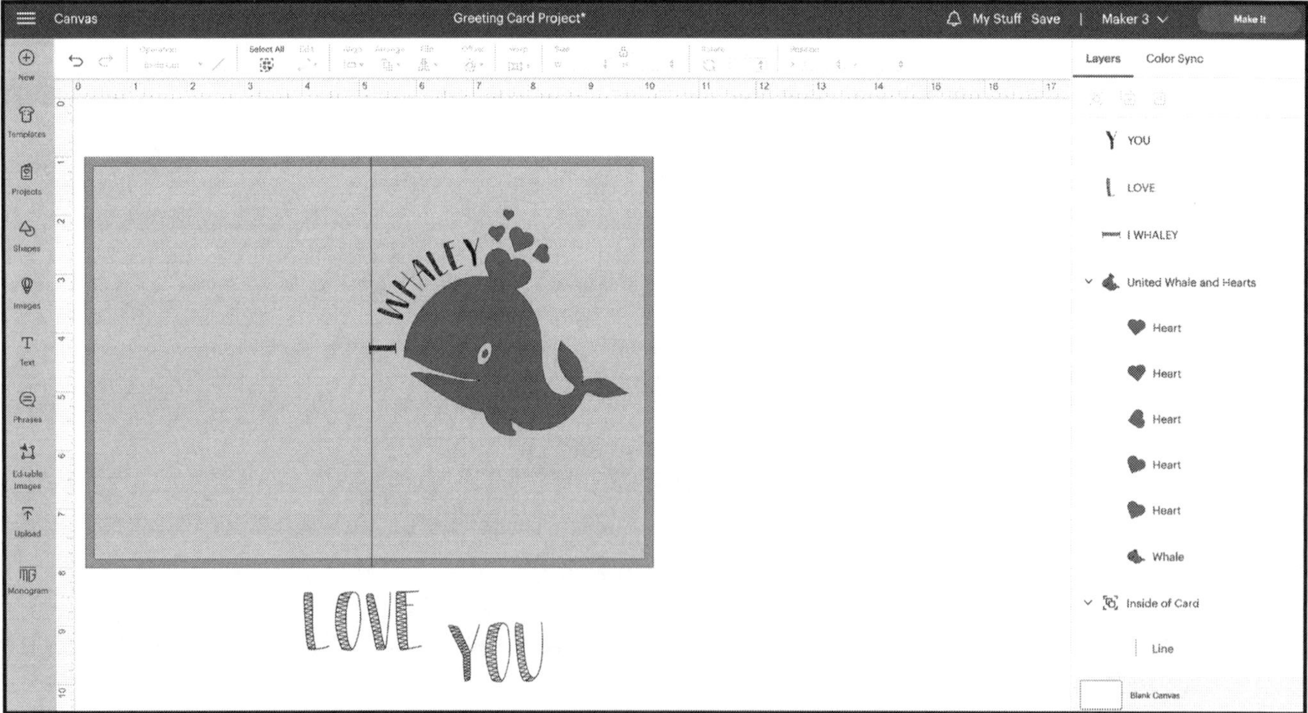

Select the two words and apply the *Bottom Align* function to get them on the same height. Then move them closer to each other—as much as feels natural to you.

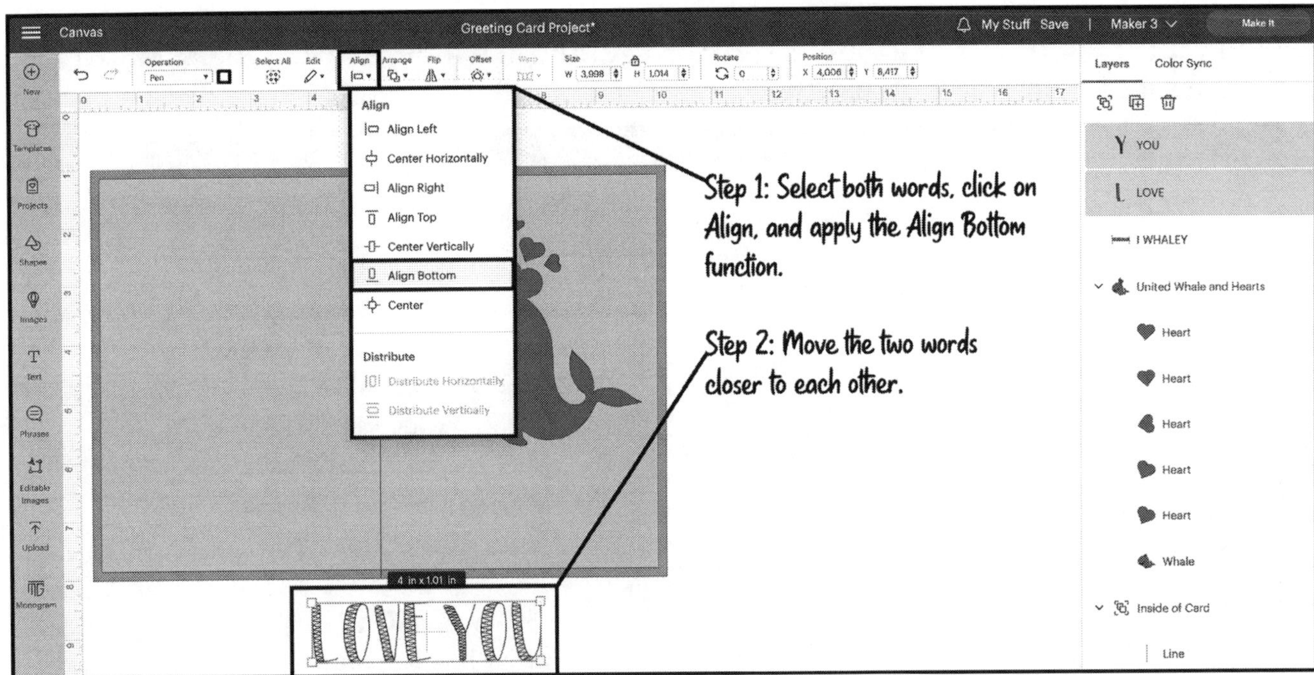

Group the two words together so they function as a unit and move them underneath the whale. Then, using the selection box, enlarge them, but keep them within the borders of the smaller rectangle.

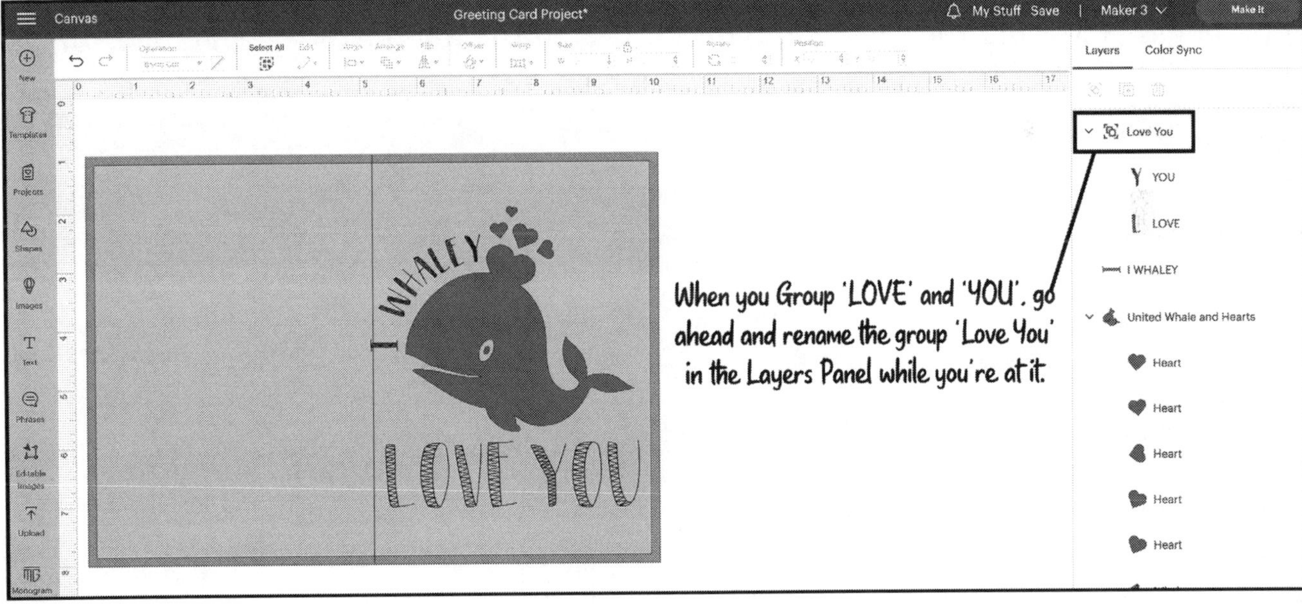

If you're designing on your phone, you'll be able to curve the 'I WHALEY' with your iOS device, but not with an Android device. If you have an Android phone or tablet, find a creative way to position the straight text around the whale. To find the *Text Curve* function on your iOS device, select the text and activate the *Actions* category in the bottom bar. You'll find *Curve* in the secondary bar.

Let's refine the design a bit. You can follow along on your mobile app using the bar at the bottom of the screen. As you can see, the 'I' in 'I WHALEY' is currently overlapping the score line in the middle of the rectangle. We need to get it away from there to prevent it from becoming part of the fold when you make card. Before we move anything, though, it's a good idea to group 'I WHALEY' and the whale, as we don't want to lose their positions relative to each other.

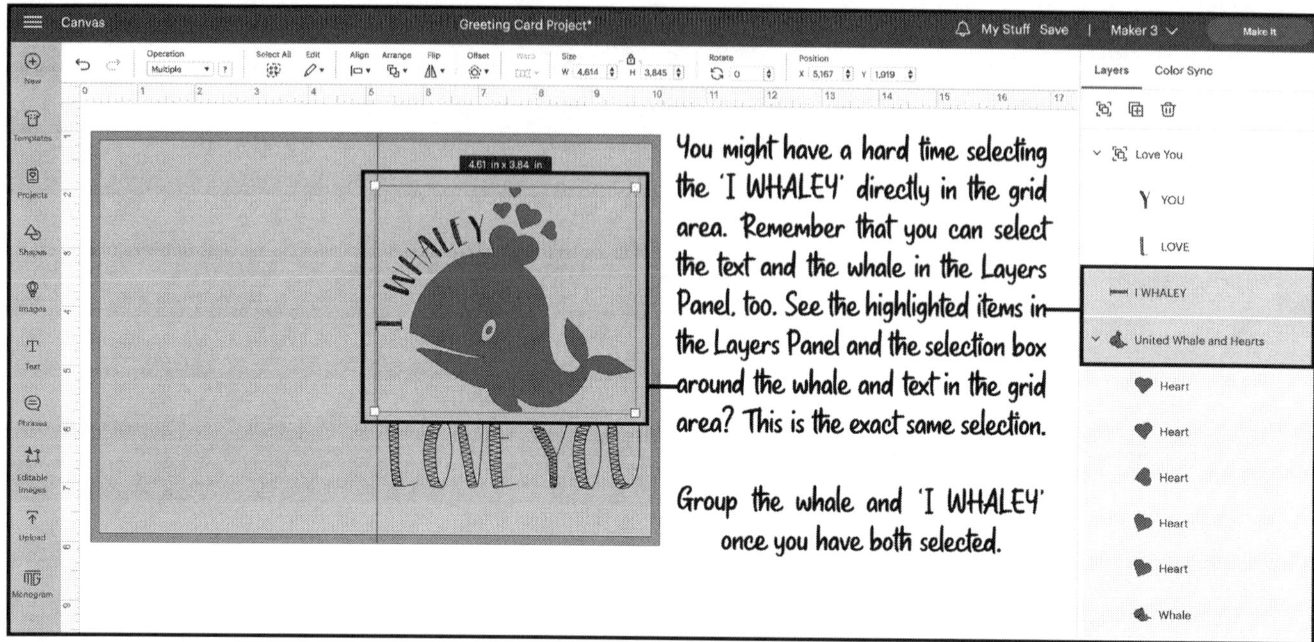

With the whale and 'I WHALEY' grouped securely, you can move them around as a unit. Reduce the selection's size to 4.5" and then move it toward the smaller rectangle's right edge. Try to get the selection more or less in the middle of the right side of the smaller rectangle.

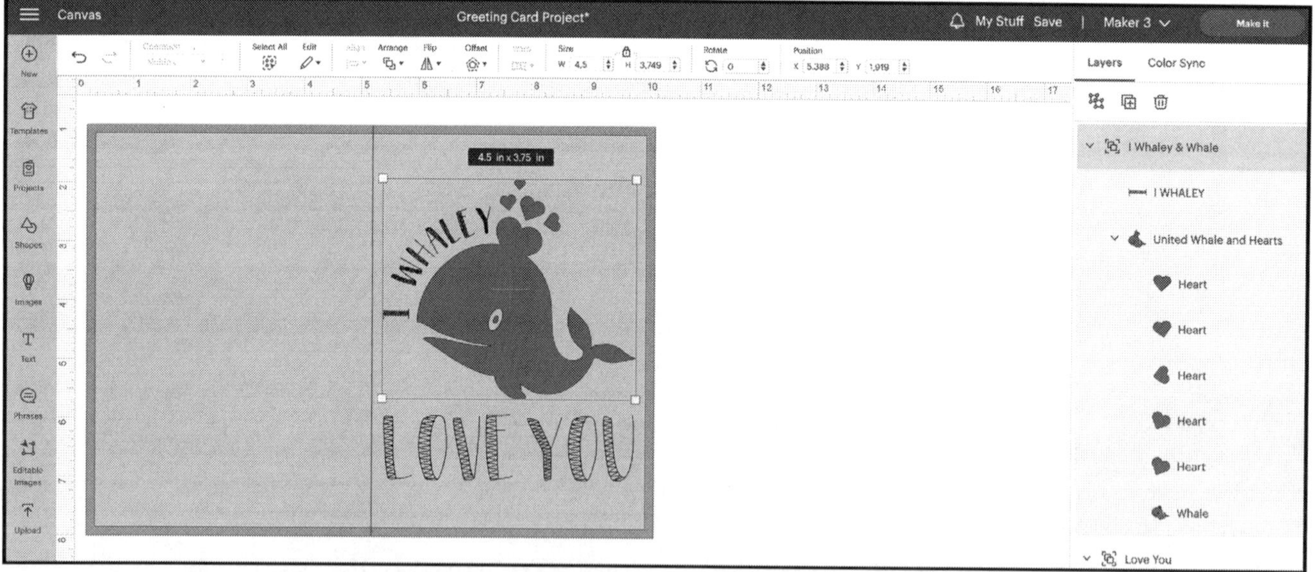

Get the 'LOVE YOU' group's positioning right. When you're happy with the overall design, you can group 'I WHALEY', the whale, and 'LOVE YOU' together. Try to position the design so it sits in the center of the right side of the smaller rectangle.

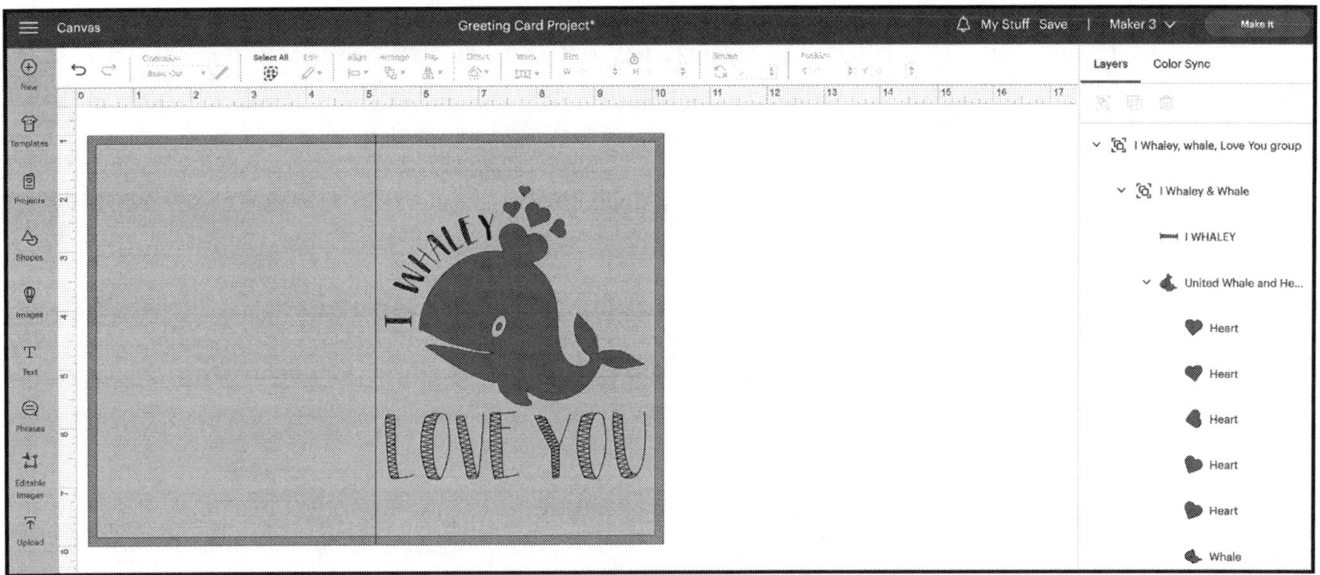

You're almost ready to cut out your card! All we need to do now to apply the *Attach* function to the right parts and then we're ready to go.

Select the smaller rectangle and move it away from the rest of the design. Since your machine needs to cut the inside of the card separately, we can't attach it to the card's cover and the design that will go on it.

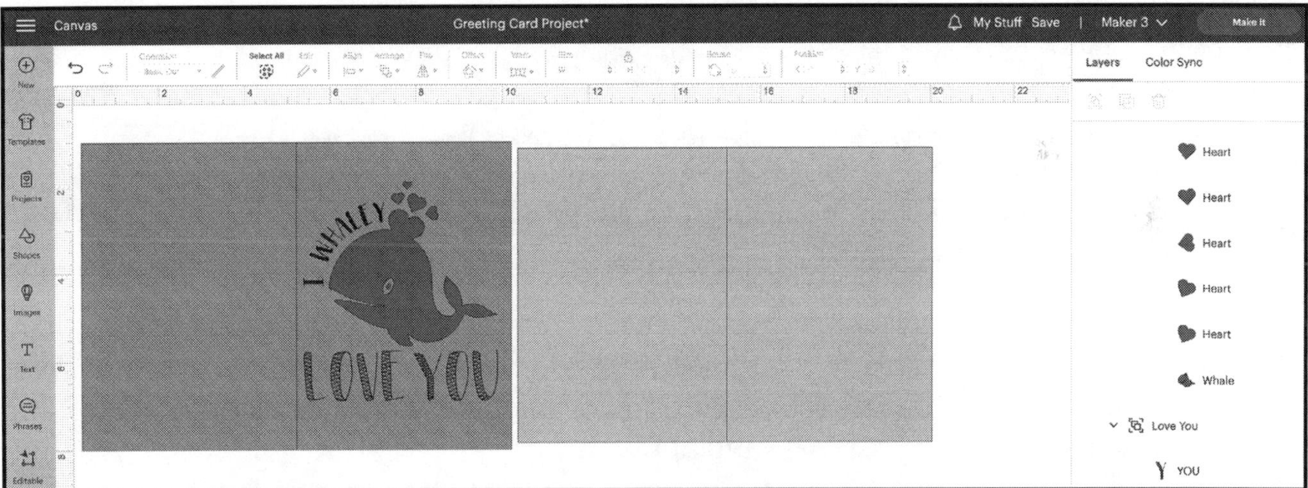

Now select the whale design and the rectangle underneath it and apply the *Attach* function. If your design now looks the same as mine below, you're all set.

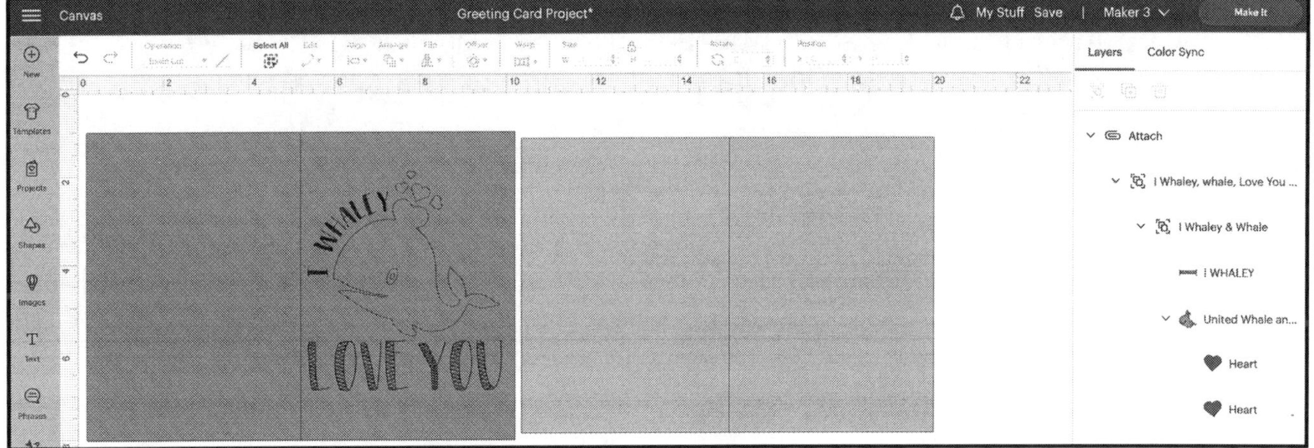

If you're doing this project with the Cricut Joy, or if you don't have a *Scoring Stylus* or *Scoring Wheel*, you need to hide the score lines from the rectangles before moving on to the *Make It* (or *Preview*) screen.

Click on one of the two rectangles. The moment you do, the *Layers Panel* will highlight the entire group of elements that are a part of it. Scroll down, keeping your eye on the highlighted items only, until you see an item named *Line*. Hovering over the item in the *Layers Panel* will make the little eye icon visible. Click on it to hide the score line. The item will now be grayed out. The eye icon will show a strike-through, indicating that the layer is now hidden, and the line will no longer be visible on the rectangle on the *Canvas*. Tap on the other rectangle and hide its score line, too.

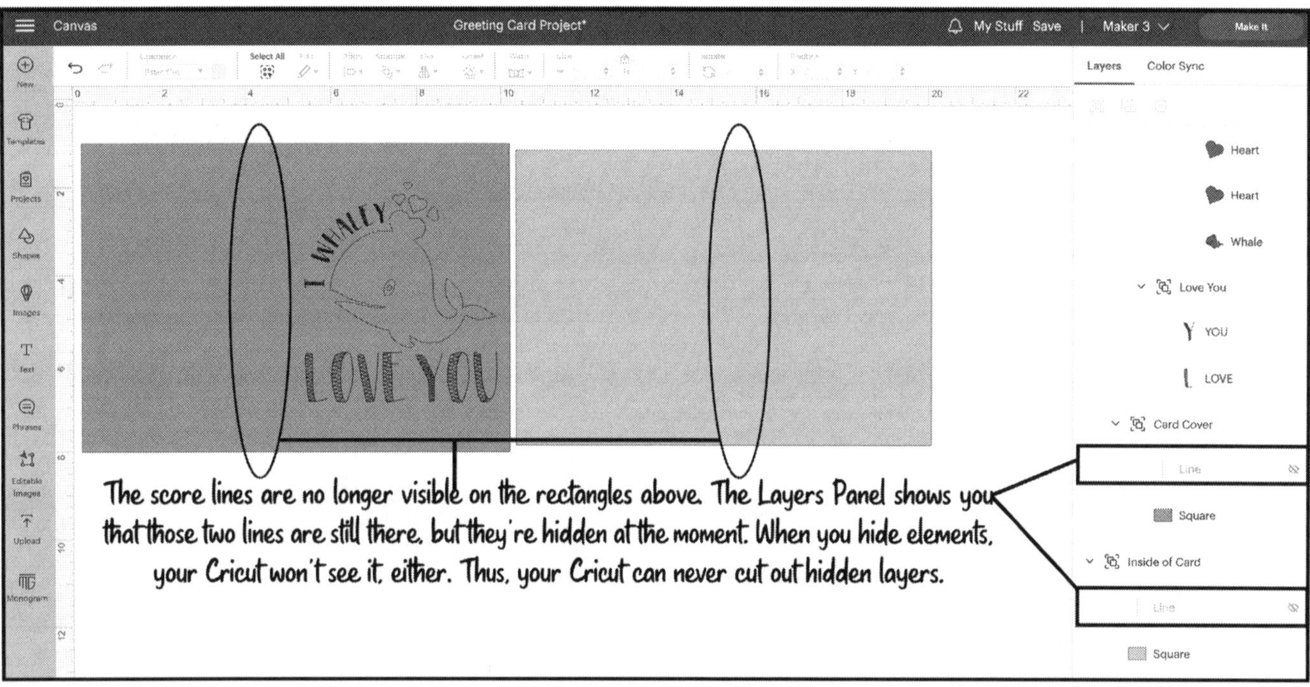

If you are going to use a scoring tool, be sure to use the *Attach* function on the smaller rectangle and score line before moving on to the *Make It* screen. Select the group (the one we named *Inside of Card* earlier) and apply *Attach*.

Sometimes, when applying *Attach* to a group of elements that contains a score line, Design Space will change the score line's *Operation* setting from *Score* to *Cut* on the desktop app. To check if this happened to your design, find the score lines in the *Layers Panel* one by one. Click on the score line (it will simply say *Line* in the *Layers Panel*) and then look at what it says under *Operation* in the *Edit Bar*. If it says *Basic Cut*, click on it and then choose *Score*.

If you're having trouble selecting the score lines on your mobile app because they're too small or narrow, you can open the mobile app's *Layers Panel* from the bar at the bottom of your screen. In the list of items that appear, find the score lines and apply the above steps (depending on your Cricut model). If you don't see the option to change the line from the cut *Cut* to the *Score Operation* on the mobile app, you'll have to *Detach* the layers, make the change, and then *Attach* the layers again.

Step 4: Double-Check Your Design

Just before you do the final step to prepare your design for the Cricut machine, double-check everything in your design.

Is everything where you want it to be? Are there typos? This is your last chance to make corrections. If you see a mistake, use the *Detach* action to separate the elements on your *Canvas*. Make your corrections and final tweaks and then *Attach* them again.

Step 5: Prepare your Cardstock and Let Your Cricut Take Over the Process

When you click or tap on the *Make It button*, Design Space will prompt you to prepare the material and cutting mat for the first of two cuts. The reason for two cuts is that we specified what should go together during the design process in the previous steps. As a reminder: we separated the smaller rectangle from the larger rectangle, while we attached the whale and text to the larger rectangle, effectively telling Design Space that we want two separate parts.

If you're working with one of the Explore or Maker series machines and you have a scoring stylus or scoring wheel, this is what your Make It screen will look like:

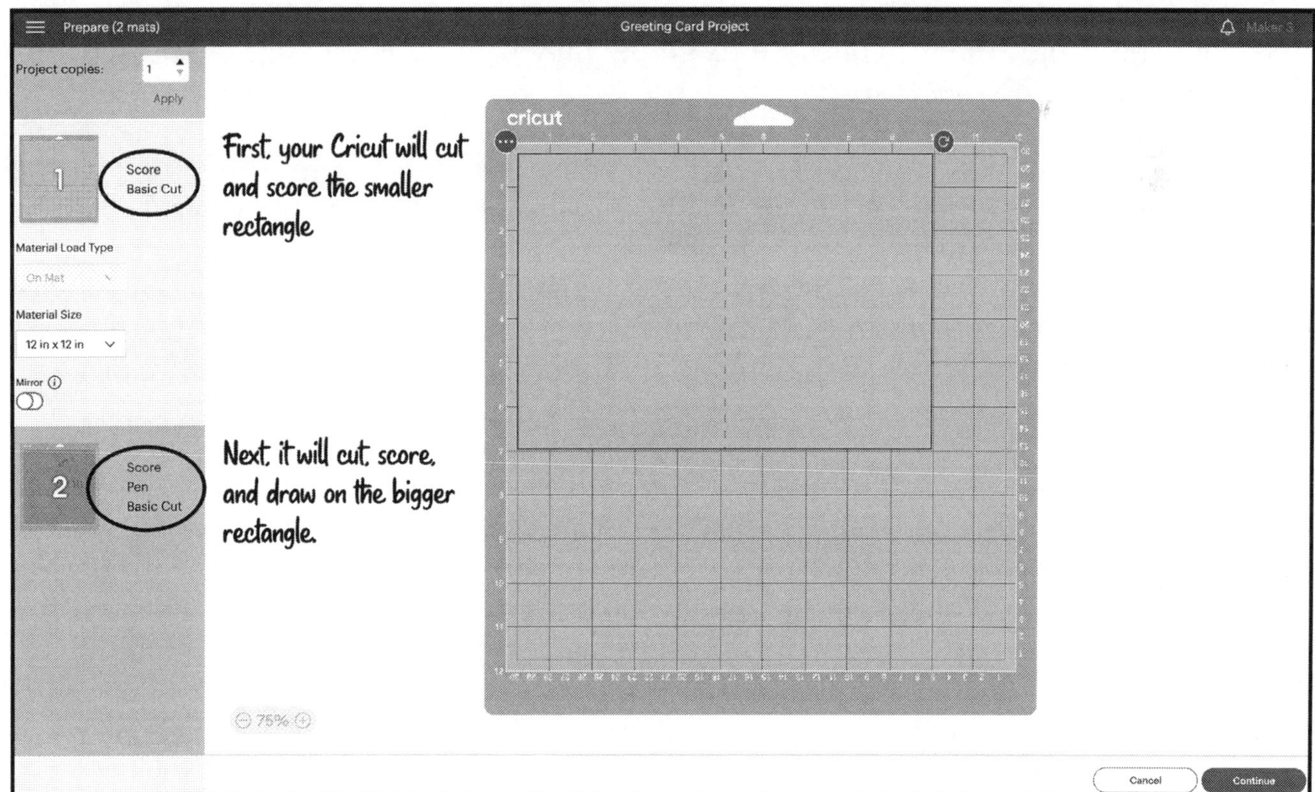

If you're working with a Cricut Joy or don't have a scoring tool and hid the score line layers earlier, the screenshot on the next page shows what your *Make It* screen will look like.

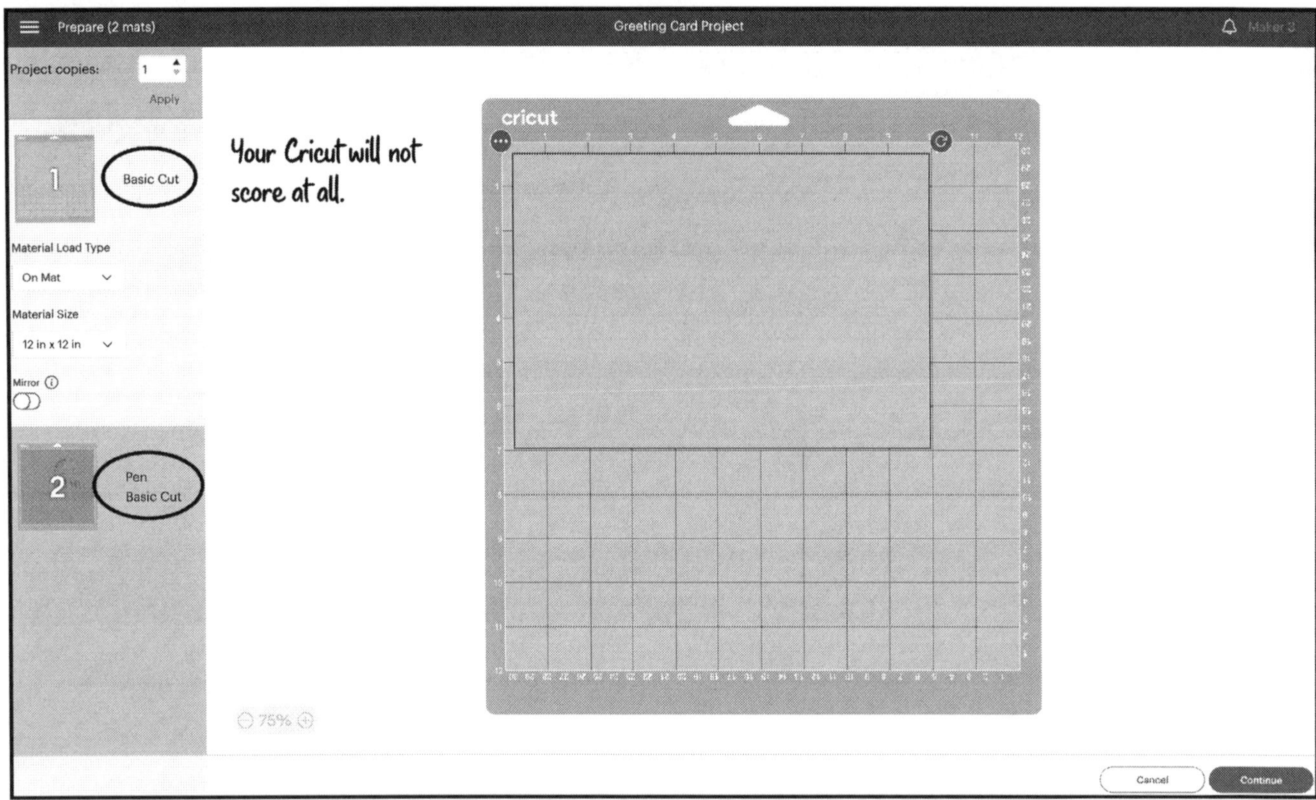

Go ahead and start the process by clicking or tapping on *Continue*. Design Space will automatically move on to the instructions for the second mat after it completes the first cut. The program will continue to guide you through each step of the scoring, drawing, and cutting processes.

If you are working with the Explore Air 2, remember to set your *Smart Dial* to the correct material setting before you start the cutting process. For this project, use the Cardstock setting. But always keep in mind that each project is unique and that you can play around with the *Smart Dial* settings to get the best results. Some people even leave their machines' *Smart Dials* on the Custom setting permanently and use the material options within the Design Space app for all their projects. As you take on more projects and experiment with ideas, you'll figure out what works best for you.

Pro Tip: Whenever your machine does a Cut project, remember that you can let it cut over the material a second time. A second cut is always useful when working with intricate designs and text with lots of nooks and crannies, as it ensures a clean cut that will be easy to weed. If you want to do a second cut on your greeting card, all you have to do is press the *Go* button again after Design Space tells you that the cut is complete.

Step 6: Assemble the Parts and Admire Your Project

Unload the cutting mat from your Cricut machine. On a clean surface, flip the cutting mat over so the cardstock rests on the table. Lift a corner of the cutting mat, then get a hold of a corner of the cardstock. Gently pull the mat away from the cardstock. Smaller parts of the cutouts may cling to the card, like the little hearts. If they don't pop out by themselves, you can use your weeding tool to remove them. Keep the whale's little eye somewhere safe, as you'll make it a part of the design again. Now that you have all the parts, it's time to assemble them.

Let's start with the cover (that's the piece with the writing and cutout of the whale). If you used a scoring tool during the cutting process, you can bend the card over and it will automatically fold where the score line runs. If you didn't use a scoring tool, bend the card slowly until the four corners touch. Align and hold them in place while you rub toward in the opposite direction toward the fold. Once the fold is made, apply some pressure on the fold to impress it.

Now do the same with the other piece of cardstock. Once you have folded it, place it inside the cover side and line the two pieces of cardstock up. Your goal is to make sure the inner cardstock covers the cutout of the whale completely. If you're happy, you can glue the cardstock pieces together. To make things easier, glue the right side of the inner cardstock to the cover first. Take your time gluing the left side, as you don't want the glue going past the cutout. Avoid getting glue on the part of the inner cardstock that will be visible when you view the greeting card from the front. As you work through this step, use your scraper tool to even out the glue in between the cardstock pieces by rubbing over the card's inside as you progress.

The final touch is to glue the whale's eye in place. Use the design on Design Space to gauge where the eye should go.

Did you complete the greeting card project? Head over to the Cricut for Newbies Facebook group to share it with your fellow crafters.

When you share your picture, use the #GreetingcardProject hashtag.

Wow! I think you can give yourself a pat on the back for everything you've learned and accomplished since starting with this book. Not only do you understand Design Space now, but you can apply three powerful methods to create projects, from using ready-to-make designs in Design Space to downloading design files and importing them into the program, to creating something from scratch.

Greeting Card Project Notes

Use this space to jot down a checklist of things you need to do this project. Maybe write down a date you'd like to complete it, too. And if you're having trouble with something, make notes and then head over to the Cricut for Newbies Facebook group to ask for help.

BONUS TUTORIAL

How To Download Fonts and Use them in Design Space

Although Cricut has many cool fonts to choose from, sometimes you just want something specific. In that case, you can download the font you like and use it for your design instead.

A word of caution, though: Cricut fonts are optimized to work with your Cricut machine, so they'll always be your best bet. Although you can use the fonts installed on your computer and even custom fonts you download, there is no guarantee the results will look good. Mostly they work fine, but be mindful that, sometimes, using a custom font will not give you the results you desire. Also, if Design Space thinks a font can cause some kind of compatibility conflict, the font will show no preview in the *Font* menu, like you see in the screenshot to the left.

If you see a blank font like this, Cricut won't let you choose it because of a possible compatibility issue.

How To Download Fonts on

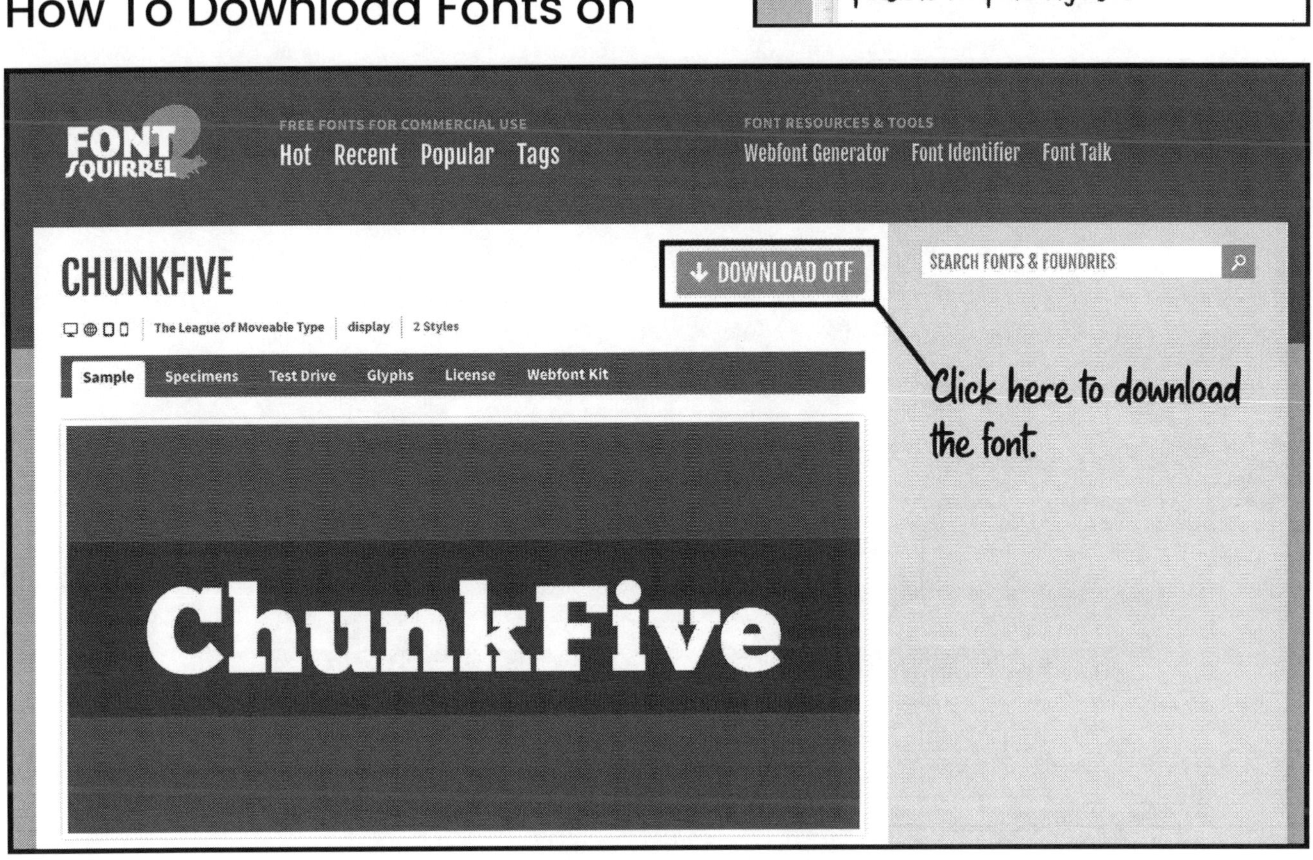

Your Computer

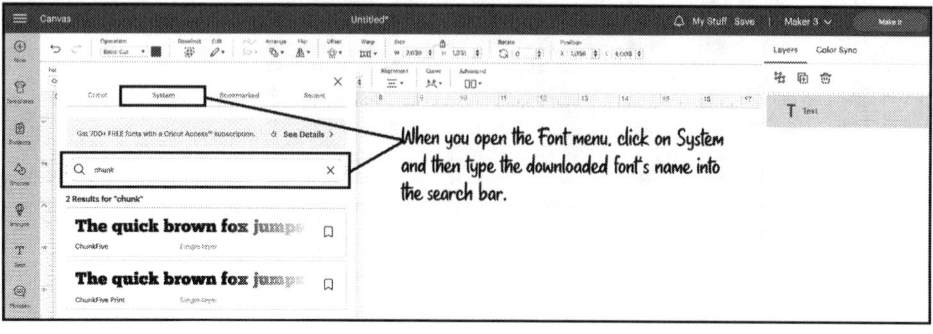

Font Squirrel is one of the best places to find free fonts as they have a huge library and their license terms are very clear. Head over to https://www.fontsquirrel.com/.

If you're unsure what you're looking for, you can browse around until you find the perfect font for your next project. However, if you know what you want, use the filters in the right-side panel of the screen to refine the results. For example, you might be looking for a display font or perhaps something handwritten. When looking for fonts to cut out, remember that they can't be too thin or intricate, as your machine might have trouble during the cutting process. And if you're looking for a font your machine can draw with a pen or marker, remember that it shouldn't be too thick.

When you see something you like, click on it. This action will take you to a download page. Click on the *Download* button (like you see in the screenshot on the previous page).

If you have an Apple computer, go to your computer's downloads folder to find the file you had just downloaded. It will be a ZIP file with the font's name. Double click on the ZIP file. After the extraction is complete, open the folder and then double click on the file that ends with *.otf*. This will open your computer's *Font Book*, where you can click on the *Install Font* button. The installation will take a few seconds, after which you can close the *Font Book*.

If you are using a Windows computer, extract the downloaded ZIP file to your desktop. Go to the *Windows Settings* menu, click on *Personalization* in the left-hand panel, and then select *Fonts* from the options that appear to the right of the panel. Resize the window a little, open the extracted folder on your desktop, and then drag and drop the font into the dotted box underneath *Add Fonts*.

Pro Tip: Whenever you install new fonts and you have an option between *.ttf* and *.otf*, choose *.otf* file. Without getting technical, this is the better option because it has more features and options than the *.ttf* font file. However, when you only have a *.ttf* font file, it will work just fine.

Whenever you download and install fonts on your computer, be sure to close and reopen your Design Space app. If you don't, the font might not show up in the program.

Open a blank *Canvas* and choose a text element from the *Design Panel*. Now open the *Font* menu and click on *System* right next to *Cricut*. This will show you all the fonts that are installed on your computer. If you type the name of the font you downloaded into the search bar, it will pop up.

How To Download Fonts on Your Mobile Device

Download fonts on your iOS device

Open your phone's App Store, search for *iFont*, and install it on your phone. After the installation, to your phone's browser and go to the Font Squirrel website. Find a font you like and tap on the download button.

Click on the download icon, tap on *Downloads*, and then tap on the file that has the name of the font you downloaded. This will open your *Downloads* folder and show the ZIP file. Tap on it to extract its contents. You'll either see a blue folder appear with the font's name or a single file, also with the font's name, called a font file. If your iOS device shows a blue folder, tap on it to open it. Inside, you will see the one or two font files and a *readme* file. The *readme* file contains information about the font's license and tells you for what purposes you may use it. If there are two font files, choose the *.otf* file instead of the *.ttf* file, as it is a newer type of file and offers more features. However, if you only see a *.ttf* file, it will work perfectly fine. If you don't see a blue folder at all, you can go ahead and tap on the font file that appeared after you tapped on the ZIP file. When you tap on the font file, a new window will open with a preview of what the font looks like. Tap on the upload icon in the lower-left corner of the screen. It looks like a box with an upward-pointing arrow coming out of it.

A carousel of apps will appear; swipe from right to left until you see the *iFont* app. If you don't see the app, continue to swipe all the way to the right until you see three dots with *More* written under it. Tap on it and then select the option that says *Copy to iFont*. This will take you to the *iFont* app, where you will see the font you downloaded listed with an *Install* button next to it. Click on the *Install* button and then follow along as your device takes you through a few steps before it completes the installation.

Next, go to your device's settings, tap on *Profile Downloaded*, then tap on *Install* on the window that pops up, and finally confirm the installation by tapping *Install* again on the new window that pops up. Now you'll be able to use the downloaded font in your Design Space app. If Design Space was open before you installed the new font, you'll have to quit and relaunch the app for the new font to become available for use.

Now, when you add a text element to your Design Space Canvas, you can choose your downloaded font when you open the *Font* menu and tap on the System option.

Download fonts on your Android device

While you can download fonts on your Android device, it's a bit hard to use them in other apps like Design Space. So, if you want to use fonts other Cricut fonts or the ones already installed on your Android device, you'll have to do it with a workaround.

You can download an app from the Playstore called *Phonto*. This font can open and use fonts you download from websites like Font Squirrel. Basically, you'll design the text part of your project in *Phonto*, save it as an image, and upload the image to Design Space. As a newbie, you might not want to go this route for your first few projects. However, keep this workaround in mind in case you ever need to create a design with custom fonts.

First, download and install the *Phonto* app from the Playstore. Next, go to the Font Squirrel website and find a font you like. Open the font link and then tap on the font's download button. When the download is complete, your phone will give you a notification. Tap on the open link on the notification. If you don't see the notification, you can go to your phone's *Downloads* folder to find it. When you open the download, you'll be prompted to install the font. Tap on the *Install* button. A window will pop up, giving you the choice to rename the font. Leave the name as is and tap on *Install.*

Go to the *Phonto* app. When the app opens, tap on the grid on the screen and then choose the *Plain Images* option from the list that pops up. Choose any of the first two options. On the new window that pops up, tap on *Color.* The last slider bar says *Alpha.* Slide the dot all the way to the left and tap on *Apply.* This will take you back to the previous window, where you can tap on *Use.* The grid will now look like a checkered board.

Tap on the *Edit* icon in the menu bar at the top of the screen. Type your word or phrase in the window that pops up and then tap on the *Font* button. Scroll through the fonts until you see the one that you downloaded, choose it, and then tap on *Done.*

Back on the grid, you'll see your text in the font that you downloaded, as well as a pop-up of various options. Choose *Size.* Increase the word or phrase's size until it almost fills the checkered part of the canvas. When you're done, tap on the *Download* icon next to the *Edit* icon, choose Save as PNG and then tap on *Save.* Now you go to Design Space and upload the image of the word or phrase you created in *Phonto.*

Pro Tip: If you use *Phonto*, my suggestion is that you save each word as a separate image file. That way, you can move things around easily on the Design Space *Canvas.*

What Will You Create Next?

I hope you had fun doing the three projects in this chapter. The aim was to get you familiar with most of the Design Space features you'll use as a Cricut Newbie and to get your creativity flowing.

If there are a ton of cool ideas inside you waiting to be unleashed, don't wait another second! Write down those ideas and get to work on your first solo project as soon as possible. The more time you spend with Design Space and your Cricut, the more confident you'll feel using it and the sooner you'll become a pro Cricut crafter.

CHAPTER 11

CRICUT TIPS & TRICKS EVERY NEWBIE NEEDS

We have the capacity for infinite creativity.
—Jackie Gleason

Now I want to help you get "Cricut wise." From maintaining your machine and tools to giving you the best places to find creative resources, you'll find it here. You may not be interested in everything this chapter has to offer right now, so feel free to browse the topics and dive into the parts that make you go *"Oh! That's what I wanted to know!"* Or, if you can't get enough of everything Cricut and want to know as much as possible before you really immerse yourself in the craft, sit back, enjoy, and absorb every gem that follows.

Cheat Sheets

Use these guides for quick referencing when you don't have the time to do research or re-read entire chunks of the book. Each cheat sheet will refer you to a page in the book where you can find more details if necessary.

Cheat Sheet #1:
Use Your Cricut Machine in Five Easy Steps

STEP 1: FINALIZE & CONFIRM YOUR DESIGN	If your design contains different layers, be sure to use the *Attach* function to keep everything in place for the cutting process. Don't *Attach* layers that you want to cut on different colors of material, like when making greetings cards with separate parts. If you have words or phrases in your design, double-check for typos before you start the cutting process. Click or tap on the *Make It* button when you're ready to make your design.
STEP 2: FOLLOW THE ON-SCREEN DESIGN SPACE PROMPTS	Design Space will ask you to specify the material you want to use for the project. If you have the Cricut Explore Air 2, remember to put the *Smart Dial* on the relevant material setting. Design Space will guide you to insert the relevant tools and/or blades into your Cricut machine based on the *Operation* settings you specified while making the design (*Cut, Pen, Foil, Score, or Print Then Cut*). The Cricut Joy has no buttons, so you will use Design Space to control the entire process.

STEP 3: PLACE YOUR MATERIAL ON THE CUTTING MAT	Make sure you have enough material for the design's size. For example, if your design is 5 x 5 inches, you need a piece of material that is at least 5.5 x 5.5 inches. Stick the material to the cutting mat best suited for it (see Cheat Sheet #2). If you are working with *Smart Materials*, you don't need a cutting mat (you can use *Smart Materials* with the Cricut Joy, Explore 3, and Maker 3).
STEP 4: INSERT THE MATERIAL INTO YOUR CRICUT MACHINE	When you insert the cutting mat into your Cricut, make sure the edges align with the guides at the machine's opening. Gently push the cutting mat into the machine until the rollers grip it. Your machine will scan the material to make sure there is enough for the cut.
STEP 5: START THE CUTTING PROCESS	Press the *Go* button on your Cricut Explore or Maker series machine. If you have a Cricut Joy, click or tap the *Go* button on your Design Space app. Design Space will keep you updated on the progress of the cut and inform you when it's finished.
WHERE TO FIND MORE INFORMATION	See Chapter 2 https://learn.cricut.com/courses/quick-start-guide

Cheat Sheet #2: Cutting Mat & Material Match-up

MAT	MATERIALS	MACHINE COMPATIBILITY
LightGrip (Blue)	Best for lightweight materials, including: Light and medium cardstock Standard printer paper Wrapping paper Vellum Washi sheets Pearl paper	Cricut Joy (4.5" x 12") Cricut Explore series (12" x 12" and 12" x 24") Cricut Maker series (12" x 12" and 12" x 24")
StandardGrip (Green)	Best for medium-weight materials, including: Heavy cardstock Glitter cardstock Embossed cardstock Adhesive vinyl Iron-On (or HTV) Textured paper Infusible Ink transfer sheets	Cricut Joy (4.5" x 6.5" and 4.5" by 12") Cricut Explore series (12" x 12" and 12" x 24") Cricut Maker series (12" x 12" and 12" x 24")
StrongGrip (Purple)	Best for heavyweight materials, including: Leather Wood (e.g., basswood and balsa wood)	Cricut Explore series (12" x 12" and 12" x 24") Cricut Maker series (12" x 12" and 12" x 24")

MAT	MATERIALS	MACHINE COMPATIBILITY
StrongGrip (Purple)	Chipboard Magnet sheets Foam Poster board Aluminum sheets	Cricut Explore series (12" x 12" and 12" x 24") Cricut Maker series (12" x 12" and 12" x 24")
FabricGrip (Pink)	Perfect for all fabric materials, including unbacked fabrics for the Maker series and bonded fabrics for the Explore series. Must-have mat for sewing crafters.	Cricut Explore series (12" x 12" and 12" x 24") Cricut Maker series (12" x 12" and 12" x 24")
WHERE TO FIND MORE INFORMATION	See chapter 2 https://cricut.com/blog/which-cricut-mat-should-you-use/	

Cheat Sheet #3: Common Design Space Terms

TERM	DESCRIPTION
CANVAS	Desktop The screen you see when working on a design project. It has a large grid surrounded by panels at the sides and a bar at the top. Mobile The mobile version of the *Canvas* takes up the whole screen, and you can access the design elements and functions from the bar at the bottom of the screen.
DESIGN PANEL	Desktop The panel at the very left end of the Design Space app when working on projects. You can access templates, shapes, images, the text tool, and manage uploads from there. Mobile You can access the same functions from the bar at the bottom of the *Canvas* screen.
EDIT BAR	Desktop The functions available in the top bar above the grid area when working on projects. You can specify whether an element should be cut, drawn, or printed before being drawn, and so on. It is also where you can adjust the size, arrange, and make other tweaks to design elements. Mobile The *Edit Bar* functions are available from the bar at the bottom of the *Canvas* screen.
LAYERS PANEL	Desktop The panel at the very right of the *Canvas* screen when working on a project. From there, you can arrange, group, and manage the separate elements that make up the design.

TERM	DESCRIPTION
LAYERS PANEL (Continued)	Mobile The *Layers Panel* can be accessed from the bar at the bottom of the *Canvas* screen.
BASIC CUT	A setting that tells your Cricut machine to cut out a design.
PEN	A setting that tells your Cricut to draw a design or design element.
FOIL, SCORE, DEBOSS, AND ENGRAVE	These are all settings you can apply to design elements if you have the specialty tools to implement them. The Cricut Joy can apply the *Foil* setting, the Cricut Explore machines can apply the *Foil* and *Score* settings, and the Cricut Maker machines can apply all settings.
PRINT THEN CUT	This feature allows you to print a design with your home printer before you let your Cricut cut it. Popular materials for this feature include stickers, bulk greeting cards, and printable vinyl.
COMBINE	A set of actions that influence overlapping layers. The options include *Unite, Subtract, Intersect, and Exclude.*
ATTACH	Not to be confused with the *Group* feature, the *Attach* feature allows you to link different elements (or layers) together for the cutting process. If your design contains many elements that make up the whole, it's the best way to keep each element in place during the cutting process. That way, you do not have to rearrange everything manually after the design has been cut.
WHERE TO FIND MORE INFORMATION	See chapter 9

Cheat Sheet #4: Popular and Newbie-Friendly Materials

MATERIAL	BEST FOR	TIPS FOR BEST RESULTS
CRICUT CARDSTOCK & PAPER	Greeting cards Invitations Papercrafts Scrapbooking designs Cake toppers Banners	Always peel the cutting mat away from the material to prevent accidental tears and curling of the paper/ cardstock. If you can't find cool ready-made designs, don't be afraid to jump in and create your own. Check out chapter 10 for a detailed tutorial on making a personalized greeting card.
CRICUT IRON-ON (HTV)	Custom hats T-shirts Tote bags Wood signs Mugs Any personalized apparel or home decor items you can think of.	Remember to mirror your design when working with this material. Always place your Iron-On upside-down on the cutting mat. If you can see the shiny side after sticking it to the mat, it's facing the wrong way for the cutting process and needs to be flipped over. Always refer to Cricut's Heat Guide when working with Iron-on and other heat-transfer materials. (https://cricut.com/ heatguide)

MATERIAL	BEST FOR	TIPS FOR BEST RESULTS
CRICUT PERMANENT VINYL	Any surface you don't plan on removing the design from, like: Signs Car decals Mugs Tumblers Coasters	Make sure the surface you want to apply your design to is clean and free of tiny particles. Rubbing alcohol is an excellent medium to apply to the surface a few minutes before you transfer the design. The *StrongGrip* cutting mat works well with glitter, shimmer, and other textured vinyls. If you want to layer vinyl (that is, if you want to stick pieces of vinyl on top of each other), it's best to use smooth vinyls as opposed to textured vinyls.
CRICUT REMOVABLE VINYL	Any surface you know of that will either need a change not too long in the future, or that you're not too sure whether you want something permanent, like: Wall decals Window decals Device decals	See the above tips for permanent vinyl.
WHERE TO FIND MORE INFORMATION	Check out chapter 10 https://cricut.com/blog/cricut-materials-cheatsheet-for-beginners/	

How to Take Care of Your Cricut Machine

Like all forms of technology, your machine will serve you well if you show it the love it deserves. This love comes in the form of proper maintenance. Let's explore everything you can do to help your machine give its best performance at all times.

Keep Your Firmware Updated

If your machine has the latest firmware, it means it is compatible with the latest software updates from Design Space and that it can handle new forms of media and other features Cricut may add. Design Space will inform you of updates in the following ways:

If you launch Design Space, you'll see a notification that updates are available.

Never ignore the prompts to do the updates. It takes a minute (or two at most) of your time and gives you the peace of mind and satisfaction that everything will work without unexpected hiccups.

If you're someone who likes to keep software programs or apps open for days on end, you can miss out on new updates.

To make sure you're working with the latest features from Cricut, check for updates at least once a week. Click or tap on the hamburger menu in the top-left corner of Design Space and select *Update Firmware*. If there are updates available, Design Space will prompt you to install it.

Note that firmware updates are different from Design Space software updates. Firmware relates to your machine's hardware, whereas the regular software updates relate to new features available in Design Space to play with when creating your designs. Every time you launch Design Space, it will automatically install the newest version. To make sure you're always working with the newest version, close and relaunch Design Space at least once a week if you like to keep your programs running.

Calibrate Your Machine

Calibration ensures that your machine delivers crisp and accurate cuts all the time. Since the Cricut Joy cuts mostly lightweight materials, there is no need to calibrate it. In fact, the option to do so is not even available for the Cricut Joy in Design Space.

If you have an Explore machine, you can calibrate it for *Print Then Cut* projects. With the Cricut Maker and Maker 3, you can calibrate your machine for *Print Then Cut* projects, as well as projects that require the *Rotary* blade and the *Knife* blade.

To calibrate your machine, go to the Hamburger menu in Design Space and click on the Calibration link. The calibration options you see will depend on your Cricut model.

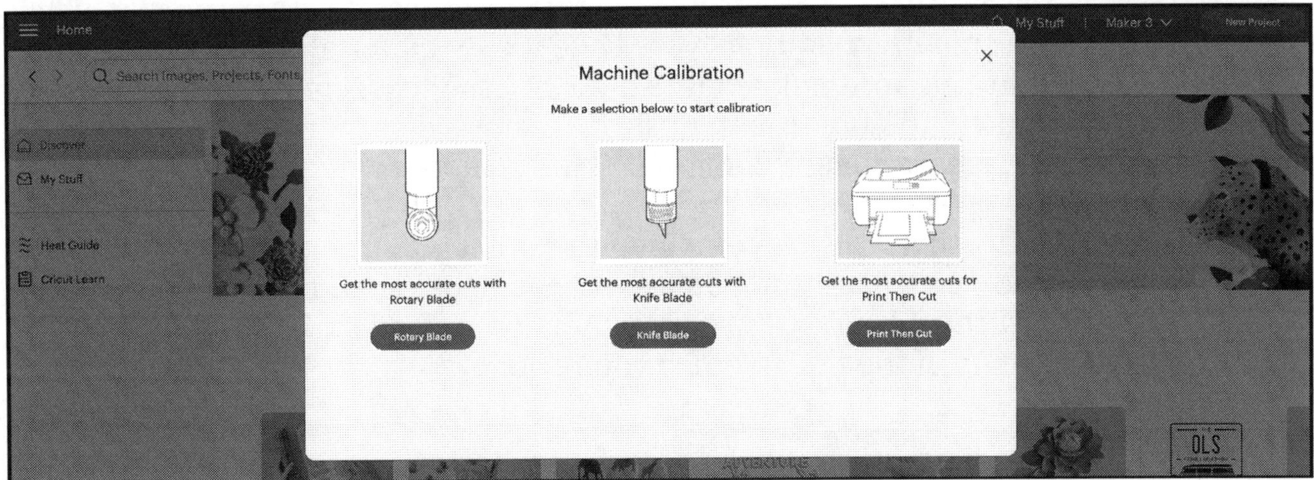

The more you use your machine, the more you will benefit from regular calibrations. For example, if you do *Print Then Cut* projects once or twice a week, you can calibrate your machine once a month. If you do such projects more often, consider a bi-weekly calibration. And if you rarely use the *Print Then Cut* feature, you can do a calibration every time you want to use it.

Give Your Cricut a Regular Clean

Your Cricut machine has a lot of nooks and crannies for dust and lint to settle in. Other than that, it may accumulate debris from the materials it cuts. If you give the dust, lint, and debris a chance to accumulate, they have the potential to hinder your Cricut's performance. Many experienced crafters say you do not need to worry about cleaning your new machine for the first eight to twelve months of using it. My humble opinion is that you should not wait at all. Instead, make a habit of scheduling a 15-minute cleaning session every month.

When you clean your Cricut, be thorough but careful not to damage those magical components. If you can, spend a few dollars on a cleaning kit and only use it for your Cricut machine. Some kits have a variety of useful brushes and extra microfiber cloths to make the cleaning process effortless. In my experience, it's best to shop for brushes made for sensitive electronics like keyboards and laptops.

Keep the following in mind when cleaning your Cricut:

- Make sure your machine is unplugged.
- When cleaning the inside of your machine with brushes, don't apply pressure. Play around with the brushes to see which one fits best at different parts. For example, a broad, flat brush works best to clean underneath the machine's shafts (or rods), while a bottle brush does the trick to get dust out of the clamps.
- You can use a baby wipe to pick up dust and other debris that fall on the bottom as you clean the inside components.
- The shaft at the back of the Explore and Maker machines has grease on it, which is important for a smooth operation every time it cuts materials. Without a regular clean, that shaft can accumulate quite a bit of crud, especially at the edges. To prevent too much buildup, use a brush to remove dirt from the edges and to redistribute the grease along the shaft. Do this on both sides.
- You can move the tool housing component manually to clean the left side of the machine, but be very gentle and don't move the housing all the way to the other side. Move it just enough so you have enough space to clean underneath and around the left-hand edges of the shafts. When you're done, move the tool housing back to its original position.
- Remember to clean your Cricut's storage compartments.
- There is an opening at the back of your Cricut where the cutting mat or *Smart Materials* move through as the machine cuts. To clean the opening, use a brush to push dust and debris out of the opening from the inside.
- If you have a can of compressed air, you can use it to remove any remaining dust after working with the brushes. Don't go too close to the machine's components and use quick bursts when working with compressed air.
- Clean your machine on the inside first, close it, and then clean the outside. If you notice scuff marks on the outside of your machine, you can spray a bit of glass cleaner on a soft, clean cloth and wipe it away. Don't soak the cloth, though.
- Stick to using baby wipes for the inside of the machine and give the inside surfaces a few minutes to dry before you close it. If you have a microfiber cloth, wipe over the machine's surfaces on the inside and outside for a final touch.

How to Take Care of Your Cricut Tools & Accessories

Cutting Mat Care

You can extend your cutting mat's life by keeping it covered when you're not using it and cleaning it when it loses its stickiness. Keeping it covered is as simple as placing the transparent sheet it came with and sticking it back on the mat after each project. However, even with the protective film, your mat will accumulate tiny fibers and stuff with use, making it less sticky over time. To get the stickiness back, you can do the following:

Luke-Warm Water Rinse

According to Cricut's website, you can place your cutting mat inside the sink, let lukewarm water run over it, and then gently scrub over the mat with a plastic, hard-bristled brush. While this is an effective method to clean your cutting mat, I don't think it's the best one for a beginner, because you can easily misjudge the amount of pressure you apply. Too much pressure can remove the adhesive coating that makes your mat sticky and render the mat useless.

Dish Soap Cleanse

Let your mat rest on a clean surface and squirt a generous amount of dishwashing liquid onto the mat. Spread the soap over the mat by gently rubbing over it with your hand. When the mat is completely covered with soap, let it rest for five minutes. After the wait, rub over the mat's surface with a gentle touch. "Gentle" is the key term here. Be mindful of the adhesive layer on the mat at all times whenever you clean it. Now you can move over to the sink and let lukewarm water run over the mat. As the water runs, keep on rubbing over the sticky side ever so gently until all the soap is washed away. Dry both sides of the mat with tissue paper and let the mat rest, sticky side up, until it is completely dry. You can cover the mat with its protective sheet once it is dry.

Don't worry that you did something wrong if you touch your mat while it is wet and can't feel any stickiness. The adhesive layer needs to be dry to work. The dish soap method is especially effective for the *FabricGrip* mat, as it tends to pick up a lot of debris from fabric materials.

Baby Wipes (my favorite method)

With all the methods I have experimented with to clean my cutting mats, baby wipes have won the race by far. It doesn't require me to leave my crafting space, and it is a little faster than the other methods. All you need is a clean surface and two to five baby wipes. How many you end up using will depend on how much debris is stuck on your mat.

Lay your mat on a clean surface, fold a baby wipe in half, and make circular movements on the mat with light pressure. I like to start in the upper left-hand corner and work my way to the lower right-hand corner. When the baby wipe becomes dirty from the debris, fold it over again and continue cleaning. Move on to the next one when you have no more folds to make; continue with the process until your mat is clean. When you're done, your mat needs about five to eight minutes to dry.

That's it. Your mat will be good as new after each clean. However, you will need to replace your cutting mat eventually, no matter what method you use to clean it. When cleaning no longer enhances your mat's stickiness, it's time to part ways and welcome a new one into your craft room.

How Often Should You Clean a Cutting Mat?

If you do a lot of projects that tend to leave more debris, like paper and cardstock, your mat will serve you better if you clean it after every four to five cuts. With projects that leave less debris, like vinyl, you can get away with cleaning your mat after every eight to ten cuts.

Accessory Care

Most crafters have multiple crafts and hobbies, and Cricut is just one of them. It is all too easy to grab the nearest accessory to "quickly do this thing." Being organized doesn't come naturally for most creative people, but that doesn't mean we can't learn the skill. This is something I had to learn, and I'm so glad I did, because now everything I use to help me craft lasts so much longer.

The rule is simple: Cricut accessories are only for Cricut crafting, scrapbooking accessories are only for scrapbook crafting, sewing accessories are only for sewing, and so on.

Cricut accessories include things like your scraper, weeder, spatula, and everything you use after the cutting process to help you complete projects. Just like your machine, they'll serve you well if they are clean at all times. How often you clean them is up to you. You can include them in your monthly cleaning schedule and do everything in one shot, or clean them after every use. For me, it's easier to give my tools a quick clean just after using them. That way, I know they're in top condition and there is no dirt that can accidentally get on the next project. Rubbing alcohol works well to remove stickiness and other dirt from surfaces and accessories, so I always have a decent supply in my craft room.

Blade and Tool Care

Your blades and tools, like the *Scoring Stylus* and *Foil Transfer* tool, can also pick up debris with use. Left unchecked, an unclean blade can tear material or not cut properly, and unclean tools can cause less than desirable results.

Every month, when you clean your Cricut machine, be sure to spend some time cleaning your blades and tools, too. You can use one of the smaller brushes in your cleaning kit to nudge out dust and material debris from your tool housings. Remove the blade from its housing and give it a good brush and rub with a soft, clean cloth, too. But please be careful not to cut yourself when doing this; those blades are incredibly sharp and can cause terrible pain... (Don't ask me how I know.)

Bonus Tip: How to Extend Your Cutting Blade's Life

Cricut blades get dull with use, and they're not exactly inexpensive to replace. Even if you have a spare waiting to take the old one's place, you should use your blade to its maximum potential.

This is where aluminum foil comes to the rescue. It sounds weird, but you'll be amazed at how this simple household item can revive a blunt Cricut blade. Remove the blade from your Cricut machine and form a ball with a piece of foil. Hold the ball in one hand and use the other hand to press down on the blade housing's plunger (the little nib on top) to expose the blade. Next, poke the aluminum foil ball with the exposed blade. You can go relatively fast when doing this. A few pokes should do the trick to give your blade some oomph again.

On average, a standard fine-point blade should last at least 12 months before it needs to be replaced. However, if you become an avid Cricut crafter who spends more time in the craft room than anywhere else, you might need to replace yours sooner.

Where to Find the Best Creative Resources for FREE

Before you visit the following websites, I would like to remind you of something we talked about earlier in the book, and that is usage rights. That is, the license terms under which you are allowed to download and use creative resources. Please, please check how you are allowed to use downloads, and please don't use anything for any purpose outside the license agreement. For example, if the usage rights say you may use something for personal reasons only, don't try to sell that design on anything, under any circumstances.

Just think of how you would feel if you had spent a ton of time creating something from scratch, only to find out some random person took your creation, slapped it on something, and is now selling it for profit. You would probably think it highly unethical, and you'd be right. So, don't ever do something similar. We creative people need to support each other by respecting the boundaries we set for each other.

Many new crafters don't know this, but using Google Images as a source of "free" images is not always ethical. If you find an image on Google that you really like, it is your responsibility to do everything within your power to make sure you can use it without infringing on the creator's or owner's copyright. One of the best ways to find out about copyright on an image is to do a reverse image search. Check out this Google article to learn more: https://support.google.com/websearch/answer/1325808. If you cannot determine the copyright of an image, don't use it because the potential trouble it can bring if the creator finds out is not worth it—ever. Besides, you would not be amused if someone else profited from your hard work, so why do it to a fellow creator?

The following websites offer free downloads and regularly update their resource libraries. Bookmark and visit them often. Even if you don't use something they offer, you might just find the inspiration you need for your own designs.

- **LoveSVG:** https://lovesvg.com/daily-freebies/
- **Craft House SVG:** https://crafthousesvg.com/collections/freebies
- **Craft Bundles:** https://craftbundles.com/product-category/free-svg-cut-files/
- **HelloSVG:** https://hellosvg.com/
- **Design Bundles:** https://designbundles.net/free-design-resources/free-svgs
- **Creative Fabrica:** https://www.creativefabrica.com/freebies/free-crafts/

The Best Places to Find Blanks for Vinyl Designs

Blanks refer to objects like mugs, t-shirts, tumblers, and towels on which you can place your vinyl, *Iron-On*, and *Infusible Ink* designs. The following places offer the best quality and prices for blanks.

Cricut

Cricut's blanks were all made specifically to work with Cricut materials, so you can always have peace of mind that you'll get top-notch results when working with their products.

Check out https://cricut.com/en_us/tools-accessories/accessories/blanks.html to see what they offer.

Dollar Tree

Visit your local Dollar Tree or check out their website at https://www.dollartree.com/ for affordable blanks.

Amazon

What can't you find on Amazon these days, right? It offers a treasure trove of blanks to pick and choose from. Head over to https://www.amazon.com/ and type whatever you are looking for into the search bar.

Here are examples of what you can look for:

- "Blank mugs"
- "Bella Canvas"
- "Blank journals"
- "Blank tumblers"

Michaels

Michaels Stores is a well-established craft and hobby chain that is now one of North-America's largest sources of all things arts & crafts. Visit their website at https://www.michaels.com/ to browse their selection of blanks, as well as Cricut products.

Target

This is another great choice for a variety of blank products at affordable prices. Go to https://www.target.com/ or visit your local Target store.

Walmart

Walmart is probably America's most well-known hypermarket and grocery chain. They're huge, and they offer a huge selection of home and apparel products, so be sure to shop around for some blanks the next time you visit them. Alternatively, check out their website at https://www.walmart.com/.

Craft Space Organization Tips and Tricks

Ah, that magical place where you lose things you need right now and find things you haven't thought of in six months or more... Your craft space or room can get disorganized and somewhat frustrating to spend time in within a blink.

The following tips and tricks came to me by chance (perhaps divine intervention) and helped me make sense of my craft room at a time I felt discouraged to spend time there because of all the clutter. They're not revolutionary, but they're certainly effective and might just help you stay sane, too.

Don't Get Stuff for the Sake of Getting Them

I get it, ideas are popping into your head almost constantly. That's just the way creative minds work. The problem is that there is only so much time to do the things we want to, so there is really no use in gathering everything you need for every new idea

One of the most profound pieces of advice I ever received was to pen down my ideas and plan accordingly. Now all I have to do is choose which projects I want to do first and then get supplies for those projects only. The result is way, way less clutter.

The other benefit of taking on crafting projects in this way is that it helps you to stay focused and actually get things done. If you have too many ideas, and you have everything you need to make them a reality, you're more likely to be struck by overwhelm and end up not doing them at all. As strange as that sounds, humans (creative types included) thrive when they are able to direct their attention to one (or as few as possible) thing at a time.

Utilize Wall Space

Instead of trying to fit all of your supplies into drawers, boxes, and other conventional places, use the walls around your crafting space to store supplies and tools you use regularly. Think of wall racks, shelves, canvas organizers, hooks, and peg boards, to name a few options. For example, the VARIERA plastic bag dispenser from IKEA is a brilliant and beautiful way to store vinyl rolls.

Label Everything

Avoid popping random supplies into random drawers and cupboards. Instead, use your Cricut machine to create labels and then organize all your storage compartments accordingly. From paper to glue, to pens, to paint, to sewing patterns, everything must have a place. For smaller and loose things, like rubber bands, glitter, beads, and pearls, you can use labeled Mason jars.

Get a Craft Cart

A craft cart can add a lot of extra storage space to your crafting room and give you an easily accessible way to have the supplies you use most of the time handy at all times. For example, you can have one cart to store Cricut supplies and accessories and another one to store your scrapbooking (or sewing or paint or other craft) supplies.

The truth is, there are a ton of useful ways you can organize your craft space or room, and what works for me may or may not work for you. But one thing is certain: an organized crafter is a happy and focused crafter. Getting your craft space ready is just as important as choosing the right Cricut machine, so spend as much time as you need to perfect that space and make it your place of bliss.

Tips to Save and Stretch those Precious Dollars

- Be a bargain hunter. Somewhere out there, you'll find Cricut supplies, tools, and accessories on a special.
- If you want to work with heat transfer materials, buy blanks like t-shirts, mugs, tote bags, tea towels, etc., in bulk.
- Measure and cut the material you need according to the size of your design. Leave a bit of space all around to make sure the entire design cuts out.
- If you have scraps of material after a cut, save it. You can use it for test cuts or smaller designs.
- Do test cuts, especially when working with new materials and machine settings. This will give you the opportunity to perfect the machine's settings for the actual project.
- Reuse transfer tape when working with vinyl projects. You can typically get away with using the same piece of transfer tape five to eight times.
- When working with thicker and heavier materials, use painters tape to secure it on the cutting mat. If the material shifts during the cutting process, it might get damaged, so be safe instead. Make sure the painters tape doesn't get in the way of the cutting blade, though.

Many experienced crafters will tell you to use generic materials and supplies for your Cricut projects to save money. Personally, I appreciate the quality Cricut offers. That's not to say other brands don't offer quality, but I guess I am biased in that regard. In the beginning, I experimented with generic materials, but once I started using Cricut's products exclusively, I just knew I had to find other, more creative ways to save my dollars. Nothing beats excellent results, and that is exactly what you'll get with Cricut materials.

Before I send you off solo into the exciting world of Cricut crafting, there's one more subject we need to chat about. After that, you'll be knowledgeable enough to give some Cricut pros advice! See you in chapter 12.

CHAPTER 12

TROUBLESHOOT YOUR CRICUT LIKE A PRO

A creative life is an amplified life.
—Elizabeth Gilbert

Where there is technology, hiccups are bound to happen, and your Cricut machine—fantastic as it is—is no exception. The chances that you'll encounter a major problem with your machine are slim. However, if it does come to that, you can rest assured that Cricut (the company) will be there to assist. In case of a major fault under warranty, they will replace the defective part or the machine for you.

If your machine does something unexpected or does nothing at all when you expect it to do something, first try the following quick fixes before you move on to troubleshooting:

1. Restart Your Machine

Whether it's a temporary memory issue or some other glitch preventing your machine from responding, a fresh start may be all that's needed. If you have a Cricut Explore or Maker machine, use the power button to switch it off and wait for three minutes before you switch it on again. With the Cricut Joy, you'll have to remove the power cord from the machine to switch it off and plug it in again to switch it on.

2. Check the Power Cord and Wall Socket

The machine might not be plugged in properly, or it could be that the wall socket is malfunctioning. If the cord is plugged in, try moving it from one socket to another to see if it makes a difference.

3. Check for Updates

It might be that there was an important firmware update for your Cricut machine, causing the current firmware not to be compatible with Design Space features anymore. Open the Hamburger menu on your app and click or tap on *Update Firmware.*

4. Close and Relaunch Design Space

There might be a software update for Design Space that will install automatically once you relaunch the program.

5. Check Your Machine for Debris or Jammed Materials

A piece of material might have torn off and got stuck inside the machine the last time you used it.

In case none of the above quick fixes work, it's time to dig deeper to find the cause of the problem and, most importantly, fix it. Let's talk about common issues you might experience with your Cricut.

My Machine Cuts Poorly or Does Not Cut All the Way through the Material

Most of the time, this issue is caused by a blunt knife or an incorrect setting on Design Space. Here is what you can do:

- Double-check that you're using the right mat for the project. Cheat Sheet #2 in chapter 11 will show you which mats work best with which materials.
- Double-check that your mat is clean and sticky enough for the project. It might need a quick cleanse before you continue.
- Make sure your cutting blade is clean and sharp. If it has become dull, try reviving it with a foil ball like we talked about on page 208. Do a test cut after sharpening the blade to see if it solved the issue. If the aluminum foil trick did not work, replace the blade with a new one.
- Go back to the material selection option in Design Space and make sure the setting you chose matches the material you're trying to cut. With the Explore Air 2, make sure your *Smart Dial* is set to the appropriate material, and if it is on *Custom*, check that you chose the correct material from the *Custom Materials* list in Design Space.

Sometimes, even if the material setting is correct and the blade and mat are fine, you may still have issues getting a clean cut. In that case, increase the blade's pressure by 2–4 from the *Manage Custom Materials* page in Design Space. After the increase, do a test cut to see if the increase was effective enough. If not, it doesn't mean that anything is wrong yet. You may need to increase the pressure up to three times for it to make a difference in the quality of the cut.

Your font or design might be too intricate and small for the blade. If the above solutions did not make a difference, assess your design and check if increasing the size helps.

As a last resort, test another material like a scrap piece of paper. If the other material cuts without issues, there might be a problem with the material you were trying to use. However, if the results are the same as with the original material and you have followed all the above steps, it's best to get in contact with Cricut's support team and let them guide you from there.

My Machine's Power Button Is Solid Red or Blinking Red

How to Interpret and Solve a **Blinking Red** Power Button

To solve the issue, you need to determine exactly when the button flashes. The most common occurrences are when you switch the machine on, when you try to update the firmware, while cutting a project, or when you load material into the machine.

OCCURRENCE	WHAT TO DO
WHEN I SWITCH ON MY MACHINE	Contact Cricut support for help.
WHILE THE FIRMWARE IS SUPPOSED TO BE UPDATING	Contact Cricut support for help.
WHEN I LOAD A CUTTING MAT OR SMART MATERIAL INTO MY MACHINE	If it is a once-off issue that did not happen with previous projects, the current project may be corrupted. Delete the project and redo it from scratch If this is something that happens regularly, your Cricut's roller bar may be blocked by dirt and/or debris. Remove the material, switch off the machine, and clean the roller bar area. It also helps to move the carriage or tool housing system from side to side a few times, but be gentle when doing so. In case the above techniques do not solve the issue, contact Cricut support for help.
WHEN I TRY TO CUT A PROJECT	Determine whether this is a once-off issue or a recurring one. In either case, you want to remove the material, switch the machine off, and move the tool housing unit across the roller bar six to ten times. Switch your Cricut on and try to cut the project again. If the power button continues to blink red, contact Cricut support for help and be sure to tell them whether it is the first time you are experiencing the issue or if it has happened multiple times already.

OCCURRENCE	WHAT TO DO
WHEN I TRY TO CUT A PROJECT (CONTINUED)	If you're working with thicker materials, like wood or leather, inconsistencies in the material's thickness may cause a pause in the cutting process, followed by a blinking red power button. Design Space may prompt you to follow instructions to clean any debris, after which you can press the Cut button again to continue. You may have to go through this a few times. But if the problem persists, contact Cricut support and explain the issue in as much detail as possible.

How to Interpret and Solve a **Solid Red** Power Button

Your machine may give you a solid red power button to tell you there is a problem with its power supply. You will either see the power button lit up red and no other lit buttons, or the power button will be red and the *Print Then Cut* sensor light will be on. In both cases, you need to follow the same steps:

1. Plug your machine into another power outlet. If the problem does not go away, follow the next steps.

2. Check that the power adapter is securely plugged into the machine and the wall outlet.

3. Make sure the power and USB cables are not obstructing the opening at the back of the machine where the cutting mat is supposed to move through as it cuts materials. (The mat may loosen or unplug the power adapter from the machine.)

4. Only use the power adapter that came with your machine. If it got damaged or lost, replace it with a new one specifically made for the model you have.

5. If you have followed the above steps and the problem persists, your power adapter may be faulty. Contact Cricut to request a replacement adapter and cord.

6. If the issue does not go away after you have replaced the power adapter, get in contact with Cricut support.

A red power button and white load button tells you that your machine's firmware needs updating. If you see the same buttons lit up after doing an update, contact Cricut support for assistance.

My Explore or Maker Machine Stops or Turns Off in the Middle of the Cutting Process

Why Your Machine Stops in the Middle of a Cut and What to Do About it

1. You might have multiple Design Space windows open. Close the additional windows and try to continue with the process.

2. Usually, if it is a once-off occurrence, it is a sign that the project file is corrupt. Delete everything, design it from scratch, and try again.

3. If it has happened before, there is a chance that other programs on your computer may be in conflict with Design Space. Close all programs except for Design Space and continue with the cut. Reopen the other programs only after the project is done.

4. Switch off your machine, disconnect it from your computer and from its power supply, wait a few minutes, reconnect everything, switch on your machine, and do the cut again.

5. If none of the above tips solve the issue, get in touch with Cricut support.

Why Your Machine Turns Off in Middle of a Cut and What to Do About it

Chances are that you were working with metal sheets, foil, or *Smart Materials* when this happened. It can happen because of a buildup of static electricity, especially if you're working in a dry environment. If that's the case, it's helpful to have a spray bottle with water in your craft room to spray mist in the air whenever you work with your Cricut machine. This will create some humidity to prevent that static energy from building up too much, but don't spray the mist on your Cricut machine. If you're working with *Smart Materials*, don't let a long roll of it drag on the floor while your Cricut cuts, as it will create more static electricity. Find a way to keep the roll on the table, or invest in a Cricut *Roll Holder* for *Smart Materials*.

Print Then Cut Issues

My Machine Cannot Read Cut Sensor Marks

In many cases, especially when you upload images that you want to cut, you may accidentally upload them as *Print Then Cut* files. So, the first thing is to be sure what you want from your machine: do you want to do *Print Then Cut*, or just a normal *Cut*? If you want to do a normal *Cut*, first make sure you're working with an SVG file. Then go back to the *Canvas* screen in Design Space and change the *Operation* from *Print Then Cut* to *Cut*. **Note:** If you try to use the *Cut* operation on a JPG or PNG file with more than one color, the program will turn the image into a silhouette and only cut the outline of the image. JPG and PNG files don't have layers like SVG files, so they're not ideal to use for the *Cut Operation*. Thus, you should always use SVG files for *Cut* projects.

If your intention is to do a *Print Then Cut* project (that is, you want to print a design on your home printer and then let your Cricut cut out the design afterward), try the following solutions.

1. The cut sensor is light sensitive, so make sure your machine is not in direct sunlight or directly under overhead lights or lamp lights.

2. Make sure you used the cutting mat's upper-left corner as the starting point to place the sheet of material.

3. Make sure the material you want to cut is free from printer and dirt marks that your machine can mistake for cut lines.

4. If you have an Explore series machine, the *Print Then Cut* feature will only work on material that is letter-size and white.

5. If you have a Maker series machine, the *Print Then Cut* feature can handle colored material, as well as lightly-patterned material. But dark colors, heavy patterns, and textures will likely give you this error.

6. When you print the design, make sure your printer settings are set to print the design on size, with all scaling options like *'fit to page'* disabled.

7. Your computer may not meet Design Space's minimum system requirements (https://help.cricut.com/hc/en-us/articles/360009556033). If that's the case, you'll have to work on a computer that does meet those requirements.

8. Calibrate your machine for *Print Then Cut* and try again.

9. Check that the *Print Then Cut* sensor light under the carriage or tool housing system is on when the machine tries to scan for sensor marks. If it is on, clean it with a small, soft brush. If it is not on, get in touch with Cricut support.

10. If none of the above options solve the issue, contact Cricut support for help.

My Machine is Not Cutting My Print Then Cut Project Precisely

This is likely a calibration issue. Stop the project, calibrate your machine for *Print Then Cut*, and try again. If the problem persists, contact Cricut support to guide you further.

Loud and Unusual Noises

All Cricut machines make sounds when they scan and cut materials. However, you'll just know when those sounds become weird. In case it happens, here's what you can do:

1. Check your pressure settings, as it may be too high for the given material. Reduce the pressure bit by bit to see if the noise abates. If it's still there after you have reduced the pressure settings three times, get in touch with Cricut Support.

2. Check if your machine's *Fast Mode* is enabled. If it is enabled, disable it and check if the noise persists when you instruct the machine to cut material.

3. Ensure you're using the power adapter that came with your machine. If you don't have it anymore, don't settle for any old or generic adapter. Contact Cricut immediately so they can send a replacement. Each Cricut adapter was designed and certified to work with specific Cricut models, and your machine can only perform at its best with the adapter that was made for it.

4. Grinding noises may be a sign of debris obstructing the carriage from moving, so inspect the inside of your machine thoroughly and remove anything you find lying around.

5. Check the belt in the back of the machine to make sure it is not loose or broken.

6. If you find something out of place, or if the noise continues after you reduced the pressure and disabled *Fast Mode*, make a video recording (with the sound enabled) while the machine cuts and then contact Cricut support for help. Be sure to give them as much detail as possible when you describe the issue, and tell them that you made a recording of the noise for them to examine.

The above troubleshooting topics do not include every issue you can experience with your Cricut machine. However, they are the most common ones you might encounter during your machine's lifetime.

If you're having other issues, check out Cricut's troubleshooting guides at the links below.

- For the Cricut Joy: https://help.cricut.com/hc/en-us/sections/360007280773-Troubleshooting

- For the Cricut Explore and Maker models: https://help.cricut.com/hc/en-us/sections/360001958073-Troubleshooting

If your machine is brand new, it is still under warranty. In that case, it's best to contact Cricut immediately if you suspect a serious issue. Whatever you do, don't fiddle with your machine, as you may render your warranty void.

Chapters 12 Notes

Use this space to jot down the best take-aways you learned from Chapter 12. Use these notes as your personal quick-reference guide whenever you want to refresh your memory ons something specific.

CONCLUSION

BET YOU NEVER THOUGHT OWNING A CRICUT COULD FEEL THIS GOOD

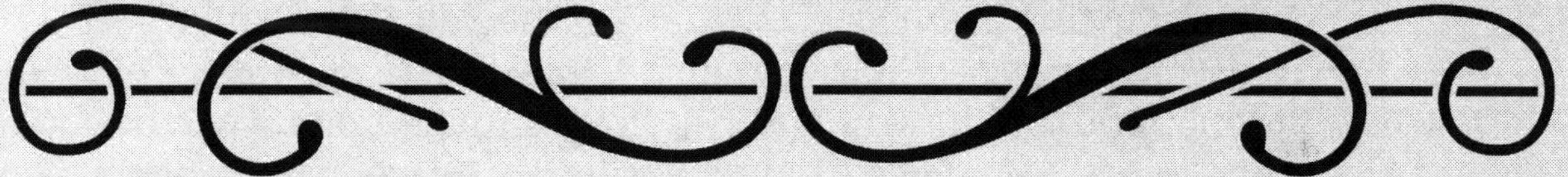

Creativity is the power to act.
—Ai Weiwei

See? I told you that you would walk away empowered and determined to pursue your passion. Now that the initial overwhelm you felt is a headache of the past, you can create with wild abandon and consider yourself a confident and proud Cricut crafter. But if the overwhelm ever threatens to sneak up on you again, remind yourself that every expert, no matter his or her vocation, was a newbie once upon a time.

You've got this!

Let's see what you've learned on your journey so far.

We took a walk down memory lane and learned about the history of Cricut, which, by the way, few pros can say they know. Also, your new knowledge of how the shoemaking industry provided a stepping-stone for the die-cutting industry can be a pretty cool conversation starter (or an awkward-silence breaker).

If someone asks you, "Why Cricut?" you can answer with confidence that it allows you to get more done in less time and gives you the perfect platform to make all your creative ideas a reality. You're not limited by tools or materials, because your machine can handle almost anything you want to try. By the way, if you're ever confronted by a "I-do-everything-by-hand" crafter who questions your prowess, simply ask her to create something using your Cricut and then wait for the excuses as to why she can't "right now." I need to point this out because too many new crafters and artists get discouraged when they come across people who insist "real crafting" is done by hand. They plant seeds of doubt and, before you know it, you've given up on your hobby or craft. Never forget that being able to use Cricut's design software, operating a Cricut machine, and making the final product takes a lot of skill, imagination, and creativity—and you've got them all. While it is relatively easy to learn how to use a Cricut machine, it's certainly difficult (grueling, even) to use it without knowledge and training. If it weren't, there would be no need for Cricut books, blogs, and social media groups. (And, of course, new Cricut machines wouldn't spend weeks or months tucked away in closets.)

We also talked about different things you can make with your Cricut, including journal covers, bookmarks, apparel designs, and typography art. You'll find many online communities and resources that will show you how to make various crafts and help you hone your skills.

When it comes to operating a Cricut machine, you now know it involves five basic steps, regardless of the model you own. It always starts with finalizing your design on Design Space and culminates when you press that *Go* button. Further, you learned about each Cricut machine's features. In fact, you know enough about their differences to guide anyone you know to choose the best model. You can even help another crafter set up their new machine. Hey, Cricut is contagious, so you'll soon have your own Cricut Newbie to guide!

Although I believe this entire book offers a valuable and hands-on learning experience, I'm especially excited for you when I think of the Design Space and Project chapters.

Design Space is an enormous obstacle for Newbies, but you received a powerful and lasting foundation to build on. Not only can you navigate the desktop version, you also know your way around the mobile app. Besides the technical know-how, you can create projects from scratch, giving you an immense advantage over Newbies who only know how to use ready-made projects. When you're ready to dive even deeper into Design Space and all it has to offer, check out my other book, *Cricut Design Space Handbook for Newbies.*

On a final note, I would like to thank you for giving yourself the opportunity to explore the exciting world of Cricut crafting. Think of this book as your personal Cricut companion, always ready to give a hand if something slips your mind. Keep it close and, more importantly, share what you learn with other Cricut Newbies. Above all, let this book be a constant reminder of how much you deserve to have a ton of fun.

Here's to you and your bright future as a Cricut crafter!

Share Your Honest Opinion of this Book

If you haven't done so already, I'd really appreciate it if you could take a few minutes to share with fellow crafters what you thought of *Cricut for Newbies*. Your opinion matters immensely, and the only way others will know if this book can change their lives is with your help.

Please head over to your favorite book review platform and share your thoughts about how this book has influenced your personal journey as a Cricut Newbie.

Join the Cricut for Newbies Facebook Group

This is goodbye, but by no means is it farewell. There's an entire community of fellow Cricut Newbies waiting to meet and encourage you, and I'm first in line. Since we're practically crafting besties now, there is so, so much more I want to share with you, from unique project tutorials to little-known Cricut secrets even many pros still haven't figured out.

Join the Cricut for Newbies Facebook Group now to connect with like-minded people and be part of a community who believes in you and what you can achieve. https://www.facebook.com/groups/cricutfornewbies

Have You Claimed Your **FREE** Gift?

If you haven't done so already, head over to www.cricutfornewbies.com to grab your FREE copy of *The Must Have Design Space Cheat Sheet for Cricut Newbies.*

Happy crafting!

Ready to Conquer the Design Space Beast Once and for All?

Although you can achieve amazing results with what you've learned about using Design Space in Chapter 9, you've really only scratched the surface. There's so much more to learn, which is why I have an entire book dedicated to Design Space, called *Cricut Design Space Handbook for Newbies.*

The book is a practical guide with screenshots, exercises, and worksheets to help you understand every feature of Design Space. It delves into the "how to" of literally everything in the program. The most exciting thing about *Cricut Design Space Handbook for Newbies* is that it covers how to work with layers in detail. Finally, the book boasts with a mega glossary of crafting terms every Newbie needs to know about.

Curious? Have a look at the book here:
https://www.amazon.com/Cricut-Design-Space-Handbook-Newbies/dp/1778127126/

Acknowledgments

Mom and Dad, thank you for sacrificing so much for me & my sisters and for always being there, no matter what. You are cherished—now and forever.

Zabed, no wife has ever loved her husband more than I love you. Your love, encouragement, and kindness keep me going on my best and not-so-best days. Words could never describe my immense gratitude to you.

Aliya, my baby girl, you're still new to this world and won't be able to read this for a few years. But when you do, I want you to know that you have added unimaginable value to our lives. You are the inspiration behind all of this.

Ela, Luna, and Rida, you three are the best sisters anyone could ask for. **Forhad**, you're a pretty cool brother-in-law! Thank you all for always giving me an ear whenever I need to talk. You're terrific.

To my nephew, **Ayaz**, I can't wait until you're old enough to read my very first book. Auntie loves you!

Melissa, you always support and encourage my ideas. You did so much for me on this journey, and I can't thank you enough.

To my CDTP family: **Caydance**, **Connie**, **Fiona**, **Renee**, **Shannon**, **Shelley**, **Sally**, **Ozge**, **Sue**, **Kimberly**, and **Jill**, thank you so much for all the support throughout this entire journey.

To my fellow publishers: **Karen**, **Matthew**, **Biola**, **Marrion**, **Kara**, **Karman**, **Leslie**, **Zhen**, and **Kellie**, I can't tell you how happy I am that our paths crossed. I am forever grateful for your wholehearted support.

Finally, I would like to thank **you**, the reader, for spending your precious time with me on these pages. I don't know your name, and I will probably never meet you, but you being here means more to me than you'll ever know. Thank you for choosing this book. I hope *Cricut for Newbies* has given you the confidence to create Cricut crafts with wild abandon.

About the Author

Delara Chowdhury is an unapologetic craft addict, smitten wife, and adoring, proud mother. She grew up in Ontario, Canada, as the middle child amongst four sisters.

The latest and coolest arts and crafts trends have always been a subject of fascination for Delara. From scrapbooking to paper-craft, to quilting, to glass-crafts, she's done it all. She is also a technology and design enthusiast. So, when she discovered the perfect combination of the two in the form of Cricut crafting, she was instantly hooked.

Delara's Cricut journey ensured many interesting, fun, happy, crazy, and sometimes down-right frustrating moments. Every one of those experiences prepared for her ultimate passion and purpose: helping Cricut Newbies conquer their machines with confidence. Today, she specializes in Cricut crafts and pays it forward by sharing her knowledge in a way so easy to understand, even your grandmother could become a Cricut pro!

You can connect with Delara by joining her Facebook Group at https://www.facebook.com/groups/cricutfornewbies or by writing to her at delara@cricutfornewbies.com